W9-BZE-263

Twayne's English Authors Series

Anthony Powell

ANTHONY POWELL

By NEIL BRENNAN
Villanova University

Twayne Publishers, Inc. :: New York

Library of Congress Catalog Card Number: 72-13381

ISBN 0-8057-1454-5

MANUFACTURED IN THE UNITED STATES OF AMERICA

Preface

This study of Anthony Powell grows out of a ten-year love affair. One of the impulses of love is to share the joy: "Read Powell's *Afternoon Men*! It's minor, but it's splendid!" When the friend a few weeks later admits only to having "liked" the novel, or complains that "not much happens" in it, one truth has to be faced: Anthony Powell is not an easy novelist for Americans to adopt. The apathy cannot be dismissed as a regional eccentricity, either, for readers as solidly American as Peter de Vries hail Powell as great, and English critics as bright as John Wain dismiss *The Music of Time* as a bore. Since other British readers, enthralled with the social richness of *The Music of Time*, dismiss Powell's early novels as "frivolous," it may be best to state firmly this book's position to begin with: two of Powell's early comic novels are among the hundred best novels of the century, and *The Music of Time* sequence promises to rival *Ulysses* as the most important novel published in English in the twentieth century.

These differences of opinion do point to the need of giving more than the usual amount of attention to Anthony Powell's background, to the family from which he took his traditions, to the friends who helped to form his esthetics, and to the times which gave his wit its ironic edge. Consequently, the first half of this book is devoted to achieving an understanding of Powell's valid, if uncommon, point of view.

The first basis of literary understanding is sympathy. Powell represents a cool, esthetic, and aristocratic culture often misrepresented in this century of the common man. For one thing, it takes for granted a love of beauty. When the partygoing world of Powell's first novel is invaded by an American publisher who repeats several times in an evening "I can't get along without beauty," we may need an un-American viewpoint, perhaps, to see that he is merely claiming to be human. Because the publisher is involved in a comic-drunk scene later, readers have been known to conclude, not without disgust, that the only character in the novel who truly loves beauty is being satirized by Powell. Far from it. The tone is that of detached amusement, not of didactic moralizing. Both the culture and the esthetic tradition oppose crude satire, whether of drunks, Americans, or people who think a love of beauty makes them somehow exceptional. An exposition of the milieu out of which the novels have come, in the trust that understanding of the culture will bring sympathy and that it in turn will lead to a better understanding of the novels, is the goal of the early chapters of this study.

A second basis must be technical, for quite as much as Joyce—but in a different way—Powell conceives the novel to be an art form. That Powell is "a writer of social comedy as revelatory and hilarious as any written by Evelyn Waugh or Henry Green"—and yet has been less widely read—has to be ascribed in part to his experiments with form and technique. As his novels set about re-posing those fundamental questions of life that American literary critics sometimes assume have been settled once and for all, his humor and irony are so tightly controlled that a reader can easily miss his most amusing and most illuminating moments. More than most novelists, Powell is a writer to be reread—that may be admitted—but his tight architectonics may be opened up ahead of time by a bit of preliminary diagramming. And the last chapters of this study aim to do just that.

I must thank Mr. Gordon Ray for having first directed my attention to Anthony Powell and for having encouraged early investigations; Mr. Arthur Mizener for asking Mr. Powell a few questions on my behalf and for words of good cheer; Professor George Murphy for suggested revisions; Miss Susanne Enos of the Falvey Memorial Library for assistance with research; the Reverend Joseph A. Flaherty, former Vice-President of Villanova University, for help in finding money to pay the typist; and Mr. Powell's publishers and agents for permission to reprint various sections of his work.

NEIL BRENNAN

Villanova University

Contents

Chronology

1814 Anthony Powell's maternal grandfather born, Edmund Wells-Dymoke, of Grebby Hall, Lincolnshire.

1847 Anthony Powell's paternal grandfather born, Lionel Lewis Powell, of The Elms, Melton Mowbray.

1864 Marriage of Edmund Lionel Wells-Dymoke to Laura de Blair Jefferson of London.

1878 Marriage of Lionel Lewis Powell to Jessie Kate Adcock, of North Lodge, Melton Mowbray.

1882 Anthony Powell's father born, Philip Lionel William Powell.

1897 P. L. W. Powell becomes a military cadet at Sandhurst.

1901 Lt. P. L. W. Powell serves at nineteen with the Welch Regiment in South Africa against the Boers.

1903 His sister Katherine marries Arthur Edmund Bonsey of Leonard Stanley House, Stonehouse, Gloucester.

1904 Capt. P. L. W. Powell marries Maud Mary Wells-Dymoke; marriage of her sister Cicely de Nyden to the Reverend Oscar Worne.

1905 Anthony Dymoke Powell (pronounced "Antony Diemoke Pole") born, December 21.

1908 Capt. P. L. W. Powell becomes adjutant of the 13th London Regiment, The Kensingtons.

1912 Death of Lionel Lewis Powell, V.D., M.R.C.S., Lt. Col. Commandant and Hon. Col., Ist V.B. Leicester Regiment. Birth of Violet Pakenham, third daughter of the fifth earl of Longford.

1914 Outbreak of World War I. Powell's father goes with his regiment to France and Belgium.

1915 Death in battle of the Earl of Longford.

1916 Maj. P. L. W. Powell awarded the Distinguished Service Order. Anthony Powell enters a private preparatory school.

1918 Lt. Col. P. L. W. Powell is made a Companion of the British Empire.

1919 Anthony Powell enters Eton.

1920 Becomes a member of the Eton Arts Society with Henry Green.

1923 Studies French near Tours in the summer; matriculates at Balliol College, Oxford, one year after Graham Greene and Cyril Connolly.

1924 To Finland in the summer with his father.
1926 Down from Oxford, he joins the firm of Duckworth as a publisher's reader and editorial assistant to "learn the business."
1928 Father resigns from the army for reasons of health. Duckworth's publishes Powell's first book, his edition of the Barnard Letters, in November. Visit to Paris, Sylvia Beach's bookshop; meets Ford Madox Ford.
1930 Powell's father becomes a barrister-ât-law in the Inner Temple. Vacation in southern France, near Toulon; begins first novel.
1931 First novel, *Afternoon Men,* published by Duckworth's in May.
1932 Second novel, *Venusberg,* published in December; dedicated to Constant and Florence Lambert.
1933 Third novel, *From a View to a Death,* published in October; dedicated to John and Evelyn Heygate.
1934 Marries Lady Violet Pakenham, December 3; honeymoon in Greece.
1935 Residence at 47 Great Ormond Street, London. Works as a scriptwriter for Warner Brothers in England.
1936 Fourth novel, *Agents and Patients,* published in January; dedicated "For Violet Georgiana." Trip to Russia. Leaves Duckworth's, becomes a scriptwriter for Warner Brothers.
1937 Moves to 1 Chester Gate, Regent's Park, London; to Hollywood by way of the Panama Canal.
1939 Fifth novel, *What's Become of Waring,* published in January, dedicated "For Edith" Sitwell. Outbreak of World War II, September 3: commissioned a lieutenant in the Welch Regiment in December; begins eighteen-month tour of duty in Northern Ireland.
1940 Powell's first child, his son Tristram Roger Dymoke, christened May 25.
1941 Attached to headquarters of the 53rd Division; becomes staff liaison officer with Army Intelligence (G.S.O.3) at the War Office in August.
1943 Promoted to the rank of major (G.S.O.2).
1944 Service in France and Belgium; attached to 21st Army Group.
1945 Awarded the Order of the White Lion of Czechoslovakia; Order of the Oaken Crown of Luxembourg; Croix de Guerre of Luxembourg; and the Order of Leopold II of Belgium. Demobilized in September.
1946 Second son, John Marmion Anthony, christened February 22. Book reviewing for the *Spectator* and occasional journalism.
1947 Joins the staff of the *Times Literary Supplement* under the editorship of Alan Pryce-Jones.

Chronology

1948 Powell's study of John Aubrey is published in December; dedicated to Malcolm Muggeridge.
1949 Acquires a Regency house, The Chantry, near Frome, Somerset.
1951 First volume of *The Music of Time* published in January, *A Question of Upbringing*; dedicated to his son Tristram.
1952 Second volume of *The Music of Time* published in June, *A Buyer's Market*; dedicated to Osbert and Karen Lancaster.
1953 Joins the *Punch* Table under the editorship of Malcolm Muggeridge in March.
1954 Powell's mother dies.
1955 Third volume of *The Music of Time* published in May, *The Acceptance World*; dedicated to Adrian Daintrey.
1957 Summer visit to Austria. Fourth volume of *The Music of Time* published in October, *At Lady Molly's*; dedicated to his son John.
1958 Summer visit to Italy.
1959 Following Malcolm Muggeridge's resignation from *Punch*, Powell becomes a book reviewer for the *Daily Telegraph*. Father dies, December 31.
1960 Fifth volume of *The Music of Time* published in June, *Casanova's Chinese Restaurant*; dedicated "For Harry and Rosie," Sir Henry and Lady d'Avigdor-Goldsmid.
1961 Visits the United States, lecturing informally at Dartmouth, Amherst, and Cornell. Some reviews for the *New York Times*.
1962 Appointed a trustee of the National Portrait Gallery. Sixth volume of *The Music of Time* published in June, *The Kindly Ones*; dedicated to Robert Wyndham Ketton-Cremer.
1964 Seventh volume of *The Music of Time* published in February, *The Valley of Bones*; dedicated "For Arthur and Rosemary" Mizener, of Cornell.
1965 Visits the United States in May. Son John attends Cornell.
1966 Eighth volume of *The Music of Time* published in September, *The Soldier's Art*; dedicated to Roy Fuller.
1968 Ninth volume of *The Music of Time* published in October, *The Military Philosophers*; dedicated "For Georgina."
1971 Tenth volume of *The Music of Time* published in February, *Books Do Furnish a Room*; dedicated "For Rupert," perhaps Rupert Hart-Davis. Two plays, with set designs by Osbert Lancaster, published together in August, *The Garden God* and *The Rest I'll Whistle*.
1973 Eleventh volume of *The Music of Time,* published in July, *Temporary Kings*.

CHAPTER 1

A Man of Family and Tradition

WHETHER genes play a role in determining an artist's career is not really a vital issue in dealing with the origins of Anthony Powell. It is enough if an artist thinks heredity is important; and Powell in a quiet way has always paid attention to heredity, to his own and to his characters'. In a review of a book about mad eighteenth-century poet Christopher Smart, Powell remarks a bit wryly that he himself had "often pondered Smart's lines.... 'Let Powell, house of Powell rejoice with Synochitis a precious stone abused by ancient sorcerers....' "[1] The incoherence of Smart's sentence allows its meanings to branch out richly, if more than a little obscurely; but its reference to the "house of Powell" points to a social entity—to a far-flung house which Powell himself views with amusement as well as affection. A family tree should always be considered—he implies in chiding a biographer—in one way or in another. That passionate radical of the 1900's Annie Besant was born in the Wood family, for instance; but her biographer "makes less of this Wood relationship than might be expected. No doubt too much can be attributed to traits of kinship," Powell admits, "but it is of interest that energies and sympathies of that sort had already shown themselves in the family.... Kitty O'Shea, the lady for whose sake Parnell wrecked his career, was also a Wood, Mrs. Besant's second-cousin."[2]

I *The House of Powell*

The "house of Powell" is of Welsh origin. After six hundred years of English domination Wales might be thought to have been thoroughly anglicized, but the vast hill-top castles still to be seen, which Edward I built to keep the Welsh in subjugation, have come to symbolize instead Welsh tenacity. Wales even has its equivalent of the Irish Republican Army, a fact brought to the attention of the world in the 1950's when the planned dedication of a dam on the borders of Wales led to a threat to blow up its dedicator, Queen Elizabeth. A short time later patriots from Scotland had to steal the Stone of Scone from the coronation chair in Westminster Abbey to get attention focused on the continuation of their own national existence. Perhaps only in Cornwall, that fourth refugee center for the Celts of the Dark Ages, has the feeling of being Celtic first been submerged by intermarriage. In Anthony Powell, there remains an island of quiet but firm allegiance to things Welsh.

As Celts, the Welsh have a self-image similar in another way to that of the Irish: as a people they are otherworldly in their attitudes—less practical than the English perhaps, but at the same time more spiritual. In reviewing *The Dictionary of Welsh Biography*, Powell questions the dictionary's principle of selection: its editor had excluded people, however famous, who were merely "of Welsh descent." "In compiling a work of this kind stringent rules must be applied," Powell agrees. "All the same, the regulation inevitably leads to some anomalies." And he finds his in the seventeenth-century school of poetry labeled "metaphysical" because of its religious bent: "George Herbert and Henry Vaughan are allowed: John Donne and Thomas Traherne excluded: yet all these poets might reasonably be held to be linked together in their poetry and thought by their Welsh origins."[3] Powell of course cannot be described as a religious artist—indeed, his novels are devoid of religious doctrine, as critics have noted[4]—yet what have been called the "spiritual realities" figure prominently in three of his novels. In evaluating their role in his art, the author's open mind on the subject should also be noted.

As a matter of fact, Anthony Powell himself would be excluded from a dictionary of Welsh biography edited so stringently. Neither of his parents was born in Wales, and he himself has had no close public association with the "Principality," although for a time during World War II he served as an officer in the Welch Regiment.

The family "Powell, formerly of the Travely and Landshipping House"—as Anthony Powell's branch of the family is called in *Burke's Landed Gentry*—was of Welsh origin and, as records attest, had "lived for at least three centuries within the adjacent parishes of Brilley, Herefordshire, and Llowes and Clyro, Radnorshire." The Travely was a house at Llowes just inside the border of Wales which the family occupied "from a period prior to 1638 until the latter half of the nineteenth century." In Powell's biography of the Welsh scholar John Aubrey he notes that Aubrey's family was not alone in having come out of Wales to settle in England: Vaughans, Powells, and Beavans had done so too.[5] And perhaps a note of melancholy is to be detected in his remark (concerning the Welsh dictionary under review) that "the famous eighteenth-century actor William Powell does not get a place because (like Garrick) he was born in Hereford."

Anthony Powell's own branch of the family had moved out from the homeland—or perhaps one should say, recalling the Anglo-Saxon invasions, back to the homeland. At the time his father was born, they inhabited an estate of some note in the annals of fox hunting: the Elms at Melton Mowbray in the Midlands of England. The Powell coat of arms depicts a lion rampant among goats' heads, and the family motto is "True to the End"; but, with the grandfather a colonel in the Leicestershire Territorials (a branch of the British army equivalent to the American National Guard), the family had a dual loyalty. In the end it was true both to Wales and to the king.

Some feeling of national kinship seems to have been a factor in inducing Powell to devote years of his life to his study of Welshman John Aubrey. As a Welshman of the seventeenth century, Aubrey had proved his otherworldliness by spending his life collecting biographical data—for biographies he could never get around to writing. Yet the service that this gentle antiquarian and his notes have rendered to British history, and to our knowledge of his era, is not easily calculated. Indeed, when Powell came in the late 1940's to choose a name for the narrator of his great novel *The Music of Time,* a narrator who is self-effacing and unambitious, he chose a name that figures often in the notes Aubrey left. Sir Leoline Jenkins was a Welsh knight who, Aubrey tells us, had a father who "was a good plaine countrey-man," and he himself had the spirit of the clan: "David Jenkins, that was prisoner in the Tower (maried a sister of Sir John Aubrey) was some remote kin to him; and looking on him as a boy towardly, diligent, and good, he contributed something towards his Education."[6] In the name of Nicholas Jenkins Powell has given a projection to this generous, curious spirit of Wales; and critics of *The Music of Time* who carp that Nick Jenkins tells us too little about himself might also note Powell's observation that, among all Celtic peoples, the Welsh are the least given to self-revelation.

II *Powell's Father*

While teaching a course in creative writing at an American university, one Englishman asked a colleague in some puzzlement: "Why do all my students imitate Joyce and Kafka?" "So that their fathers won't understand them," he was told. If this quirk is typical of the American writer, Anthony Powell is quite un-American. Even his first novel, *Afternoon Men,* written years before he became a father himself, contains as father figure one of the most admirable characters in the novel. He is George Nunnery, the father of the heroine: "You must meet old Nunnery. . . . He's one of those brilliant men whose mind has become a complete blank," a rather blank-minded character exclaims. "All the brains and understanding there and never the least danger that they are going to become a nuisance" (64). And George Nunnery's daughter insists that all the young men courting her come to meet her father: "You'll like him. . . . He's a curious little man with a walrus moustache . . . a retired failure, you see" (89). At the time Powell published this novel in 1931, his own father might have been described in terms akin to these. Although himself the son of a colonel, Powell's father had reached only the rank of lieutenant colonel—though his career at several points had seemed promising enough—before ill-health forced him to retire.

Philip Lionel William Powell, as he was christened, entered the army from Sandhurst in 1901, his obituary reports; and he "served when he was nineteen in the South African War as a Second Lieutenant, First Battalion, The Welch Regiment, receiving the Queen's Medal."[7] In 1904 he was married and he became a father the following year; yet, like his own father, he was destined to have only one son. Anthony Dymoke Powell, born late in 1905, thus spent the years of his childhood, which are in theory most formative, in a military environment. In 1909 his father was appointed adjutant to the 13th London Regiment, known as the Kensingtons; and, until the regiment went overseas at the outbreak of war in 1914, the boy saw army life from inside. What he saw impressed him.

Since the creation of Gilbert and Sullivan's "very model of a modern Major-General," in *The Pirates of Penzance,* the army officer in literature has not often been treated sympathetically. Although James Gould Cozzens in *Guard of Honor* (1948) and Ernest Hemingway in *Across the River and into the Trees* (1950) have regarded the problems of military command with sympathy, their sympathy came late and has not been widely shared.

However, Powell has created some of the most likable army officers in modern fiction, from Captain Hudson, who writes biography in a clean style in *What's Become of Waring,* to Major General Aylmer Conyers, whose modesty and wisdom sound recurrent chords in *The Music of Time.* To understand the value system underlying Powell's art, it may be well to examine more closely his relation to the British army and his attitude toward it. Neither is simple.

III *Army Life and Powell's Novels*

The sixth volume of Powell's great work *The Music of Time* takes us in a sense to the beginnings of his army experience, to the household of Captain Jenkins near Aldershot, the great British military base. It is the day the Great War begins, and within a few weeks Captain Jenkins has left his family for the duration. Powell's own father and his regiment were in Belgium within ten days of the outbreak of the war. Captain Powell was later promoted to brigade major of the 95th Infantry Brigade, was mentioned in dispatches, and in 1916 was awarded the Distinguished Service Order. When his son spoke thirty years later deprecating the medals he himself had been awarded by the Luxembourg, Belgian, and Czech governments after

World War II he was not being falsely modest; he was merely aware his own medals were honorific in comparison. And young Powell saw more than empty honor in the professional family. In *The Music of Time* (6.51) the children of seven families receive private tutelage from Miss Orchard; six of their fathers are killed in the war (6.74); only Captain Jenkins survives.

After World War I, Powell's father was awarded a C.B.E., that is, made a Companion of the British Empire, and was appointed to the staff of the War Office. Although Anthony Powell was away at school during much of the following period, his vacations took him back into military society; and, when his father was appointed an attaché to the British Military Mission to Finland in 1924, he experienced embassy life abroad. He was introduced to Marshall Mannerheim, the savior of Finland; and he had, he recalls, a brief talk with him.[8] No doubt it was during this period that Anthony Powell's familiarity with the Baltic countries began, the familiarity that informs his second novel, *Venusberg*. On the other hand, there seems to be no indication that he accompanied his father to China in 1927, when his father was transferred to the Shanghai Defence Force. Unfortunately, in China Colonel Powell's health broke down; invalided home, he retired from the army the following year.[9] At least as late as 1936, however, Colonel Powell was still attending reunion dinners with his former comrades of the Welch Regiment; there seems little doubt of his devotion to the service.

Examining passages where Anthony Powell speaks in his own voice, we also find little question as to his devotion to the service. A history of the school from which his father graduated with an officer's commission is reviewed by Powell with an eye on the problems of the school as seen from the top, and he notes first the complexities involved. For Sandhurst, as for West Point, the main problem was and is to devise a system of education "to train the less bright specimens in a manner that insures their efficiency in carrying out demanding, tedious, often soul-destroying duties," Powell says, "while, at the same time, such glittering specimens as have fallen into the net must not be deprived of all originality, breadth of view and mental energy by the grind of early routine."[10] Among the glittering specimens, we might mention Winston Churchill, who graduated from Sandhurst about the time officer candidate Powell arrived.

Armies long maintained tend to form, within the larger society of the civilian world, a quasi-closed society of their own and therefore to develop their own rules and traditions. Children of American army families speak of themselves as "Army brats," for instance, which to the outsider seems a harsh sort of self-denigration; but the phrase, part of a tradition, is used with affection and pride. British army life in the time of Powell's youth tended to be similarly clannish, in part because vast distances often separated the army branch of a family from its "civilian" relatives. Stringham's mother in *The Music of Time* shows an insider's knowledge upon meeting the narrator (and discovering that he is on his way to the West of England where his father is stationed) by speaking of her first husband as "a soldier" and by asking Nick Jenkins, in his last year of public school, if he is "going to be a soldier, too?" (1.61). Her first husband, Lord Warrington, was a general; but the word "soldier" is used with pride by those associated with the service, however disparaging it may seem to outsiders.

As a matter of fact, the larger world has its own illusions about life in the army, as a character points out in *The Music of Time*: "It's a misapprehension to suppose, as most people do, that the army is inherently different from other communities. The hierarchy and discipline give an outward illusion of difference, but there are personalities of every sort . . . weak-willed generals and strong-willed privates" (7.108). Few better introductions to "the idea of society" could have been devised, in fact, for the future creator of English literature's most complex society. Even in the American army, "society" is more complex than the outsider at first realizes. A Capt. George Patton may one year live next door to a Maj. Omar Bradley; and, while Patton, as a millionaire, may travel from post to post with a string of polo ponies, Bradley—his superior in rank but a man dependent upon his salary—may count himself lucky to have a new Ford from time to time. And a year later both may meet with equal rank in a situation in which wealth is irrelevant.

In the British army the situation is further complicated by the intrusion of family connection and aristocratic title. The poor brother of an earl of ancient lineage may be the commanding officer of a regiment in which a rich beer magnate's son commands merely a platoon. From drill parade, where only rank would count, to leaves in Paris—where wealth would tend to bed the lieutenant at the Ritz and, lack of it, the colonel in a dingy Hotel d'Angleterre—the network of relations between them would have almost infinite ramifications.

IV *Class Structure and Tradition*

The myth that in Britain all people are either "U" or "Non-U" —either "in" as members of the Upper Class or "out"—is one that Americans have swallowed to the detriment of their understanding of what the later novels of Powell are trying to do. Our assumption is that the United States, being a country where all men are created equal, has managed to elude the invidious pigeonholing by class that our ancestors fled. That Americans have created a classless society is part of the "American myth," Powell remarks, "an extraordinary piece of unreality. . . . Who, having spent 24 hours in the United States, could possibly suppose there is no 'rank and social distinction'?"[11] Americans have agreed. One of them, Louis Auchincloss, sees great complexity even within American society:

> Most people who write about society, whether they are novelists or sociologists or simply gossip columnists, make the basic error of assuming that there must be some consistency in its standards. They take for granted there are rules which govern the qualification of those seeking admission, that if one has been gently born or if one can play polo . . . one may tap with confidence at any closed gate. When the rules are not seen to apply, the observer concludes that they once did, but have since broken down. . . . What Proust alone had the patience to piece out is that any society will apply all known standards together or individually, or in any combination needed, to include a maverick who happens to please, or to exclude an otherwise acceptable person who happens not to. Nor are society people conscious of the least inconsistency in acting so. They keep no records, and they have no written constitution. Why should their rules be defined in any way other than by a list of exceptions to them?[12]

Another feature of society as much to be noted in the army as elsewhere is status variability in time. After pointing out that even Catherine the Great gossiped about Madame de Staël and her "disadvantageous marriage," Powell adds that "It is interesting to note that Mme de Staël's father had begun life as a bank clerk, her mother as a governess: and that it is not only in modern times, as is sometimes implied, that careers began to be forged by talent and industry."[13] The Establishment as it is called—the power structure in Britain as seen from below, with church, militia, and civil service dominating the country and in turn being dominated by an established upper class—has been widely attacked in England since World War II. What Powell observed in the army of his childhood was rather a flexible "establishment" in which the possibility of escalation in rank was a perennial factor wrecking any simplistic societal pattern.

"If genealogy is anything else but simply and solely the truth about ancestors, it is worthless," Powell insists. Although the study of genealogy is "commonly thought of as a pursuit best adapted to keeping the various classes of society apart," it is a study which reveals "how extraordinarily close the classes are—and have always been—together." Powell traces the class system back to the military aristocracy who owned their lands through service to the king; heavy cavalrymen were expected to assemble for combat in person: the knights, as troopers; the barons, as officers. Yet even in those days in England there were no "legal and absolute class barriers."[14] Any survey of his remarks on class must reach the conclusion that the only "establishment" Powell supports is a flexible "establishment" in which transits take place both up and down. Chateaubriand was the "younger son of an immensely ancient Breton family," Powell remarks, a family having the "long pedigrees and short purses of Wales of the past, a less feudalised, but somewhat similar Celtic community where younger sons . . . might easily return to tilling the soil."[15]

Powell and his friend Evelyn Waugh take a similar view of the obloquy that has fallen over the idea of class. Both attribute it to oversimple compartmentalizing, to the "in or out simplism." "After the Civil Wars and the Revolution of 1688," Powell says, "the great Whig lords were in the saddle, whose concept of the social order was that a gulf should yawn between themselves and the mere gentry . . . ." These magnates "had little interest in the strict regulation of a privilege—that of bearing arms—

which they and the poorest gentry shared."[16] Waugh speaks in a similar vein of the irresponsibility of apartheid as a simple cleavage, with pigmentation "fantastically . . . the determining factor, in which Cardinal Garcias and the Hottentot savage are equal on one side; you, gentle reader, and the white oaf equal on the other."[17]

Some of Powell's critics have failed to help their readers in this matter of class. Even a critic born in England and writing in *The New Yorker* has pointed to *The Music of Time* as promulgating a view he identifies, oddly, as Powell's—a "view that the human race is divided into two sections—one that counts, consisting of Old Etonians, and one that doesn't, consisting of people who are either grubby or comic and who didn't attend the school."[18] Even the first volume of *The Music of Time* makes it abundantly clear, however, that four boys can graduate from the same public school into four widely different and quickly shifting social positions, with only one of them (Stringham) being wholly "in" but being at the same time the one most on the way "out." Understanding of such a complexity can come only after we admit the truth: in Powell's view, society is almost infinitely complex, and there is no simple key to its door, Etonian or otherwise.

V *Snobbery?*

What distinguishes Powell as a novelist in this egalitarian age is his open admission that he likes the upper classes as well as—perhaps a bit better than—other classes. Often Powell seems in his own mind to be merely redressing a balance, pulling on an undermanned team with Yeats, Waugh, and Joseph Conrad. "But if Dostoevsky is applauded . . . for satirising decadent Russian nobles and officials, why should it be unfair for Conrad to make fun of decadent revolutionaries?" he asks. "After all, you can be . . . a decadent trade unionist, as easily, for example, as a decadent aristocrat. Decadence is no respector of social position."[19] Similarly, when Marcel Proust is accused of being a social climber, Powell notes the French novelist's origin in "a rich, but irredeemably middle-class family"; admits that Proust's urge to know dukes may not be a "particularly attractive" form of climbing; but argues that "it is not the only sort of social penetration. People sometimes seem to forget that, and lose a sense of proportion. After all, it is not unknown for the ambitious to climb in such hierarchies as, say, the Church or the Labour party."[20]

Aldous Huxley has observed wisely that the label "snob" has been too simply applied to genetic snobbery which "is elsewhere on the decline." "All men," he argues, "are snobs about something," be it about their taste in art, their gas mileage, or their capacity with booze. "The value of snobbery in general, its humanistic 'point,' consists in its power to stimulate activity. A society with plenty of snobberies is like a dog with plenty of fleas; it is not likely to become comatose."[21] Much of the humor in Powell is missed if we do not notice that he shares Huxley's double view: that snobbery as a part of human nature is not something to be detested but something to be observed with irony and tolerance; and it is to be observed far more variously than is sometimes supposed. The man who prides himself on hating snobs, of the social kind, is merely exposing his own brand of snobbery—his feeling of superiority as a man with a "broader mind" than other men.

However, when Thomas Hardy's dull wife is seen in a memoir parading her middle-class pretensions before her novelist husband, Powell finds an exhibition of snobbery not easily stomached.[22] An aristocracy without culture is more nauseating. Finding irony in the title selected by the Marqués de Villavieja for his autobiography, *Life Has Been Good,* Powell describes the book as "a hideous little gift monument to the complacency, pretentiousness, and intellectual bankruptcy of society in the sixty years preceding the war."[23] The class into which a man is born is not the only class that counts with Powell, and his concern with strata of intelligence and culture can also be traced back to family roots.

VI *Family Roots*

Precisely what status Powell's own family had in military society is not easy to determine. Gentlemen do not parade such matters and consequently are often misunderstood. One comic novelist much admired by Powell and his friends, P. G. Wodehouse, has been described—as if the character Jeeves were his alter ego—as entering Bloomsbury by the servant's entrance.[24] But Powell chides the first full-length study of Wodehouse for failing to tell its readers "that Mr. Wodehouse himself belongs to a cadet branch of an unusually ancient family, holding one of the oldest baronetcies extant (of which he could, in theory, be the heir), later submerged in an earldom. In other words, the nostalgia for an aristocratic world of fantasy has some obvious basis. . . ."[25]

Powell's own name is to be found in Debrett's *Peerage*, and his tastes must be described as aristocratic; but he does not classify himself as an aristocrat. "On the whole aristocrats do not become novelists," he says in discussing Lampedusa's *The Leopard*. "I use the word 'aristocrats' here purely as a convenient term to describe persons who are the actual holders of comparatively ancient titles together with landed possessions of considerable extent and an ancestry connecting them closely with other families of the same sort."[26] Powell defines his own social position much more modestly—as we see when he takes to task the biographer of an American novelist's "wife" for having made "great play with the grandeur" of Nora Crane's earlier marriage to a Captain Stewart of the Gordon Highlanders: "Captain Stewart was a younger son whose father had been made a baronet for military services in India. Stewart himself later received a K.C.M.G. for his work in what is now Kenya. To talk about the Stewart family opening 'charmed circles of London society' and Harrington Gardens being 'fashionable' is surely to lose sense of proportion." He describes the Stewart family as "a typically honourable, hard-working Services family. It seems worth making this point, because in some ways the story would have been *less* extraordinary if the marriage had been more dazzlingly aristocratic and racketty."[27]

On the other hand, though Powell's father came from "a typically honourable, hard-working Service family," he had married a girl whose ties to the English aristocracy were centuries old: "Maud Mary, daughter and eventual heir of Edmund Lionel Wells-Dymoke, formerly of Grebby Hall, Lincolnshire." Perhaps wealth was involved too. When the colonel's will was probated in 1960 after an "unremunerative" army career, as well as one as a barrister that must have been brief, beginning as it did when he was nearly fifty, he left an estate on which the inheritance taxes came to about a quarter of a million dollars.[28] It is not likely that young Anthony Powell ever felt financially desperate. It also seems clear that, at least in his school days, he was not permitted to feel affluent. There were impeccable family connections, without much room for grandeur.

Powell's contemporary Evelyn Waugh, in contrast, came from a family less well connected and less wealthy; but he cut a brighter swathe through Oxford society by adopting so liberal a financial policy that it grayed his father's hair.[29] Powell's experience seems to have been more in keeping with the modesty of his social pretensions. We might note, however, that in *The Music of Time* the bungalow that the narrator's family rents in 1914 is staffed by four servants: a chef, a parlormaid, a housemaid, and a gardener, with the occasional added services of the gardener's wife and a male "striker"—a regular army soldier acting as valet and handyman. Yet Captain Jenkins considers himself poor in relation to his guest General Conyers (6.41).

VII *Comic Glamor?*

Powell's sense of the comic in his novels has often been marked by his linkage of glamor with the comic. In *The Music of Time* one character even gains social power among royal friends by bizarre practical jokes. Such a mingling of glamor and comedy is unusual in British fiction, but the root of it in Powell's novels may be discerned in his own family history, in the marriage of Lt. L. P. W. Powell to Maud Mary Wells-Dymoke.

Many claim to have come to England with William the Conqueror. But as one English historian of the Dymoke family observes, "few indeed, even of our best families, can trace their lineage so far back and with such certainty as the Dymokes of Scrivelsby."[30] Robert Marmion, who married a niece of Baldwin II, King of Jerusalem, had received the Dymoke estate of Scrivelsby from Henry II's son Prince Henry around 1170. Nine generations later in the War of the Roses his descendant Sir Thomas Dymoke formed the Kingmaker's Plot with his brother-in-law Baron Willoughby d'Eresby and restored Henry VI briefly to the throne; and both Dymoke and d'Eresby were beheaded for treason in 1470. Loyalty, or treason, of a different sort was displayed a century later when Sir Robert Dymoke was imprisoned in the Tower of London as a recusant and died there for his faith in 1580. The title by which he entered history has an irony of its own, however: he is known as "the Martyr Champion."

The Championship of the Kings of England had come down with the possession of Scrivelsby through the centuries: each coronation time the head of the Dymoke family mounted the king's charger to enter Westminster Hall, where the Coronation Banquet was being held, to do his duty. Samuel Pepys describes the ceremony that marked the Restoration of the Stuarts, the coronation of Charles II in 1661. The sight of thousands of people inside lining the galleries excited Pepys:

> But, above all, was these three Lords, Northumberland, and Suffolke, and the Duke of Ormond, coming before the courses on horseback, and staying so all dinner-time, and at last bringing up the King's Champion, all in armour on horseback, with his speare and targett [shield] carried before him. And a Herald proclaims "That if any dare deny Charles Stuart to be lawful King of England, here was a Champion that would fight with him"; and with these words, the Champion flings down his gauntlet, and all this he do three times in his going up towards the King's table. To which, when he is come, the King drinks to him, and then sends him the cup which is of gold, and he drinks it off, and then rides back again with the cup in his hand.[31]

An old ballad celebrates the winning of the hand of Margaret de Ludlow, the Marmion heiress, by Sir John Dymoke in the fourteenth century:

> And ever since, when England's Kings
> Are diadem'd—no matter where—
> The Champion Dymoke boldly flings
> His glove, should treason venture there.[32]

But, as we have seen, not all were able to define "treason" to their monarch's satisfaction.

Not all Champions added to the dignity of the family either. When the Champion of James II in 1685 got off his horse to kiss the king's hand, according to William Prynne's diary, he "fell down all his length in the hall . . . whereupon the queen sayd 'see you, love, what a weak Champion you have.' To which the King sayd nothing, but laught, and the Champion excused himself, pretending his armour was heavy, and he himself was weak with sickness." Pretending? He died within the year. A finer mixture of pomp and comic circumstance was seen at the coronation of George IV in 1821. According to the London *Times*, "The knightly appearance and gallant deportment of the Champion obviously gave considerable pleasure to his Majesty, who, taking the goblet . . . drank to the bold challenger, with a corresponding air of gaiety. The Champion, on his part, having received the cup, drank to the King, but pronounced the words 'Long live his Majesty King George IV' in somewhat of a schoolboy tone."[33]

On this occasion the "knight" was a young Mr. Dymoke acting on behalf of his father, a clergyman for whom so martial a duty would have been unseemly; and, riding steel-shod on the parquet between the Marquis of Anglesea and the Duke of Wellington, he may have been understandably nervous. Yet in an age of railways and steam engines, the picture of an armored knight riding into Westminster Hall to do battle was too quixotic to be missed by English wits; and satiric verse gave the coup de grace to the ceremony—at least for the rest of the century.[34] And by 1895, after scores of coronations, only seven of the jeweled gold cups remained at Scrivelsby; for the family had had its economic difficulties.

VIII *Cultural Heritage*

One of these difficulties oddly enough had a literary origin. A standard analysis has it that class is determined by difference in "rank, wealth and education"; and, when we turn to the intellectual and cultural status of Anthony Powell's family, we find a mild distinction, too. The Dymokes figured modestly in literary history when Shakespeare's contemporary Samuel Daniel ("tipped by some as the Rival Poet" alluded to in Shakespeare's sonnets) dedicated his own sonnets in 1602 "to his patron, Sir Edward Dymoke,"[35] the son of "the Martyr Champion." But about that time Sir Edward's younger brother Talboys was writing a play which proved far more expensive; it satirized his tyrant uncle, the second Earl of Lincoln, and resulted in a fine of £1000. "The huge fine upon Sir Edward, representing at least ten or twelve thousand pounds according to present values," a scholar observed in 1934, "must have been an important cause in the financial decline of the family."[36] Though the family was also impoverished by its loyalty to Charles I at the time of the Puritan Revolution, literary creativity had exacted more than its usual price.

Literature came into Powell's childhood through more lines than the genealogical, of course. Discussing a group of six once famous but forgotten literary works, Powell could recall having been exposed at home to three of them.[37] At least one copy of the Countess von Arnim's witty *Elizabeth and Her German Garden* was found "in every house of my childhood."[38] The fact that his father was admitted as a barrister-at-law to the Inner Temple within a year or two after retiring from the army attests also to a prior development of more than ordinary verbal and analytic skills. The home life of Anthony Powell as a child seems to have been culturally as well suited as his ancestry to the development of an artist who values the traditional virtues and the classic disciplines of art.

VIII *A Novelist of Manners*

Society as seen in the Welsh diaspora, or from the viewpoint of the Champions of England, or from the variegated life of the peacetime British army—society as a viable idea seeped into Powell's system as if by osmosis. He felt it whole and in its intricacy, something absorbed from childhood. As much as any twentieth-century British novelist he was prepared to write of its intricacies, its comedy, its manners. Though decades were to elapse before he found himself specifically a writer in the comedy-of-manners tradition, life had schooled him unconsciously to be the modern re-creator of the comedy of manners in the twentieth century's own form, the novel.

Mannerisms and eccentricities of course only point up the rich stuff of ordinary human nature on one level, and growing up in an advantageous position for their observation, Powell from youth had the unconscious knowledge that the way people behaved was important and that human balance was precarious. Failures to behave well—the rustic, the gauche, the uncouth—were comic, but equally comic were those obsessively concerned with behaving well: the hypocrite, the trend-seeker, the snob, the Emily Post devotee. It is between these poles of inept behavior that the comedy of manners takes its median way, well mannered but without stress, and Powell's family had provided the orientation. Yet it was only as *The Music of Time* got under way that Powell's unique talent came to be recognized.

Not until 1971, as a matter of fact, did the next logical step take place and Powell extend his talent to the creation of a play in the comedy-of-manners tradition. His first play, *The Garden God*,[39] might not at first seem to fit the comedy-of-manners tradition, as a matter of fact, but its scene (an archeological "dig" on a Greek island) functions as an open-air drawing room, its cast is highly educated, socially oriented and witty; and plot, dialogue, and style follow the tradition. Touched with fantasy twice, when the statue of Priapus admonishes the characters for their failures in the arena of love, the play retains its roots in social realism: wit and common sense lead to a reasonably happy resolution for the principals and for love, the garden god's concern. Both the inadequately restrained and the overly constrained, both the promiscuous television personality and the virginal archeologist provide amusement and are directed to better ways.

Powell's second play, *The Rest I'll Whistle*, is more overtly in the comedy-of-manners tradition. The setting of the first two acts is the Great Parlor of Trefwardine Court, a manor house on the border of Wales preserved as a national trust. Two people—an American professor and the curator's wife—arrive on the same day that the curator's daughter and a servant lad decide to leave. The professor appears uncouth, pushing his way into the house in pursuit of the rumor that the Welsh poet Henry Vaughan had once stayed there, and the curator's wife promises amusement of another sort, for she is a not-quite-reformed alcoholic.

Ironically, it is the American who proves in the end too well mannered; the suave and witty curator has a ruthless inner core and, encountering the professor in the Vaughan Room in the last act, foils his proposed elopement with his daughter to America. The curator turns out to be both the better scholar and the more flexibly mannered. But looking back from these plays, we see that Powell's novels had been skirting the comedy-of-manners tradition from the beginning.

CHAPTER 2

The Fox Hunters of Faringdon Folly

SCHOOL life for Powell seemed less benevolent at the start. About the time World War I began, he was sent to a preparatory school in Kent which he later compared to the infamous private school in Charles Dickens' novel *Nicholas Nickleby.* It "reflected in some degree the atmosphere, if not the conditions, of Dotheboys Hall."[1] As a consequence, when Powell arrived at Eton in 1919, he entered a world so different that it seemed an escape.

I *The Masters at Eton*

Eton College is organized as a series of some twenty-five houses, each quartering forty or fifty boys ranging in age from ten to eighteen. Powell had "the good fortune to be sent to a very 'bad' house," he says; he was amused by "the unusual personality" of the housemaster. Powell recalls him with affection as "bursting like a sea-lion into boys' rooms when they least expected him, playing the Wall Game with almost homicidal violence, giving imitations of Mr. Gladstone, performing on the harmonium at prayers in the evening while we sang *All Things Bright and Beautiful,* or hurrying feverishly through the passages with some huge volume illustrating the History of Footgear through the ages."[2] We might note that the schoolmaster Le Bas is similarly regarded with amusement early in *The Music of Time* (1.26-51), and later predominantly with detached affection (3.170-97).

It struck Powell as odd that men at Eton, who could have earned fortunes merely by walking across a music-hall stage, should teach unruly boys the classics: "It is true that sometimes masters proved unequal to the grueling course they had to run and left to be cabinet ministers or to become political bosses in truculent Balkan kingdoms, spheres where the maintenance of discipline came easily after what they had been through." But Powell's study of "peculiar mannerisms and eccentricities of appearance" seems to have begun at Eton; and again Powell, as a future comic novelist, was lucky: "There was a long-standing tradition at Eton that masters should be a little odd . . . the school was on the whole admirably staffed."[3]

One of the members of the staff in 1919 was Aldous Huxley, whose first story about the school, *The Farcical History of Richard Greenow* (1920), became a favorite with the boys at Eton. The headmaster of Aesop College in Huxley's story is himself a comic figure, but later the tables were to be reversed. Tall, gaunt, begoggled, Huxley was driven out of the teaching profession by callous boys—or so Cyril Connolly claims, perhaps rightly. Huxley later depicted Eton from the viewpoint of a schoolmaster in *Antic Hay* (1923), and a certain amount of revenge is secured, this time upon the pupils. His young schoolmaster Gumbril balks at reading interminable papers that echo the same Protestant clichés about Pio Nono, and he finds even more onerous his task as chapel monitor: "On the opposite side of the chapel two boys were grinning and whispering to one another behind their lifted Prayer Books. Gumbril frowned at them ferociously. . . . Their faces at once took on an expression of sickly piety" (9). At that moment the organ blasts forth, and Gumbril, uncomfortably seated, gets the idea for pneumatic trousers that effects his removal to the less ferocious world of London finance. Thirty years later Anthony Powell was to conclude another story of school days in the same chapel, with his narrator in *A Question of Upbringing* feeling "rather moved as the hymn rolled on"—and with a master frowning, as a group of boys "began to chant a descant of their own . . . not entirely disagreeable" (1.51).

Despite this difference in point of view, Aldous Huxley may well have been among the mentors whom Powell recalls with approval for saying to the boys, "If you don't learn some sort of civilized behaviour, England will become uninhabitable for everybody" (152). As a critic Huxley was saying much the same thing in the *Athenaeum* in that period. Whatever the source, such counsel seems to have been as influential in shaping

Powell the novelist as his education in the classics. His counsellors had wit enough to defend their own tradition, and the witticism of G. K. Chesterton, that Peterloo was lost on the playing fields of Eton, was countered by the headmaster's quiet but factual reply that the only Etonian present with the army that bloody day was cashiered for sympathy with the workers. Fifteen years after leaving Eton, when asked by a friend to contribute to a group of exposés of the British public school system, Powell took his title "The Wat'ry Glade" from Thomas Gray's fond "Ode on a Distant Prospect of Eton College" and exposed only his quite benign attitude toward the school—one benign enough to cause the editor who published it to express some disappointment.[4]

II *The Students at Eton*

Staff and curriculum at Eton differ only slightly from those of other English public schools. Admittedly, the school has the unusual policy of alloting each boy a room of his own; its library is excellent; and older boys at Eton do have an unusual degree of self-government. But such advantages can work for better or worse. What most distinguishes Eton from other schools is the student body itself. When, among the characters of *The Music of Time,* we meet the son of an earl who has been out all day trying to get his own son enrolled in "a public school," Americans may be shocked when they realize that the son is yet only a few months old (5.75). To be admitted is not easy; to get into the better schools is success in itself.

That mere entry into Eton connotes a certain status becomes understandable when the statistics of British power are surveyed: "A Labour Party study in 1963 found that 35 out of 107 directors of London's top financial houses were Old Etonians, as were 46 out of 149 directors of the large insurance firms."[5] Even in the arts "Etonians have been far more prolific than the products of any other public school, scoring 57 against Harrow's 28" in one random sampling, with other schools lagging far behind.[6] Yet the number of openings at Eton in any one year is severely limited; it is perhaps only natural that students accepted at Eton should feel chosen. The odd thing is that Powell, soon after entering Eton, joined a group who felt that Etonian students by and large had been poorly chosen. No other factor in Powell's life seems of more importance than the constitution of this small group, the "foxhunters of Faringdon Folly."

A dozen of Powell's contemporaries at Eton have since become famous in the arts and another dozen well known in political or commercial circles. Frank Pakenham, who was to become First Lord of the Admiralty and Powell's brother-in-law; Harold Acton, novelist and art historian; Robert Byron, the art critic and explorer; Cyril Connolly, most distinguished perhaps as editor of the *avant-garde* periodical *Horizon*; Bryan Guinness, the brewer and poet; Oliver Messel, the stage designer; George Blair, better known to the world under his pseudonym of George Orwell; and Henry Vincent Yorke, better known as the novelist Henry Green, are merely those closest to Powell personally. All affected his art in one way or another. But the ones to affect it the most were those who became fellow artists and close friends.

III *The Eton Society of Arts*

In 1920 half a dozen students, repelled by Eton's single-minded exaltation of sports and abetted by the headmaster, decided to band together. "I fled the company of those in my house," Henry Green recalls in his autobiography, "to a set then beginning to form. They were to be known by the term, which at school spelt leprosy, of 'the aesthetes.'"[7] This Society of Arts, as it was more officially called, came into being as a club to hold weekly debates on topics related to art; but, according to Henry Green, debates were few and wild speeches many. Such feelings as have led other artists to pen manifestos the members expressed in the pages of the *Eton Candle*, a magazine they founded and brought to national attention by soliciting contributions from Aldous Huxley, Osbert Sitwell, and Max Beerbohm.

The *Eton Candle* was edited by young Brian Howard, a man of great literary promise. His classmate Cyril Connolly recalls Howard as belonging "to a set of boys who were literary and artistic, but too lazy to gargle quotations and become inoculated with the virus of good taste latent in Eton teaching... and who gained much from Eton because of the little they gave. There was Harold Acton, a prince of courtesy, his brother William, Robert Byron... the two Messels, Anthony Powell... and Henry Green, who described them in his novel, *Blindness*." Connolly's cleverness had earned him a place in Eton's top club—and he snubbed Howard when invited to tea, perhaps wisely since the invitation was part of the plot of the Society of Arts to get one of its own elected to "Pop." The plot failed for the time being, but Connolly gave himself a failing mark in the affair. "They were the most vigorous group at Eton," he admitted in later years, "yet my moral cowardice and academic outlook debarred me from making friends with them."[8]

The hostility of the school forced the members of the Society of Arts into yet closer association; and perhaps, by inducing them to cast about for some method of self-defense, it intensified their sense of the comic. Green's novel *Blindness* (1926) might be cautiously explored in this connection. "It is 'the thing to do' now to throw stones at me as I sit at my window," the narrator of *Blindness* records in his diary, disgusted at the philistia of Noat ("Really, it might be Eton!"). "However, I have just called E. N. a 'milch cow' and shall on the first opportunity call D. J. B. a 'bovine goat,' which generally relieves matters. These epithets have the real authentic Noat Art Society touch, haven't they?" (9). In *Pack My Bag*, Green later stated that the Eton Society of Arts was provocative by plan: "we hoped to arouse more than disdain, we were out to annoy by being what we called 'amusing.'... We took a fearful joy in making fun of all that we thought the school held sacred.... We tried to show that we were proud [that] we were no good at football or cricket" (170).

This aggressiveness was supported not only by shared tastes but by self-respect, several of the members being, even then, Green insists, "well on in their age in literature, in their knowledge of painting and most of all in the point of view... towards the life led about us. We were witty already even by the low standard which was set by wider circles afterwards and which we were to know when we said goodbye to Oxford" (156). "We made humour one of our symbols," Harold Acton recalls in his *Memoirs of an Aesthete,* and fought esthetic crusades under the banner of the comic (119). The nostalgic essay on Eton that Anthony Powell contributed to *The Old School* suggests a more pacific attitude on his part—and he did later resign from the club—but he laments that he "was not in the division that bribed a tramp to sit with them during a Greek lesson, nor . . . one of the three boys who went to see their tutor one Sunday morning and found a glass of milk and a slice of cake on a plate by his desk. One drank the milk, one ate the cake and the third broke the plate. Perhaps the story has no lesson to teach," Powell adds, in the esthetic tradition, "but for some reason it has always amused me. There is something stimulating about it" (159-60).

At Eton the literary, social, and political attitudes that characterize the group in adult life took form. The beautiful and the comic were co-determinates in their appreciation of the arts. Typically the narrator of Green's *Blindness,* becoming "an absolute slave" of Gogol's *Dead Souls,* resolves solemnly to "keep this book for ever by me if I have enough cash to buy it with" (28). In the esthetic tradition of Oscar Wilde and Max Beerbohm, they were dandies: "I have fallen hopelessly in love with the ties in Bartlett's window. I shall have to buy them all, even though they are quite outrageous . . ." (18). It became a mark of their identity to express themselves fearlessly, even with a sort of joyful insolence. Typical was the occasion when three of them, dressed as Etonian dandies, intervened in a political election: "We found all the Socialist working-men-God-bless-them drawn up in rows on either side of the street, so we three went down the rows haranguing. We each got into the centre of groups, and expected to be killed at any moment, for there is something about me [the narrator] that makes that type see red." In apprehension, the police forced their way in and "marched us off, I shaking every man's hand that I could see. So we returned shouting madly. It was too wonderful; never to be forgotten" (23-25).

The central endeavor of the Eton esthetes was to sap the school's power "to turn the really clever . . . into people who pretend for all they are worth to be . . . mediocrities." In this campaign Harold Acton was standard bearer. Acton had come to "provincial" Eton from a villa above Florence, from a childhood acquaintance there with art critic Bernard Berenson: he had already traveled around the world. While still in his teens, he had met many of the great figures in contemporary art—Jean Cocteau and Sergei Pavlovich Diaghilev, for instance —as well as such peripheral figures as Lord Berners of Faringdon and Lady Ottoline Morrell of Garsington. Flamboyant of manner and brilliant of speech, Acton's natural preference was for the associates of Oscar Wilde; and, while an Eton schoolboy, he charmed Reggie Turner, one vacation, by reciting from memory long passages from Wilde. It was only natural, therefore, that Acton should appear "unnatural" at Eton.

In *Blindness,* Henry Green has the Secretary of the Noat Art Society remark that the average Noatian "cannot bear us as a set," and loathes "a person who glories in his eccentricity, which of course is true of all of us." But the Noatian regards Ben Gore "as really and actively evil, and I don't blame him as he does not know B. G., whose appearance is well calculated to sow the seeds of doubt and dislike in any righteous person" (6). Acton returned for his last year at Eton trailing a renewed acquaintance with others who had known Oscar Wilde, such as Max Beerbohm and Ada Leverson. He also chatted about meetings in Florence with Norman Douglas and the Sitwells, a spectrum which broadened the life of art for his friends at Eton.

When Powell left Eton in 1923, he bore away neither the grudge of Cyril Connolly, who expanded a theory later "that the experience undergone by boys at the great public schools is so intense as to dominate their lives and to arrest their development," nor the disdain of Osbert Sitwell, who describes his education for *Who's Who* as having been acquired during vacations from Eton. Powell claims to have been more fortunate: "The whole of my life at Eton was spent in well-deserved obscurity. I have no triumphs to look back on and I think myself lucky to have reached at last the House Library," the senior group who "managed" the house. "It was . . . possible for someone like myself, quite ludicrously bad at games and none too high up in the school, to achieve this distinction by intrigue on the part of friends" (154). But in these words there is a pose of indolence. Powell must be considered in John Wain's observation that "Eton has always lavished the resources of a superb humanistic tradition on its more forward pupils, making them free of a full-blown, sophisticated literary culture that either sinks them altogether or . . . gives them that characteristic Etonian brilliance, a kind of shimmer on the surface of everything they write."[10]

IV *Balliol College, Oxford University*

At Oxford, Powell found himself with the esthetes still, though not all of them matriculated as he did at Balliol College. Balliol has still perhaps as high a reputation as any college of Oxford University, and Powell entered it only a year behind the novelist Graham Greene, a fellow history major; but the Balliol Powell expected to experience no longer existed. "The Balliol of Jowett, the Balliol of the victims of the Somme, the Balliol of Graham Greene are three quite different institutions worthy of a brief 'Decline and Fall'" Cyril Connolly has remarked; and Powell agrees: "When I went up to Balliol in 1923, some vestige of the former greatness of the college remained, at least in the minds of those unconnected with the university."[11]

Benjamin Jowett as don and Master had educated great public leaders; after his death the sons of his pupils held their own, until the Somme, that early battle of World War I that wiped them out as a group. Evelyn Waugh, in a biography of one of them describes "the Etonians and their friends" of that generation as forming "yet another set in Balliol, an especially flamboyant and rambustious one. They took possession of the Anna (the Annandale Society, a dining club), and after their dinners took possession of the College, sending 'waterfalls' of crockery down XIV staircase, serenading Gordouli of Trinity, and chasing nonentities out of the quad." Waugh insists that their exclusiveness was not based on genetic class: "There were perfectly well-born men excluded from the 'Anna' while two Rhodes scholars were boon companions." Their own justification for their existence was their courage and their love of art. Oscar Wilde had dedicated a story to Billy

Grenfell's mother, and "They talked well. All of them loved poetry and many of them wrote it."[12] But one of their tutors, A. D. Lindsay, looked with disapproval on the antics of Grenfell and his friends; and, when he succeeded as Master in 1924, he "drove the aristocrats out of Balliol as effectively as the 'Anna' had chased the nonentities out of the quad."[13]

Anthony Powell looks upon A. D. ("Sandy") Lindsay, Master of Balliol (1924-49), as a Balliol disaster. He had had a reputation even among the future "victims of the Somme" as a dull tutor; yet the parents of the "Anna" aristocrats induced him to accompany their sons on summer travels abroad. In this regard, he resembles the don Sillery in *The Music of Time;* and yet, also like Sillery who is revealed to be a fellow traveler in the 1930's, Lindsay "was a thorough-going 'under-dogger' all his life."[14] As a Balliol student of more conservative bent, Powell's emotional conflict with "the Balliol of Graham Greene" was inevitable.

V *The Larger Oxford Life*

Powell, however, fell in love with Oxford itself. "It is right," Powell says, "that Aubrey's bones should lie at Oxford—the place that he used to long to see 'with the longing of a woman.' "[15] Yet when we wonder that Powell's major work, *The Music of Time*, should have, in the first ten volumes, devoted only two chapters to Oxford, perhaps the explanation is to be found in the brilliance of Evelyn Waugh's earlier depiction of their epoch together there in *Brideshead Revisited* (1945). Of all the attempts "to evoke for non-Oxonians the fusion of ancient traditions and . . . ultra-modernity which formed the quality of mid-twenty Oxford," Christopher Sykes insists, *Brideshead Revisited* is best. "People may believe that in this book he cannot be attempting a serious picture of this ancient seat of learning, but the picture is true."[16] Lord David Cecil has made almost the same claim for L. P. Hartley's *The Sixth Heaven* (1946). Wherever that laurel should be bestowed, by 1950 the Oxford-memoir-novel field was crowded.

Later volumes of *The Music of Time* do allude to esthetic Oxford. A poet named Mark Members who was at the university in the 1920's is said to have profited from the esthetes and to have passed on to psychoanalytic literature. More amusingly, we meet Hugo Tolland, the narrator's youngest brother-in-law, who is an Oxford esthete—one out of his time in the 1930's:

> "Even Sillery says Hugo goes too far. . . . He drives all the other dons quite mad. . . . The other undergraduates are very disapproving too. Apart from anything else, aesthetes have gone completely out of fashion at both universities these days. I told Hugo when I saw him the other day that he was hopelessly out of date."
>
> "What did he say?"
>
> " 'My dear, I love being *dated.* I hate all this bickering that goes on about politics. I wish I'd lived in the *Twenties* when people were *amusing.*' " (4.34)

The tone is that of Anthony Blanche in *Brideshead Revisited*, but the architecture is Powell's own.

The leader who set the tone of "Aesthetic Oxford" in the 1920's was the former Eton esthete Harold Acton. Although a dandy, Acton had more than a trace of toughness in his composition. When an Eton friend had invited him to luncheon at the Carlton Club on a visit to London, and there had pointed out an effeminate youth as being both an Oxford student and an esthete, Acton was disgusted: "There was already sufficient prejudice against art in England. . . . If that eunuch represented Oxford aestheticism something would have to be done about it soon." Peace might have come to the crasser world, but "those who loved beauty had a mission still, to combat ugliness and exterminate false prophets."[17] Accordingly, upon reaching Oxford, Acton founded *The Oxford Broom*, with the financial aid of a young relative of Mrs. Bernard Berenson—an "esthetic" broom to sweep away what Acton called "*fin-de-siècle* cobwebs." That autumn Duckworth's published Acton's first book of verse, *Aquarium* (1923), which had been solicited from him at Eton at the suggestion of the Sitwells. As a poet who had been "published" and as the founder of a new Oxford magazine, Acton was the outstanding man of his year at Oxford; and, chanting his poems through a megaphone from a Christ Church College balcony to crowds passing below, he did nothing to lower this panache.

"Oxford in the middle twenties vibrated with a fantastic ephemeral life that unaccountably burst into being, burnt for two years with a fierce brightness, then suddenly died," Daphne Fielding recalls.[18] The Earl of Birkenhead, in a memoir of his sister, connects the Bright Young People she was to lead in the late 1920's to the same golden Oxford days when "they drank milk and ether . . . ate Lobster Newburg from bronze Roman baths and wore with almost the significance of a livery high-necked sweaters."[19] Claud Cockburn in his autobiography also catches the orchidaceous coloring of the epoch. Both he and Acton describe, with the authority of cohorts, their envelopment of The Hypocrites Club. The club title itself was a multiple jest, coming as it did from the Greek for "Water is best" and, perhaps, from Beerbohm's story "The Happy Hypocrite." The club, housed in a "ramshackle" building in a slummy section of town, was admirably staffed. "A figure from the music-halls of Sickert's day served drinks," and "the small house tottered night after night; the deafening din could be heard a mile away."

Nothing became the Hypocrites Club better than its fall. Robert Byron and John "Widow" Lloyd, a recruit who in later years was to be best man at Powell's wedding, organized a fancy-dress party with "a piano in one room, a barrel-organ in another, and a combined zither and xylophone in the next" to supply music "for every taste." An Eton cohort who had gone to art school in London instead of to Oxford, Oliver Messel, "came up expressly from the Slade to assist with the decorations"; and he suspended "still lifes" of lobsters in the place of chandeliers and painted the walls to agree with their unStracheyan cult of the Victorian. Girls were invited, and "the party was uproariously gay, but rumour transformed it into a shocking orgy, and . . . the club was closed by the Proctors." Even its death the members converted to legend by giving "a funeral dinner at a hotel in Thame," a town about as far to the east of Oxford as Faringdon is to the west, from which the "leading members had driven back to Oxford riotously in a glass hearse."[20]

VI *The Fox Hunters of Faringdon Folly*

The aristocrats of Brian Howard's set at Oxford kept horses and rode in local fox hunts; and Howard, to establish their identity as the Hearts, had designed racing colors for them all, each with a heart motif. It was perhaps this perambulating symbolism as they galloped off to fox hunts that drove Acton to invent the "foxhunters of Faringdon Folly."

Reading Nancy Mitford's novel *The Pursuit of Love,* the reader is intrigued by Lord Merlin, a character living near Oxford. He appears as an artist as well as a patron of the arts, and he squanders chunks of his fortune on a rather unusual genre of art—comic architecture.

Osbert Lancaster has since given attention to this neglected form of the comic, pointing out its conscious as well as its more prevalent, unconscious forms. But while Osbert Lancaster was still a schoolboy in the early 1920's, Lord Merlin appears to have taken his rare, esthetic view. The "folly" he erects on a hill not far from Oxford is in the tradition of that eighteenth-century millionaire eccentric William Beckford, builder of the bizarre and extravagant mansion of Fonthill. Lord Merlin builds his "folly" because the idea amuses him; and its weird mingling of architectural forms, floodlit in blue by night, is artfully calculated to outrage the neighboring gentry. Constructed of marble, it is "topped with a gold angel which blew a trumpet every evening at the hour of Lord Merlin's birth . . . 9:20 p.m., just too late to remind one of the B.B.C. news." More than one fox-hunting neighbor turns vitriolic at the very mention of Merlin's Folly.

Yet it is through the eyes of the daughter of one such neighbor, a girl not yet confirmed in her parents' philistia, that Nancy Mitford presents this "internationally known" esthete. Brought to call by a social happenstance, the girl is delighted at the overflow of flowers in his villa, the birds of paradise flying through the rooms, and the sense of music. But she is shocked to discover in the dining room, not the decadent fellow guests she had dreamed of—dressed in oriental silk and wreathed in incense or opium smoke—but bright-cheeked young men clad in the pink coats of the fox hunter. Instead of the promised entrée into a bucolic Limehouse, she feels for a moment as if she has merely returned home. At last she ventures to ask the young men where they plan to hunt. The young men look pained.

> "We don't," they say.
> "Oh, then why do you wear pink coats?"
> "Because we think they are so pretty."[21]

Nancy Mitford was later to reveal that the character of Lord Merlin was based upon that of a neighbor of her youth, the neighbor Lord Berners to whom she dedicated her next novel: *Love in a Cold Climate* (1949). Testimony only slightly less explicit points to the identity of "the young men." Her dedication of the third novel of the sequence to Evelyn Waugh is suggestive, but in an autobiographic sketch she speaks of coming to meet—as she left childhood—"people who were not ignorant at all . . . a set . . . which included Messrs. Henry Green, Evelyn Waugh, John Betjeman, Sir Maurice Bowra and the brilliant Lord Berners (who appeared, at his own request, in *The Pursuit of Love*, as Lord Merlin)."[22]

The bizarre home of Lord Merlin near Merlinford in her novel—with its trick loud speakers, Watteau originals, collapsing walls, Dada extravagances, naked skulls, and absurd placards ("As Lord Merlin was a famous practical joker, it was sometimes difficult to know where jokes ended and culture began. . . .")—finds a counterpart in memories of the home of Lord Berners near Faringdon. Daphne Fielding, for one, recalls Faringdon House in her autobiography as having "many eccentric properties, from pigeons sprayed with wonderful colours to a hideous Japanese mask which reiterated from its megaphone of a mouth a ludicrous string of invitations to imaginary events in high life and a notice in the garden, 'Beware of the Agapanthus.'" John Betjeman's wife Penelope, she adds, at a later period used to lead her "white Arab pony called Moti . . . up the steps of Gerald's house into the drawing room, where it remained for tea."[23]

Merlin's Folly is also matched in several particulars by the folly Lord Berners built near his house at Faringdon (also a half-hour drive west of Oxford and only a short distance from the estate where Nancy Mitford lived as a child). Lord Berners erected the folly when he came into the title and resigned from the diplomatic corps after World War I. Since it too was designed in a comic spirit and became a landmark for the west country, it might be taken as a totem of what was to come in the careers of the young men in the pink hunting coats. To the names listed by Miss Mitford must be added, however, those of Harold Acton—who tells in *Memoirs of an Aesthete* of having had the idea of wearing the pink coats "aesthetically" to taunt fox-hunting undergraduates—and Anthony Powell.

What sets the sham fox-hunters of Faringdon apart from similar groups in literary history is that they are known by no manifesto; they have not advertised their coherence. Virginia Woolf's diary reveals her irritation with many a hostile critic who generalized about Bloomsbury since every writer of that circle was in truth unique; but her diary also reveals the comfort she found, when depressed, in "belonging" to Bloomsbury and all the word "Bloomsbury" connoted in the 1920's of talent and a recognized identity. This comfort Powell's friends in large measure denied themselves. After leaving Oxford at any rate, they evinced no desire to attract attention to their cohesion, perhaps because they learned while still at Oxford that to formalize a group was folly—for the artist.

Reading history, Waugh became interested in what had come to be called "the Oxford coterie"—the circle of friends around William "Topsy" Morris and Edward Burne-Jones who, as students at Oxford seventy years before, had "decided to devote 'Topsy's' considerable fortune to the endowment of a monastery from which they should wage 'a crusade of Holy War against the Spirit of the Age.' " But their "formulation," made public, did them harm as artists. In his study of the Pre-Raphaelite Brotherhood and again in his biography of Rossetti, Waugh quotes the seasoned judgment of Mrs. Millais: "It is the forming of yourself into so large a body and all the talking that has done the mischief."[24]

And any history of the Oxford Aesthetes, written at the time, might have omitted Powell. He had drifted to the periphery and his position resembles that of E. M. Forster in Bloomsbury: spiritually the kinship exists, and yet the artist is somehow—spatially? financially?—detached. Waugh includes Powell among the friends of his later days at Oxford, though he adds him to the list "not because of any intimacy I then enjoyed with him. . . . At Oxford we stood on friendly terms though barely in friendship."[25]

Scholarship may have played a role in this estrangement. Soldiers returning from the war had brought to Oxford considerable "indifference to academic success," and their mood spread. "The result was that . . . there has [never] been a time in Oxford's history when its undergraduates were so wholly indifferent about their degrees," Christopher Hollis concludes. "I do not think that I exaggerate when I say that the greater number of undergraduates who have won intellectual success in after-life—Evelyn Waugh, Alan Pryce-Jones, John Betjeman, Tony Bushell, and others—all went down without degrees."[26] In this respect, Anthony Powell was an exception. When he left Oxford in the summer of 1925, it was with degree in hand.

Perhaps Powell's more scholarly attitude may also account for a cryptic entry in Waugh's diary where he records, for Monday, November 12 (1924?), an evening of drinking, at a later stage of which "my recollections became blurred. I got a sword from somewhere and got into Balliol somehow and was let out of a window at sometime having mocked Tony Powell."[27]

The alienation on the other hand, may have arisen from the increased pace of life of the Esthetes, and from a financial drain that Powell's own parents would not tolerate. Certainly his spirit had undergone no depression. Of a German baron who was then a student at Oxford, Powell recalls "a confused memory of being one of several undergraduates helping to lift his not inconsiderable bulk into—or out of—an Oxford college."[28] And later years were to spread the group spatially while reuniting it esthetically, for Green went to Yorkshire to work in one of his family's factories, Waugh went west to Wales to endure schoolmastering, Powell went down to London to make his way in the publishing world, and all turned to writing comic novels.

CHAPTER 3

A Tory in Bohemia

HENRY GREEN'S first novel deals with young men at a public school; Evelyn Waugh's with young men at a university; but the first novel of Anthony Powell deals with another world altogether. All five of Powell's early novels derive from the London art world. Powell's young men move from London, it is true, to a seaside cottage for a while in *Afternoon Men* (1931), to the grimmer world of a Baltic capital in *Venusberg* (1932), to the fox-hunting country of the west in *From a View to a Death* (1933), to the nightclubs of Paris and Berlin in *Agents and Patients* (1936), and to the brilliance of the Riviera in *What's Become of Waring* (1939). But in each case the painter, or film scenarist, or publisher's reader, or fugitive plagiarist has been formed by the bohemian London that he leaves behind—and that draws him back. Moreover, in Powell's greater work, *The Music of Time,* painters who also have not attended a public school and music critics who have not attended a university play vital roles; and the London bohemia of the 1920's, where Powell met such people, is as important in his development as family or school—and just as complex and just as fascinating when seen in relation to his art.

I *The World of the London Publisher*

When Anthony Powell "went down" from Oxford after the summer term of 1926, he entered a publisher's office "to learn the business." His new position was a form of apprenticeship: Powell was to work as publisher's reader, deciding which of the manuscripts sent in were worthy of publication, and as editor, improving the style and correcting the manuscripts chosen, in exchange for a small salary and the opportunity to learn the higher mysteries of the book trade—the ways of dealing with author, printer, and bookseller.

The publishing firm he joined was to contribute, however, to his feeling of social complexity and thus to the creation of *The Music of Time*. Duckworth's had been founded in 1898 by Gerald Duckworth, a recent graduate of Eton and Cambridge, and by A. R. Walter, who afterward became secretary to the Cambridge University Press. Gerald Duckworth, as a younger brother of George Duckworth, Lord of the Manor of Frome, had landed connections. As the son of Julia Prinsep, he also had connections with Bloomsbury. When he was eight, his widowed mother Julia married Sir Leslie Stephen and became, a few years later, the mother of Virginia Woolf. On the other side, his elder brother George (whose landed wealth may have underwritten Gerald's venture in the publishing business) married Lady Margaret Herbert, a daughter of the Earl of Carnarvon; and George Duckworth for twenty years was chairman of the wine committee in the Travellers' Club, the first club of social importance to which Anthony Powell was elected. Evelyn Waugh was to marry a niece of Lady Margaret Duckworth, and the Duckworth publishing firm had offices at 3 Henrietta Street, a few doors down the street from the publishing firm of Chapman and Hall, where Waugh's father was the managing director during Powell's decade on publishing row.

Much of Powell's work was dulling routine, but life at Duckworth's widened his acquaintance with the arts. No family was more in England's literary eye in the 1920's than the Sitwell family of Renishaw Hall, for instance; and all three Sitwells had transferred their publishing activities to Duckworth's about a year before Powell joined the staff. Osbert Sitwell had already had some contact with the Eton esthetes, contributing to their magazine and inviting Harold Acton to Renishaw Hall (later he visited him in Peking), and his stature had grown in the world of art. In *The Sweet and Twenties*, so Beverley Nichols reports, "Osbert's epigrams echoed round the town . . . rather, one imagines, as Wilde's must have done, thirty years before" (50). Edith Sitwell (to whom Powell was to dedicate a novel) had gone up to Oxford to read her poem *Façade* through masks designed by Oliver Messel and to a jazz accompaniment, one of the major esthetic "outrages" of the time. And Sacheverell, the youngest, collaborated with Powell's close friend Constant Lambert—the former writing the poetry, the latter the music—for *Rio Grande* in 1931. The nature of the Sitwell-Powell relationship is suggested by Evelyn Waugh's allusion to Powell as he records, as an instance of Sir Osbert's generosity to the young, that he once offered a young man who worked for the publisher of his early books—"now a fine novelist"—his London house to give a party for his friends.[1]

What Powell admired in the Sitwells besides humanity was what he found in T. E. Hulme: a "reaction from what might be called Bloomsbury and Bertrand Russell; an opposition with plenty of wit and energy, that was at the same time not itself philistine."[2] He protests one commentator's "describing Sir Osbert Sitwell as 'Bloomsbury,' even though Sir Osbert may have attended parties sometimes in that district. The Sitwells, if we are going to speak collectively, surely represent, aesthetically speaking, something very different from the former Bloomsbury Group; if not, indeed, the precise converse."[3]

Moreover, the Sitwells, like Harold Acton, provided a link socially to an era of the past that had long fascinated Powell (and the Oxford esthetes in general): the period of Wilde and Beardsley. Ada Leverson, whom Wilde had called both The Sphinx and "the wittiest woman in the world," was in her old age a favorite of the Sitwells and was often taken under their wing socially.[4] "I used myself to meet The Sphinx sometimes years ago," Powell recalls. "The vision of her remains as a little old lady, always in black, swathed in stoles and veils, picking her way, as she smiled gently to herself, through an infinitely rackety pack of persons most of whom were at least forty years younger."[5] A selection of correspondence, *Letters to the Sphinx from Oscar Wilde*, was published by Duckworth in 1930.

The publishing world when Powell arrived in London in 1926 reflected what he calls "that odd sense of intellectual emancipation that belonged, or, at least, seemed . . . to belong, to the art of that epoch" (2.16). And Henrietta Street stood on the south flank of "the now legendary bohemian world of Fitzroy Street, and writers as disparate as Edmund Gosse and Aleister

Crowley, Norman Douglas and Stephen Gaselee."[6] Fitzroy Street was in part a Bloomsbury outpost since Roger Fry and his Omega Workshops were located there; but it was also the locale of Walter Sickert and the Fitzroy Tavern; and around the area prowled eccentrics of a type Bloomsbury did not often see.

Weirdest in some ways was Aleister Crowley whose dark rituals at the Abbey of Thelema at Cefalu (in Sicily) had been reported to the world at large. There, so it was said, he had ritually murdered Raoul Loveday, the "Adonis of Cefalu." This was a rumor that Crowley did not discourage in London; and when Betty May, the Jacob Epstein model who had married Loveday, came in 1929 to publish her memoirs—*Tiger Woman: My Story*—they were published by Duckworth's.[7] As the publisher's representative, Powell met Crowley about this time, and Crowley treated him to luncheon in the Strand, exhibiting, for all his sinister qualities, "something ludicrous about him, especially his accent . . . probably derived . . . from . . . Nonconformist sects."[8] Crowley was fond of enigmatic, portentous formulas—"Love is the Law, Love under Will"—and he had already attracted the attention of Somerset Maugham, whose novel *The Magician* (1908) is perhaps as faithful a capturing of Crowley as his novel *The Moon and Sixpence* (1920) is of Gauguin. Crowley was to enter Powell's fiction as one of the components of Dr. Trelawney in *The Kindly Ones* (1962).

At Duckworth's, Powell was able to aid his friends and no doubt the company as well. Evelyn Waugh remembers that when he was, in 1927, "very hard up and seeking a commission to write a book, it was Tony who introduced me to my first publisher."[9] Waugh's biography of Dante Gabriel Rossettti was published by Duckworth's in May, 1928, but when Waugh offered the firm the manuscript of his now famous first novel *Decline and Fall* a few months later, it was declined. According to Harold Acton, "Duckworth's dare not publish *Decline and Fall* without copious bowdlerizations, and I am glad I persuaded Evelyn to stand firm. It is odd to look back on the spinster prudery of our publishers in the nineteen-twenties, reputed to be so naughty."[10] Embarrassing as this snarl must have been for Powell, he could do nothing about it at the time; only a decade later with the appearance of his own fifth novel *What's Become of Waring* did the experience find an outlet in art. In Waugh's second novel, *Vile Bodies* (1930), reaction to the censorship found an earlier expression, in the caricature of a publisher who takes it upon himself "to 'ginger up' the more reticent of the manuscripts submitted and 'tone down' the more 'outspoken' until he had reduced them all to the acceptable moral standard of his day" (33).

Powell's experience in the publishing world was to find artistic shape in *Books Do Furnish a Room*, as well as in *What's Become of Waring*, and in both the tone is one of exasperation. Duckworth's erratically rejected the volume of hagiographic verse that Harold Acton had written at the urging of Norman Douglas, for instance, yet accepted the verse of another Oxford friend Bryan Guinness (who later, as Lord Moyne, was to found the Guinness Poetry Prize). Lady Pansy Pakenham's first novel was published by Duckworth's in 1931 and her biography of King Charles I in 1937, but the first book of Powell's close friend Constant Lambert—*Music Ho!* (1934)—was published by Faber and Faber.

A publisher's reader never has decisive power over what is to be published, of course, but Powell did have a key role in what has been called "the Firbank revival." Having wanted to read the much-talked-about novels of Ronald Firbank while at Oxford and having found them difficult to obtain—"due in some degree, no doubt, to their attractive production and the artists who had illustrated them"—Powell pursued them in London "and, since they were hard to find . . . suggested that my firm might reprint some of them. No great enthusiasm was stimulated by this proposal," Powell recalls. "Even when it was found that a capital sum had been left in his will to guarantee the expenses of republication, a limited edition of one hundred copies was felt to meet the case. There was genuine surprise in the office when this edition was 'over-subscribed' . . . before publication to the extent of twice that number. 1929, therefore, may be said to have been the year of the Firbank revival."[11] At that time Powell was unknown; and Arthur Waley, the Oriental scholar, was asked to write the introduction to the collected edition. In view of Powell's role in the revival, it is fitting that when Duckworth's came to publish a second collected edition thirty years later, the firm asked Powell to write the introduction.

It was fitting, yet a bit surprising, for all had not been sweetness and light between Powell and Duckworth's. Although the firm arranged the publication of Powell's own first book, his edition of the Barnard letters in 1928, and did between 1931 and 1936 publish his first four novels, his fifth novel, *What's Become of Waring*, was published by another company after his decade with Duckworth's had drawn to an end.

II *The World à Clef?*

Evelyn Waugh has suggested that Powell's early novels such as *Afternoon Men* and *What's Become of Waring* were based directly upon experience—as if a key might be used to reveal the "real" man behind the character. "I have known Mr. Powell for forty years and we have countless friends and acquaintances in common," Waugh remarks in his survey of the first six volumes of *The Music of Time*; but "in this sextet, as distinct from the books which captivated us before the war, I have recognized no character or incident 'taken from life.'"[12] There is, of course, an element of truth in Waugh's observation. In the later novels a more delicate relationship between the experience and the art that it provided the materials for is achieved. His observation is also misleading, however, if the reader assumes that Powell even at the beginning of his career was transcribing his experience directly into fiction in the manner of the later D. H. Lawrence or the early Thomas Wolfe.

Powell and Waugh both complain of the annoyance that novelists alone among artists seem to suffer in this regard. "There cannot be a novelist, from Petronius onwards," Powell says, "who has not been repeatedly forced to explain that characters in a novel are something on their own," and Waugh adds that "It is impossible to persuade a few novel-readers who are not themselves writers that novelists do not 'put people into their books.'"[13] Speaking of Harold Acton in his autobiography, Waugh complains that "there are characters in my novels—'Ambrose Silk,' 'Anthony Blanche'—whom people to his annoyance and to mine have attempted to identify with him."[14] Acton had earlier exonerated Waugh: "Our friendship has withstood many buffetings from malicious mutual acquaintances who insist on identifying me with the more grotesque of his characters. It is only natural that a novelist should borrow idiosyncrasies from his friends, for . . . his is an applied art and he cannot rely entirely on his imagination."[15] Waugh's Ambrose and Anthony are compounds in which Brian Howard certainly figures as importantly as Acton; but neither is either, simply.

The Oxford esthetes agreed that it was rude—and as D. H. Lawrence demonstrated, socially destructive—to portray friends or acquaintances in any simple, "true-to-life" way. The good novelist, they argue, is the one whose imagination penetrates its material, digests it, and transforms it. Powell praises a biographer of Marcel Proust for making it clear that "much earlier identification" of the characters in Proust's novels "has been done in too crude a manner. Proust would not only use traits of more than one individual (together with much management of circumstances) to make up characters of his novel; he would also redistribute the characteristics of one person in 'real life' among several *dramatis personae* of his book. In other words, he wrote a novel rather than a thinly veiled fictional account of certain people who actually existed."[16] The French novelist's method of "compositing" a character—taking a manner of speech from one person he had known, a habit of mind from another, a nose from another and "creating" a fourth (the method that led Proust to remark that, if there is a key to the characters in *A la recherche du temps perdu,* there are seven or eight keys)—is a method that could produce grotesqueries. The secret seems to lie in the imaginative fusion, in the feel for what features are compatible, what combinations strike us as "real."

Thus, *What's Become of Waring* as the story of a publishing firm is not to be read as a factual depiction of Duckworth's from the inside. Powell from the beginning was trying for the imaginative fusion, and the "brotherly" feud he depicts in that novel bears so many resemblances to the situation Frederic Warburg found when he began as a publisher's reader in London about the same time for the firm of Routledge and Kegan Paul—with co-directors, one wielding power from the northwest corner of the main office; the other, in opposition, from the southeast corner[17]—that one must suspect at the least some blending of the two publishing situations. Trade gossip would have acquainted Powell richly with the Routledge-Kegan Paul details. Certainly the character of the publisher who has come to hate books, all books—a comic figure in both Powell's novel and Warburg's memoirs—is not a unique figure in the publishing (or the teaching) world; nor is the office feud rare in business generally since split authority not uncommonly leads to absurd vendettas. But the fact remains that, after leaving the employ of Duckworth's—and after the death of Gerald Duckworth in 1937—Powell took his own novels elsewhere, to Cassell's before and to Heinemann's after the war.

III *The World of Music*

If Powell's school friends did most to form his tastes in art, new friends and acquaintances—the musicians and painters he met in his London years—did the most to provide its materials. Perhaps the dispersal of Oxford friends to the antipodes of China and Wales did much to effect Powell's entry into this world. "The hiatus between coming down from the university and finding some place for myself in London had comprised," the narrator of *The Music of Time* recalls, "an eternity of boredom" (5.15). Whether or not the passage may be taken as reflecting Powell's own experience, he soon made the acquaintance of two musicians of importance in the creation of his novels, Constant Lambert and Philip Heseltine.

Constant Lambert is probably best known today as a music critic. Powell has often referred to his one book *Music Ho!* (1934) as "very brilliant" (it was republished in a Penguin edition in 1948), and years after Lambert's death Powell continues to quote his judgments—that the biographer Enid Starkie "tidies Baudelaire into a bore," for instance, or that the Joyce of *Finnegans Wake* is like a man who is "too shy to write a love letter except in the form of a crossword puzzle."[18] Powell speaks of Lambert as "an old and close friend of mine . . . of tremendous brilliance,"[19] and others seem to have agreed about the brilliance. In the 1930's Wyndham Lewis formed "a congenial little group," the editor of his letters records; and Lewis, "far from monopolising the conversation, in a . . . civilised fashion kept it going from one to another, inciting Lambert in particular to sparkling brilliance of wit."[20]

As an artist Lambert may have had some influence on Powell's art, despite the dissimilarity of their media. Like the character Moreland in *Casanova's Chinese Restaurant* (1960)—and like Powell—Lambert was intrigued by the classic austerity of the new Russian ballet. "In 1926 Diaghilev chose his ballet, 'Romeo and Juliet,' as his first work by an Englishman and produced it at Monte Carlo." Lambert was then only twenty-one, and in the following year he gained further accolades when Nijinsky danced in his *Pomona*.[21] His art bears other affinities with Powell's, to judge from descriptions of it. The piece *Music for Orchestra*, which he at one time considered his best, might be thought to resemble *The Music of Time* in being "an extremely intellectual, almost wintry work, remarkable for its bold architecture."[22] And in reporting that Lambert had been taken up by "an advanced set," the suggestion was made, in 1931, that Lambert's social success might be due to the fact that his music reflects "the post-war generation . . . touching the surface of the emotions but leaving the depths undisturbed,"[23] a description that would apply as well to Powell's *Afternoon Men* (1931) and to the novels that followed.

But if Lambert enters the world of Powell's fiction, it is not merely as an individual but as a character in a net of personal relationships. Moreover, Powell's greatness as a novelist was to lie less in his ability to create isolated characters than in his ability to trace social patterns. Other novelists have become identified with one social pattern or another, of course—Dickens, with the orphan buffeted about in an alien world until the adoptive guardian is found; Anthony Trollope, with the clergyman stickily involved in the politics of the cathedral close; Somerset Maugham, with the irrational but powerful attachment of one person for another who has nothing to offer in return—but Powell has made another pattern his specialty: that of the hostile friendship.

We might describe the hostile friendship as the involvement of people who on some grounds detest one another but are so drawn together on other grounds that, despite the pain, they find it difficult to separate permanently. Such is the initial human relationship between Atwater, a museum official, and Pringle, a painter, in Powell's first novel, *Afternoon Men* (1931): "From the first they had felt a certain mutual antipathy, but at the time they met in Paris at the Coupole Bar, by contrast and comparison fellow-countrymen had seemed more nearly tolerable. . . . For some reason the acquaintance had persisted . . . long after the earlier reason for putting up with each other's vagaries had been forgotten" (2).

The most comic of hostile friendships in the first novel, however, is that of Pringle and another painter named Barlow, formerly a fellow student at the Slade and now a rival, who tries persistently to inflict his will upon Pringle: "Pringle had the best of it in the end, because he used to lend Barlow money and ask for it back at awkward times, but Barlow in periods of affluence publicly contradicted everything that Pringle said and forced him to do things he disliked. His greatest triumph had been to make Pringle buy an expensive saloon car, but while he was away in Paris one Christmas Pringle had sold it" (6). In *The Music of Time* such "illogical" but only too real human ties are traced in patterns on a dozen planes. And Powell may have first become aware of the comic possibilities of the hostile friendship as he observed during his early years in London not two painters, but two composers, Lambert and Philip Heseltine.

Heseltine was of good family by descent and was a composer and music critic by profession; yet his social reputation grew quickly seedy, and, if he survives in the history of art, it will probably be in the history of the novel. D. H. Lawrence met him during World War I, Heseltine's biographer tells us, before he "translated himself into the hearty, bearded composer Peter Warlock; he was at this time an Eton-and-Oxford aesthete, with grandiose ideas, chewed nerves, and violent affections and antagonisms—the Halliday of *Women in Love*."[24] Lawrence and Heseltine spent several months in Cornwall together, but within the year Heseltine had rejected Lawrence as a writer who had " 'no real sympathy' " with other people and who sought only "converts 'to his own reactionary creed.' " He taunted Lawrence by sending him mock reviews of Lawrence's forthcoming novel and then reported to the composer Frederic Delius that Lawrence was "quite comically perturbed." The only mode of "creating" novels D. H. Lawrence seemed to know was to "live it up" for a while, then "skimpole" the friends who had lived it up with him. He had already been threatened with libel actions; and, fearing that Heseltine would recognize himself as Halliday and sue, he wrote before *Women in Love* was published to ask legal advice: "Ask Don if he thinks any part libellous—e.g. Halliday is Heseltine, the Pussum is a model called the Puma, and they are taken from life." In the end, Lawrence changed the color of Halliday's hair; but Heseltine managed to extract damages from Lawrence's publisher anyway. All of which shows, the advocates of Lawrence conclude, that "Heseltine . . . was callow, maladjusted, and unhappy; and he had a barb of cruelty in him."[25]

Heseltine's dogmatic and violent character made him an attractive subject for novels dealing with London's bohemia. Aldous Huxley was to "use him" in *Antic Hay* (1923), a novel in which "The composer Philip Heseltine ('Peter Warlock') is easily recognizable in the character of Coleman."[26] By growing a beard and adopting his own pen name "Peter Warlock" as more in keeping with his new self. Heseltine had changed his personality from that of a shy, ineffectual youth to that of an articulate, masterful "womanizer"; and, in catching this later character in Coleman, Huxley delighted Heseltine. To some degree Huxley had caught his very words: Cecil Gray recalls having been with Huxley at Verrey's Cafe in Regent Street in 1922 when Heseltine came in punning brilliantly: "Where the hormones, there moan I"[27]—a line Huxley assigns to Coleman in a similar locale.

Heseltine reveled in pugnacity, and he especially enjoyed feuds with other musicians and critics: "I do not think there was a single one of eminence," his friend Gray reflects, "who was not at some time or other the object of his aversion and the recipient of his insults and abuse."[28] In several memoirs of "the Heseltine circle," as his group came to be called, we see the homicidal violence that Huxley relates to Rimbaud in glamorizing him. Powell relates it to Algernon Swinburne in disparaging him. "A comparatively small amount of drink overcame Swinburne," Powell notes, "whereupon there was an almost instantaneous change from lively conversation to utter intoxication. In this and certain other respects—the violently anti-Christian outbursts, the dancing, the scenes like Swinburne's kicking top-hats about in the cloakroom of the Arts Club—one is reminded of the composer, Peter Warlock (Philip Heseltine), also a passionate student of the Elizabethan period. No doubt they belonged to a somewhat similar psychiatric type."[29]

But there was also a compulsive openhandedness about Heseltine that helped impoverish him. From the memoirs of the woman painter Nina Hamnett who knew him well we recognize, in the cottage that Heseltine rents at Rab Noolas, near a pub as a summer place for himself and his friends,[30] a possible model for the cottage the character Pringle rents for himself and his friends in *Afternoon Men.* And in the relationship between the two composers Heseltine and Lambert we perceive the genesis of the friction that novel depicts between the painters Pringle and Barlow. But, as obviously as Powell may be relying, in Waugh's view, upon recognizable events and personalities, he is already splitting and regrouping details imaginatively; he gives to Barlow the aggressive belligerence of Heseltine and to Pringle his reluctant openhandedness.

We might also look to Heseltine for the origin of a type Powell depicts repeatedly, one perhaps the converse of the lonely romantic figure struggling against a callous society to bring beauty to birth. The Tory in Powell could see that, as often as society victimized the great artist, the second-rate artist victimized society; and of all the painters, composers, and writers in his early novels, the only one given anything that looks like a halo is the biographer in the last novel, who is an army officer by vocation. Professional artists in Powell's early novels are more often power-hungry predators, devotees of Nietzsche.

Glancing around the studio of the painter Barlow in *Afternoon Men* the visitor saw "some books. Not many. One of them . . . was *Thus Spake Zarathustra*" (49). Little is said about Zarathustra's connection with Barlow's unscrupulous, predatory conduct in regard to Pringle's girlfriend; but, significantly, Barlow brings the book along to Pringle's cottage, where he finds the girlfriend compliant and is discovered with her by Pringle. Barlow is sitting with the book in a deck chair when he learns that Pringle has not, after all, commited suicide (198). The connection between the philosopher and the painter's conduct is only implicit, but it is hardly mistakable. In Powell's third novel, *From a View to a Death,* he draws an even more detailed study of the artist who considers himself, as a superman, above common morality. (In fact, fearing that Americans would not recognize the words of the traditional final dance song at English hunt-halls and would miss the ironic significance of the title *From a View to a Death,* the American publisher retitled it, a bit crassly perhaps, according to its theme, *Mr. Zouch, Superman.*

In constructing this portrait of the Nietzschean "womanizer" Mr. Zouch, Powell was no doubt to some extent using Heseltine as a model. Heseltine's early idol, Delius, was "the avowed disciple of Nietzsche, the champion of the manly, pagan virtues as opposed to those of Christianity," Cecil Gray tells us, as he recalls their "common admiration of Nietzsche. True we had . . . but a very patchy acquaintance with his works and had by no means understood all we had read, but we discerned in him—in *Zarathustra* especially—an attitude and opinions that appealed to us." Gray had been the first to bring a Fascist black shirt back from Italy to wear around London in the 1920's; and Heseltine had been vigorous in denouncing those who attributed World War I to the permeation of Nietzschean ideas in German ruling circles.[31] Powell's fiction was to have its fun with such Nietzschean devotees.

IV *The World of Painting*

The title of Powell's great work *The Music of Time* suggests the world of music, but the title comes from the world of the pictorial arts, from Nicolas Poussin's painting *A Dance to the Music of Time.* Powell also alludes to paintings and painters more often than he alludes to music or composers, and as a novelist he views the world with a painter's eye. Nick Jenkins' first view of his first girlfriend, for instance, is of an "arrangement of lines and planes: such as might be found in an Old

Master drawing, Flemish or German perhaps, depicting some young and virginal saint" (1.74). And periodically through *The Music of Time* character groupings stand as if time frozen in the way a painter would visualize a set piece.

In reviewing *The Memoirs of an Art Addict* by Peggy Guggenheim, Powell reveals how deeply ingrained this habit of perspective is when he points out that her memoirs missed "a great opportunity for a genuinely original piece of action painting" when she failed to record the night "when Jackson Pollock entered the party given by the late Jean Connolly."[32] At such parties, Powell gained a quite unsentimental appreciation of the painter's world, and consequently Rudyard Kipling's *The Light That Failed* was not the kind of book that he would write. "The art world is one of a toughness to make an Al Capone hesitate to join in its commercial transactions," Powell observes, "transactions to which piquancy is given by the fact that beauty and scholarship play a part. Finer feelings need not disturb the agents who put through a smart deal in steel or rubber."[33]

One of Powell's closest associates at Eton, Oliver Messel, had gone to the Slade School of Art instead of to Oxford. As we have noted, he visited Oxford to help decorate the Hypocrites Club; and he may have been instrumental later in broadening Powell's acquaintance in the London art world; but he seems to have drifted out of Powell's life for reasons not at the moment apparent. A Slade student closer to Powell was Adrian Daintrey, dedicatee of Powell's novel *The Acceptance World* (1955) and a guest at Powell's wedding in 1936. Daintrey's autobiography *I Must Say* (1963) paints in words one of the richest scenes of the epoch available outside of Powell's novels; and the scene links Donald Maclean the Communist with Powell the Tory, Soho with Petworth.[34]

Another painter well known to Powell was Nina Hamnett, who "brings with her wherever she goes a nostalgic breath of the old spirit of Montparnasse and Fitzroy Street in the 'twenties.' "[35] The daughter of an army officer, she had, ironically enough, first received professional tutoring in the art of painting from the father of Constant Lambert, Lambert's father being then an instructor at the London College of Art. Some of the raffish models and feminine painters of *The Music of Time* must owe something to her, as may the former artists' camp follower Betty Passenger who neatly sees through Mr. Zouch in *From a View to a Death*. Nina Hamnett was obviously fond of Powell: her second volume of memoirs contains her "Drawing of the Novelist, Anthony Powell, made in 1927," four years before his first novel was published.[36] That Powell was fond of her may be inferred. "What an unfailingly zestful individual she was," the *New Statesman* remarked in citing the passing of her as a "Bohemian landmark" in 1956: "You may say that her neglect of her talents—especially perhaps as a portrait painter—was tragic. Nevertheless, she had a time-defying capacity for living in the moment that amounted almost to a form of higher mysticism. She would preside—in a room much of which was taken up by a motorbicycle—from a bed made of orange boxes, over a tea party that included a Negro boxer, an Irish jockey and two poets."

Wild as Nina Hamnett's conduct may have been, she had what Powell found in Constant Lambert and in Rosa Lewis of the Cavendish Hotel: bohemian attitudes firmed by a genially conservative backbone. "A friend reveals encountering her in Charlotte Street late on the night of the abdication of Edward VIII. With her disregard of convention and her ready sympathy, he expected to find her defending the lovelorn [king]. Not she. 'He's let us all down, my dear,' she explained, tossing her head. There spoke the Colonel's daughter and former pupil of the Royal School, Bath."[37]

One of the features of John Aubrey that attracted Powell was that he had joined two worlds in the seventeenth century, each attractive, as he moved "familiarly through the more or less bohemian world of intellect and fashion on the outskirts of the court," from painters' studios in London to the great country houses. Like Powell an only son, "Aubrey had a lonely childhood. He used to amuse himself by drawing, or watching workmen on the estate."[38] And the opening scene in *The Music of Time*—that lantern-lit scene of workmen moving as if in a quadrille—is composed as if by a painter's eye not without cause. Evelyn Waugh reports of his own William Morris period that "Three years after going down from the university I tried to learn cabinet-making at the L.C.C. [London County Council] school in Southampton Row. There in the same drawing class I found Tony, who was studying typography."[39] This meeting was in 1928, before either had found himself artistically. With Waugh, Powell was seeking artistic expression while oscillating through a special world, from bohemia to county society.

"There was between the wars," Evelyn Waugh records, "a society, cosmopolitan, sympathetic to the arts, well-mannered, amusing, above all ornamental in rather bizarre ways, which for want of a better description the newspapers called 'High Bohemia.'"[40] From one point of view this society might seem déclassé; indeed, Powell's future sister-in-law Christine Longford spoke of it as a mildly disreputable refuge: "there was always Bohemia: studio-parties, very nice and jolly, but not quite socially O.K."[41] From the opposite point of view, there was a certain resentment about the intrusion of high society into the artist's world. "The correct thing to do, for intelligent young people with a fixed income and no particular vocation, was to call themselves 'artists' and live in Chelsea studios," Robert Graves recalled. "There they gave 'amusing' parties and played at being Bohemian. Bohemianism was understood to mean a gay disorderliness of life, cheerful bad manners, and no fixed hours or sexual standards. . . . Their chief influence on art was to make the rents of studios rise so high that real artists could no longer afford them"—or so Graves concludes a bit irritably.[42]

The lure of this High Bohemia where art and society come together, where Chelsea and Mayfair overlap, finds its way into the makeup of several figures in Powell's novels. Blore-Smith in *Agents and Patients*, lured to London by the promise of "Life," is inveigled by some sharpsters into substituting film-making for Art, the cinema being "the art form of tomorrow." Other wealthy or aristocratic young men and women are lured toward High Bohemia, notably Mary Passenger in *From a View to a Death*; but the portraits of Eleanor Walpole-Wilson and Lady Norah Tolland in *The Music of Time* are most detailed. The diplomat's daughter and the earl's daughter alike withdraw almost completely from high society, without quite being able to join wholly into bohemian society.

V *The World of High Society*

Nor were the ties of Anthony Powell solely with bohemian London. Family connections and school friends drew him at least occasionally in the 1920's to the West End, to the world of high society; and it was there that he was to marry and settle down. With perhaps no direct autobiographic correspondence, Powell has the narrator of *The Music of Time* move in a similar direction at roughly the same period of history. Nick Jenkins falls in love with a debutante, the sister of a youth he had known only slightly at school, as he walks with her one afternoon in Kensington Gardens. He sees her briefly when she comes in from the country that Christmas; and the following May, as the London Season begins, he comes to know her better: "one afternoon, when I was correcting proofs in the office, Barbara rang up and asked if I could dine at Eaton Square that evening for the Huntercombes' dance" (2.24). The Season, stretching in London from late spring into early summer, is the time for coming-out parties; and in the late 1920's the guest lists at debutante balls, reported on the Court Page of the *Times,* often list, among those present, the future wives of Henry Green and Evelyn Waugh, along with Nancy Mitford and Lady Mary Pakenham. Young men without title are not normally listed; yet one may presume that Powell was now and then among them.

At that time the most eligible young men, heirs to titles and eldest sons of bankers, were known, Lady Mary Pakenham recalls in her memoir *Brought Up and Brought Out,* as The White 400. But these young men did not flock to the Pakenham townhouse until several years later when her younger sister Violet at eighteen entered "circulation." The wedding of Anthony Powell and Lady Violet Pakenham took place early in December, 1934, at All Saints' Church in Ennismore Gardens, London. It was not a large wedding as society weddings go, but the reception was held at 12 Rutland Gate, and the modest guest list included Lord Dunsany and Lord Dynevor, General Pennington, the Countess of Jersey, and artists and writers in abundance.[43] After a honeymoon in Greece, the Powells resided in Great Ormond Street and "had the good fortune to acquire

George Moore's former cook, Clara Warville, who herself contributed a chapter to Mr. Joseph Hone's excellent Life of George Moore . . . a woman of mature age and great personal charm."[44]

VI *The World of the Cinema*

Powell seems to have shifted occupation from publisher's reader to movie scriptwriter in stages about this time, for he did his first work for Warner Brothers Studios in England in 1934 and left Duckworth's for good in 1936. Presumably the need of increased income accounts for the change, though the departure of the Sitwells (for the publishing companies of Macmillan and Faber and Faber) in 1935 suggests some change in Duckworth management that possibly could have been antipathetic to Powell. The new profession accounts for his first visit to the United States, a trip as a script consultant to Hollywood in 1937.

He later described Hollywood as a "distressful place," but he met there one of the men he most admired in a literary way, F. Scott Fitzgerald, who at the time was "helping to make a film called *A Yank at Oxford*" and needed an authority on Oxford slang.[45] Sheila Graham "saw Fitzgerald for the first time on July 14, 1937, and I met him a few days later at luncheon in the M.G.M. commissary and found him a most enjoyable contrast to Hollywood life."[46] "He was charming, an amusing talker, yet serious almost to the point of making one feel he might easily be shocked by some hastily expressed opinion. He drank milk, looked washed out, but somehow gave the appearance of inner vitality against the zombies of the movie-world."[47] But what Powell calls the "grimness of a script-writer's position"—of dealing every day with tycoons who pursue "their passion for the obvious with a love greater even than the love of money"—led him, after a side trip to Mexico to sample the wines, back to England.[48]

The film writer's life led to Powell's fourth novel, *Agents and Patients,* and it also plays a part of some magnitude in *At Lady Molly's.* "I've got to get up early tomorrow and write filmscripts," Jenkins says at the end of a pub-crawl near the end of the latter book. "Good God," Ted Teavons exclaims.

Their introduction had been effected at the beginning of the volume by a fellow scriptwriter named Chips Lovell, who later was to become Nick's brother-in-law. Powell's own introduction to the world of cinema scriptwriting seems to owe much to an Eton and Balliol friend, John Heygate. Heygate was later to inherit his uncle's baronetcy, was a few years older than Powell, and was also a novelist by inclination as well as a scriptwriter. Among his novels, *Decent Fellows* (1930) seems to reflect his experiences at Eton, and *Talking Picture* (1934) deals with experiences shooting a film on location in Germany.

With Heygate we may see again in Powell's life not only an individual but the individual as part of a pattern crisscrossing in society. On the strength of the publication of his first book by Duckworth's, Evelyn Waugh had married in 1928; the marriage lasted less than two years; and in 1930 his former wife, also named Evelyn, married John Heygate. In 1933 Powell dedicated *From a View to a Death* "For John and Evelyn." Their linkage in the dedication was not, as it turned out, an augury of permanence. In 1934 they attended Powell's wedding, but two years later were divorced; and each remarried almost immediately. Nevertheless, the Honourable Mrs. Nightingale (as Evelyn Gardner was then called) became godmother to Powell's second son in 1946.[49]

As a scriptwriter, Powell seems always to have worked in that limbo of collaboration that inhibits any ascription of credits or debits. That the work affected his novel-writing style, as some critics have implied,[50] is of course possible; but this attribution needs sober questioning. Years before he became a scenarist, it should be noted, his first novel not only had the subtitle *Montage* but used montage in its presentation of scenes (as certain novels had been doing for years). And in his second novel, *Venusberg*, we find that the total action is ultimately reduced in the protagonist's mind to a reel of film (180-81)—and before any behind-the-camera experience on the author's part.

Upon his return to England, Powell became a book reviewer for the *Spectator*, and book reviewing in the decades since has been one of his principal activities. Having begun in 1936 with reviews for the *Daily Telegraph*, he wrote for the *Spectator* until 1939 and revived that connection after the war. In 1946 he joined the staff of the *Times Literary Supplement* where a number of his reviews appeared anonymously. In 1953 he switched to *Punch* (again with editorial duties as well), and in 1958 he returned to the *Daily Telegraph* as an editor. Summing up this aspect of his career, Powell has reviewed, on the average, nearly a book a week for thirty years. To Americans, this emphasis on critical writing may seem an occupational anomaly; but the English have done much to combine the professions of critic and creator. Indeed, Powell started reviewing years later than either Orwell or his Oxford contemporaries such as Waugh and Greene.

International politics were closing in on all writers in the late 1930's, however. Powell completed his fifth novel as Neville Chamberlain returned from Munich waving his umbrella and announcing "Peace in our time!"—after an accord with Hitler which even then was labeled "infamous." The first half of Powell's career had come to a close, and with it an era. London seemed gone, as *The Music of Time* records, with old friends out of town or in uniform. World War II settled in drearily. "In this atmosphere writing was more than ever out of the question," the narrator of *The Music of Time* recalls; "even reading could be attempted only at short stretches" (6.206). But the five novels Powell had already published would have insured for him a place in the history of the English novel. His art was not on a gigantic scale, but it had been well formed.

CHAPTER 4

"The Subtle Web That Makes Us Mind"

THE early novels of Anthony Powell were so well formed that the passing decades have only added to their luster; and, collectively, they have another characteristic of fine art: the ideas that shaped them and the concepts of art that guided the shaping were of a piece. Any compulsive need to establish a congruence between a writer's worldview and his esthetic principles would be meretricious, of course; but T. S. Eliot set a precedent when he found himself philosophically and defined himself as "classicist in literature, royalist in politics, and Anglo-Catholic in religion."[1] Powell might have defined himself similarly. That he did not do so may be explained by T. S. Eliot's later regret that his formula was, although true enough as a loose generalization about his views, not exact enough; moreover, it had been the product of a habit of mind from which he was already withdrawing. Such a conservative position was sympathetic to Anthony Powell in 1928, but the habit of mind, even then, was not.

I *Art and Reality*

Considering how deeply Powell's generation had absorbed Eliot's "Prufrock," it may seem odd that Eliot's formulizing bent of mind was one it had learned to avoid. Yet Powell had not needed the later Eliot, Wittgenstein, or Hans Küng for that matter, to point out that the clear categories that language seems to afford can trap a man into oversimplifying his beliefs, overstating his theories—and overlooking the reality. At Eton, while reading Wilde and Max Beerbohm, the Oxford esthetes had agreed that what was most interesting about a person was the mask he wore, that language too was a kind of mask, and that the relation between mask and reality might be deceptive. Most important, they learned that to be conscious of this deceptiveness was to avoid the greater deception: the world's deception of mistaking the mask for reality.

New theories of optics had led to the Impressionist movement, and the movement had helped develop in Wilde an attitude toward nature, and man's limited perception, that makes him still of interest as a thinker. "Wilde belongs to the modern age. If anything," Powell declares, "he lived before his time";[2] Wilde does so in his advice to avoid mistaking the mask that all things wear for the mystery within—or the surface for the reality. This doctrine seemed paradoxical at the time, and Wilde often dealt with the idea outrageously. His pronouncements about the consequent "necessary superficiality" of art (in the brilliant essay "The Decay of Lying") are not, it must be admitted, persuasive out of context. That "The only real people are the people who never existed" seems mere nonsense.

Fortunately, in book reviews of an earlier vintage, Wilde expressed the arealistic view more soberly: "There is an element of imitation in all the arts . . . and the danger of valuing it too little is almost as great as the danger of setting too high a value upon it."[3] "What is the use of telling artists that they should try and paint Nature as she really is? What Nature really is, is a question for metaphysics not art. Art deals with appearances. . . ."[4] To understand art wholly, Wilde implies, is to understand existence, and that may be beyond man's capabilities.

As a member of the Eton Society of Arts, Powell may have been influenced in his attitude toward knowledge (or in his epistemology) also by the thought of Aldous Huxley, who argued publicly in 1926 much as Wilde had, that "Art is not the discovery of Reality—whatever Reality may be, and no human being can possibly know. It is the organisation of chaotic appearance into an orderly and human universe."[5] The artist seen in this light is a kind of scientist, if scientist is taken to mean not one who knows but one who explores an unknown reality. "For what is a work of art," Miss Nathalie Sarraute adds in agreement, "if not a break through appearances towards an unknown reality?"[6]

II *The Triumph of Rationalism?*

The chief assumption of rationalism, as it came to dominance in the early eighteenth century, had been that man's vocabulary is, at any given time, adequate to cope with reality. This belief derived from a faith so deep it was not recognized as such: it was part of an assumption that man's conceptualizing apparatus is equal to any demand which the universe might place upon it, abetted by the illusion that the universe every day was "proving" to be simpler. Or, as Alexander Pope gave voice to this mood of the Enlightenment, "Nature and Nature's laws lay hid in night./ God said, 'Let Newton be!' and all was light."

The triumph of Rationalism in the modern world is traced by Powell back to that eighteenth century when Newton was "deified" because his world view "fitted in with the notions of the Whig historians."[7] Powell's own view is better suggested by the sequel to Pope's verse written by Sir John Squire two hundred years later: "It could not last, The Devil, hollering 'Ho!/ Let Einstein be!' restored the status quo." In this reversal of world view, from light again to dark, there is comic potential certainly; and the new universe seems as germane to the spirit of comedy as the eighteenth-century "universe" had been to the spirit of satire. From cosmic rays to π-mesons, our "reality" of matter is wildly different from Newton's "reality." With a feel for the history of science, Aldous Huxley in the 1920's had drawn the obvious connection between such "new truth" and the literature of the absurd: "In the sub-atomic world practically all our necessities of thought become not only unnecessary but misleading. A description of this universe reads like a page from Lewis Carroll or Edward Lear."[8]

Intellectual humility in the face of the shifting "realities" of the universe also seems only sensible to Powell, and this attitude provides another reason for his attraction to that seventeenth-century observer of life, John Aubrey, "a man who has half-explained to himself the follies of the world; who has failed; and yet achieved something"(115). To see intellectual humility as a value also elucidates the structure of *The Music of Time,* for there the narrator follows a similar path: he forever speculates about the world, forever is proved wrong in one crucial particular or another, and yet he gets somewhere. Perhaps no work of fiction since *Alice in Wonderland* has more firmly delineated man's insufficiency in matters of the intellect, and Powell's does so without losing his sense of humor.

Tying together the threads of humility in the intellectual world and conservatism in the social world with comedy in the literary world, Powell approves of John Aubrey also as a man who was modest, though, in comparison to others, "very well informed; and, just as vanity is a source of weakness that can make even the most gifted appear ridiculous, so a degree of dignity and strength is inevitably conferred upon him by his modesty" (15). Such modesty Powell found to be more Tory than Whig, more British than French. "Poetry in France has always suffered from a too great insistence on logic and rationalism," Powell observes,[9] disgusted with the "awful banality" of Victor Hugo's "wooden psychology." "To some people life presents itself as a web of infinite subtlety; to others a picture daubed in the crudest colours."[10] The narrator of *The Music of Time* confesses that he, too, in youth, had imagined life in crude compartments, with paired abstractions—such as love and hate, work and play—to "think" about; but in the course of time, love and hate grew "tenaciously inter-related," and work and play merged "into a complex tissue of pleasure and tedium" (2.159). He had come to perceive the subtlety of the web.

III *The Mystery of Human Nature*

The adult figures in Powell's novels who still think in juvenile categories, who compartmentalize their fellows with neat labels and solve the problems of the world with the latest theories, whether of Freud or Marx—and who exhibit hostility toward those who point out facts that "complicate matters"—are all figures of fun. But Powell perceives them as figures of fun at a deeper level than Evelyn Waugh does—not so much on the ideological level as in terms of their primary failure, to understand themselves.

Typical of Powell's characters is the painter Isbister in *The Music of Time.* When social criticism is fashionable in the 1930's, Isbister tries vainly and unconsciously to combine flattery of rich clients with socially acceptable criticism of them (3.118). Paradoxically, or so it might be thought, egotism hinders characters such as Isbister and Widmerpool in the acquisition of self-knowledge, for the ego blinds a man to the true nature of other people and of himself. Men famous in the history of art suffer from the same myopia, however; Isbister is not unlike Mark Twain, for instance: "Cocksure, materialistic, anti-religious, anti-capitalist, he could not avoid in due course—like so many persons of his kind—becoming involved in truckling to the causes he was ostensibly attacking." Twain too failed to perceive his inconsistency: "He had no power whatever of self-examination. He cannot tell you what he himself is like; he cannot tell you what other people are like."[11]

Contemplating another American author, Powell points to Jack London's egotism to explain his lack of interest in individuals, his belief in Anglo-Saxon racial superiority, his total lack of humor, and what Powell—alas!—calls his "typically American lack of interest in the subtleties of human nature."[12] But failing to be interested is "typically human," Powell implicitly admits: "James Joyce's ferocious egotism, with all his gifts, prevented him from achieving that grasp of other people's personalities so much required by a novelist"—and he therefore "was committed to producing some eccentric version of his own life."[13] And John Galsworthy "lacks the pitiless knowledge of human nature to be found in, say, Proust or even James."[14]

Of the technical innovations that make Powell's novels more baffling than most, one of them derives from Powell's view of human nature. Characters are habitually depicted as acting with an insouciant but systematic inconsistency. Since the contradictions found, when layers of the self peel off, intrigue Powell, and since he finds contradiction inherent in human nature—perhaps its chief distinguishing feature—he depicts a man of intelligence who is not at all a hypocrite but whose professed aims and deeds may yet vary amusingly. Or he presents a sympathetic soul whose theories and emotions may contradict one another without his being aware of any internal discrepancy. The hallmark of Powell's technique is his juxtaposing these variants without explicit comment upon them.

Although some natural bent in Powell may lead to this technique, it is rooted in his observation of his fellow men; and he detects such failings in the subtle web among the obscure and celebrated, friend and foe. Regarding the Victorian poet Arthur Hugh Clough, he notes that Clough's "inability to commit himself arose to some extent from a kind of innate unworldliness, which Clough combined with regarding himself, in some respect, as knowing a good deal about the world."[15] The novelist George Gissing is a similar example; "In theory, the arch-exponent of realism . . . he was at the same time unable to face a too brutal closeness to reality."[16] More amusing is the case of the English poet who horrified Victorians with the immorality of *The Rubáiyát of Omar Khayyám*,–for Edward Fitzgerald felt that the French were so "innately immoral" that he would have had France divided among the other powers, as Poland had been.[17]

The people admired most by Powell do not escape self-contradiction: they merely escape ignorance of it. Shakespeare in his sonnets shows "a self-knowledge that a lesser mind of that period would not have possessed. Shakespeare knew what was happening and resented it bitterly."[18] Stendhal "himself was well aware of his own political inconsistencies. . . . Fastidious as an individual, he liked the idea of democracy at a distance. Temperamentally (and economically) drawn to Bonaparte, he was also well aware of Bonaparte's many odious characteristics. One must, I fear, accept such contradictions," Powell concludes, "as different sides of Stendhal, which he never managed to fuse."[19] "A poet who craved a life of action . . . an amorist never entirely at ease with women. . . . Nothing could have been less ordinary than Byron," Powell points out; but Byron's "larger-than-life qualities and defects show in a hard light what human beings are really like."[20]

Looking at human nature again in the hard light of the twentieth century, with its concentration camps and "liquidation" centers, William Golding states that he was impelled to write *Lord of the Flies* (1954) to rebut the sentimental view of humanity's natural goodness found in such Victorian novels as R. M. Ballantyne's *Coral Island*. But even before World War I, the narrator of *The Music of Time* and a good friend had felt a similar "animosity towards . . . *The Coral Island*" (6.82). To know oneself truly is to know human nature with its capacities for evil as well as for good; and the admirable character of General Conyers in *The Music of Time* is due, we are told, to his "good-humoured, well-mannered awareness of the inherent failings of human nature; the ultimate futility of all human effort" (4.71)—including any effort to change the primary fact, the inherent imperfection of human nature.

Powell's keen interest in memoirs of the more searching kind derives from his fascination with the insolubility of human nature. The Swiss diarist Henri Frederic Amiel, for instance, gains Powell's recommendation for his self-deprecatory humor, for his spiritual toughness (quite in contrast to the self-pity of Rousseau), and for his deep awareness of the problem of evil (in contrast to Victor Hugo's all-crime-stems-from-environment-or-heredity sentimentality). To such qualities of mind as Amiel's, Powell attributes the acuity of his observations about his chief theme—the mystery and vexation of all personal relations.[21]

Powell's early novels make tentative explorations of this mystery in the tightly knit way of the better Greek dramas; but human beings, to be fully seen, need to be unrolled, so to speak, in time. When Powell found a form adequate to deal with the linear complexities after World War II, he produced a novel that had much the tone of the memorials of Amiel and Aubrey; and Nicholas Jenkins, like John Aubrey, goes quietly through life, marked by an "easy-going laziness, an inquisitive interest in people, blending . . . unaccountably an unworldliness with a deep appreciation of the world's ways" (115).

IV *The Mystique of the Aristocracy*

John Aubrey's "habitual interest in the eccentricities of human behaviour" (231) is associated by Powell with Aubrey's bias in political life toward the aristocracy—as if understanding of human nature led one automatically to political conservatism. Aubrey's sympathies were not with the "moveable, moneyed aristocracy" of the sort represented by Sir Magnus Donners in *The Music of Time* but with the rooted aristocracy of great old families. While the narrator of *The Music of Time* questions the theory of a fellow scriptwriter that "Realism goes with good birth" as being "hard to substantiate universally," he feels in that theory some validity: "By recognizing laws of behaviour operating within the microcosm of a large . . . network of families . . . individuals born into such a world often gain an unsentimental grasp of human conduct; a grasp sometimes superior to that of apparently more perceptive persons whose minds are unattuned by early association to the constant give and take of an ancient and tenacious social organism" (4.18-19). Such families are often connected to great country houses, the "stately homes" of England—Petworth, Hackwood, in life; Glimber, Trubworth in *The Music of Time*—and the houses themselves become for Powell, as they do for Waugh, symbols of the aristocratic traditions that made England great (6.128). The first love affair of the narrator in *The Music of Time* is consummated in such a house, "a kind of refuge," he feels, "for beings unfitted to battle with modern conditions. . . . In these confines the species might be saved from extinction" (2.68).

Internationalist though he was in principle, Aldous Huxley in 1920 felt "proud of belonging . . . to that nation which has produced more eccentrics than any other of the tribes of man"; and he praised the aristocracy for its habit of extending its "protection to eccentric and heretical members of other classes" and for making of the great country house "a sort of Red Indian Reservation." "In a little while the advancing armies of democracy will sweep across their borders and these happy sanctuaries will be no more. . . . And eccentricity, new ideas, culture—one doesn't see much room in the new world for these," Huxley concluded. "The prospect is melancholy, dims one's liberal ardours."[22] In the 1920's Powell agreed. When Widmerpool, the rising young industrialist, defeats the narrator's patron, the aristocrat Stringham, what is "suggested [is] a whole social upheaval; a positively cosmic change in life's system" (3.209); and the effect, though not labeled, is one of melancholy.

Status in this high aristocracy is not always understood, Powell points up in explaining Lord Byron's defection from his wife Annabella: her "background from the point of view of being well born" was "impeccable," he observes; but Augusta, "although always hard up for money, came from a much 'smarter' more dashing aristocratic world"; and, though a baron, Byron "always had uneasy memories of a childhood in rooms at Aberdeen, and could hold his own . . . as a snob."[23] To this "high aristocracy," represented in the Byron story by Augusta, royalty in England pays respect; and in *The Music of Time* members of the Royal Circle, such as Lady-in-Waiting Frederica Budd (the narrator's sister-in-law) and General Conyers (a friend of the narrator's family) lack status in relation to Stringham. Americans may find perplexing an upper-class disdain of royalty, but Queen Victoria herself experienced it—even in public occasionally. Max Beerbohm has his young duke in *Zuleika Dobson* (1911) express it more charitably: "I admit the Hanoverian Court is not much. Still it is better than nothing." Since 1688 there had existed a disdain of the line of the boorish Georges, and to this Jacobite tradition the Oxford esthetes belonged.

On the other hand, any ruling class needs correction since corruption goes with power; and John Aubrey's comedy *A Country Revel* was designed to provide it. As Powell summarizes Aubrey's plot, "Gentlemen and ladies of the old school are contrasted with the bad-mannered, drunken, irresponsible louts" of the newer, more emancipated gentility. On the other hand, "Sow-gelders, carters, dairymaids, and gypsies . . . indicate in no uncertain terms that his criticism of the upper ranks of society was intended to imply no sentimental idealisation of the lower class." Aubrey's critique of the upper class is thus a critique like Powell's from the viewpoint of the upper class: "Squires who have left their wives and co-habit with scullery-maids stagger through the acts in the company of heiresses who have succumbed to the physical attraction of grooms" (289). Agreeing with Beerbohm and Waugh again in believing that literature needs moral values—but the less explicit the moral, the better—Powell lessens the satiric sting of Aubrey and presents merely the comic picture: the world as it staggers, observed for better or worse.

Powell's novels have been read as satires of the upper class perhaps because of the belief that a writer makes fun only of his opponents, and Powell does have fun with noblemen such as Lord Erridge. But Beerbohm in *Seven Men* provides a better key to Powell: "One can't really understand what one doesn't love, and one can't make good fun without real understanding." That dictum would make the best Tory satirist a Tory, and the only label Beerbohm himself accepted was that of Tory-Anarchist, a term which is illuminating when applied to Powell. Powell agrees, dismissing one Tory cartoonist for lacking " 'that streak of Radicalism proper to political caricaturists of the right as of the left.' In the last resort," he adds, "the caricaturist is an artist to whom his own side is as funny—though perhaps not so detestable—as his opponents'."[24]

Furthermore, although the Tory of "left-wing caricature" is "always facing the past, [and is] against reform, entirely unenlightened," the thinking Tory—such as Samuel Johnson or Benjamin Disraeli—is "in many way precisely the reverse."[25] Such an enlightened Toryism as Powell's, undercut with Tory criticism, is as viable a basis for a work of art as any other, however "unadvanced" it may seem in an age when leftist critics have been known to condemn artists for depicting the upper classes at all (1.203).

V *Powell and the Intellectuals*

As for an "aristocracy of the intellect," such as H. L. Mencken was advocating in America in the 1920's, Powell has hardly a modicum of sympathy: "Even if it is agreed that something of the sort would be desirable, if attainable, it is hard to see how, in practice, any attempt artificially to build up government of the kind Nietzsche outlines could result in anything but an approximation of the Third Reich."[26] The key is the word *artificially*; for Powell believes, as did T. S. Eliot, in a hereditary but flexible or "permeable" upper class, rather than in a fluid elite. This upper class, despite its imperfections, by its hereditary nature retains integrity; it is less efficient, perhaps, but also less likely to run wildly wrong. While echoing with apparent approval Amiel's undemocratic view that "The majority is necessarily composed of the most ignorant, the poorest and least capable" ("opinions . . . not of a kind to find wide popularity . . . although time has not lessened the potency of much of their judgment"),[27] Powell also views intellectuals as a class with considerable skepticism.

For one thing, intellectualism came to have a leftish connotation as early as 1911. We see the trend when a conservative exclaims, in Conrad's novel *Under Western Eyes,* that he too is "a thinker, though to be sure, this name nowadays seems to be the monopoly of hawkers of revolutionary wares."[28] Politically, Conrad was a good prophet, as even people who scorned his political naïveté in the 1940's were ready to admit by the 1960's;[29] and, in Powell's view, Conrad's success came from his firm grasp of human nature, and his consequent regard for tradition and moral values. Although, as a fictional study of the uprooted and revolutionary mind, Conrad's *The Secret Agent* is "surely one of the best," his novels in his lifetime brought him small fame and less money. Say what one will of the self-protective nature of the Establishment, Conrad's Tory poverty is in sharp contrast to the affluence of such radicals as Bernard Shaw and H. G. Wells; and there is greater irony in the fact—an unfortunate fact for the world, Powell notes—that "Conrad's estimate of where social revolution . . . would lead has proved to be . . . a shrewder, more accurate one than that of more idealistic literary contemporaries."[30]

That the rootless intellectual, who would re-create society from scratch, might unwittingly create a nightmare has become a literary commonplace in an era in which Huxley's *Brave New World* and George Orwell's *Animal Farm* and *1984* vie for popularity; but thinkers of a conservative bent like Conrad had said as much decades before World War I. Powell has commended Amiel, Baudelaire, and Jacob Burkhardt for having long ago recognized the advent of Rousseau as a key to world disaster. Burkhardt's concept that "the great harm was begun . . . through Rousseau with his doctrine of the goodness of human nature" was, in Powell's opinion, what enabled Burkhardt to predict "with startling acumen the modern authoritarian state."[31] And the dawn of the authoritarian state came as the French Revolution, "the most disastrous event ever to rend Europe,"[32] went its way from the enthronement of a Goddess of Reason, to ethical chaos, to tyranny. Romantics such as William Hazlitt hailed Napoleon as the savior of the revolution—indeed, Napoleon became a dictator, Powell says rather acidly, "dear to the near-quisling British Whigs of his own time."[33] "One of the few encouraging facts of history," however, he adds, in discussing the Duke of Wellington's final victory at Waterloo, is the sight of "a sense of duty, respect for established institutions, and an admirable dry wit triumphing over a lust for power, moral irresponsibility, and a taste for vulgar stage effects."[34] The cause of the French catastrophe was, in Powell's opinion, less the poverty of the French peasants—they were among the richest in Europe—than the permeation of the French upper classes of the time "with the ideas of 'the Left.' "[35] The upper classes were not used to Ideas, and their will was sapped by the verbal intoxicants of Diderot and Voltaire.

VI *Powell and Bloomsbury*

Dominating the intellectual atmosphere of Britain at the time Anthony Powell came to maturity were liberal intellectuals who had established a center near the British Museum, the focal point that gave them the label "Bloomsbury." The economic theorist Maynard Keynes, the art critics Clive Bell and Roger Fry, the biographer Lytton Strachey, the novelist Virginia Woolf the painters Duncan Grant and Vanessa Bell, the publisher Leonard Woolf (who had gone to Burma with fourteen volumes of Voltaire in his trunk)—these were the stars of the group; and a supposedly close association with E. M. Forster, T. S. Eliot, and others who had no focal point of their own tended to make "Bloomsbury" a term of power in the literary world. As World War I ended, Keynes went into the Cabinet; and a new Establishment, rooted in the nonconformist liberal thought of their scholarly nineteenth-century parents and buttressed by the turn-of-the century agnosticism of G. E. Moore at Cambridge, spread its aegis over London.

Upon his return from Burma, Leonard Woolf had become, Powell says, "a member of 'Bloomsbury,'—that community which had about it something of a small religious sect in the attitude of its adherents towards each other and the outside world." To Leonard Woolf, the Dreyfus case (1894-1906) was "a kind of cosmic conflict . . . between the establishment of Church, Army, and State on the one side and the small band of intellectuals who fought for truth, reason, and justice on the other." Powell adds, after quoting this sentence, that it seems to him "a typical piece of 'Bloomsbury' over-simplification, characteristic of a view of life which divided the world into 'good' intellectuals (provided they were of the approved sort) and 'bad' outsiders." Powell's technique is to introduce the fact that "complicates matters": "Of course the acquittal of Dreyfus was a triumph of justice over injustice, but in point of fact Major Picquart, a soldier... first sought justice for Dreyfus at great risk to himself.... It is surely a completely inadequate picture to suggest that the conflict was untinged on the Dreyfusard side by all the normal impurities... or that the panorama was not an infinitely complicated one."[36] Denial of the subtlety of the web is, therefore, the first treason of the intellectuals.

Bloomsbury, as it came to birth in the Edwardian era, was characterized by its rejection not only of everything Victorian but also of anything prior to the Age of Reason. In defining their intellectual unity, Geoffrey Keynes said it emerged from a joint and entire repudiation of "customary morals, conventions and traditional wisdom."[37] All this freedom from prejudice seemed quite scientific; it took a younger generation to see the "new liberty" with a comic eye. Powell on his part wonders whether Bloomsbury's "self-righteousness and intellectual arrogance" had been "justified, either by their personal behaviour or by their contribution to art and letters?"[38] Virginia Woolf's egotism kept her from having "the smallest idea of how the rest of the world lives, even in the case of those who came quite close to her."[39] For Conrad Aiken, "writing in 1927," to find Virginia Woolf "oddly old-fashioned" seems to Powell acute; he praises a biographer for administering "a terrific and well-deserved excoriation to Lytton Strachey for innuendo and literary vulgarity"; and he finds "much to be said" for Wyndham Lewis' angry war of the 1930's "on the intellectual dictatorship of the mainly pretty second-rate team that 'Bloomsbury' was then putting into the field."[40]

VII *The Mysteries of the Spirit*

Among Victorian "baggage" discarded by Bloomsbury was religion, and the leading American critic of Powell seems to suggest that in this regard his thought might be near to Bloomsbury's. In praising Powell's "enormously intelligent but completely undogmatic mind," Arthur Mizener adds, quite rightly, that Powell's mind is "in every respect undistorted by doctrine." But he does so in a context which contrasts Powell with contemporary English novelists such as Waugh and Greene who are "preoccupied . . . with the theological inadequacies of modern civilization"[41]—and thereby Mizener risks leading the reader into misunderstanding.

Powell finds Christianity less doctrinaire than a reader might infer. "The Christian religion, in the last resort," he says, "does not attempt to explain the extraordinary patterns of human behaviour and destiny. There is a stage in such matters when its churches say no more than 'God moves in a mysterious way.' Mystery, on the other hand, is denied by the atheist Marxist, who, ignoring what does not fit into his scheme, crams all human life . . . into a measuring vessel of economics."[42]

In response to a Bloomsbury suggestion that the atomic bomb has altered life forever, Powell replies that "the human predicament" seems to have remained just what it was before Hiroshima; and religion, instead of being finally "played out," remains the target of "the common (or house) bore."[43] Praising Rose Macaulay for her piety, he also expresses regret that England lacks writers who are "deeply religious, deeply interested in philosophy, yet calm, open-minded."[44] Obviously, Powell finds no necessary incompatibility between the religious impulse and an open mind.

As a matter of fact, Powell seems closer to W. B. Yeats when it comes to spirtualism—and to "gifts which, for want of a better word, must be called 'psychic.' "[45] Powell refutes Richard Garnett's implication that "Aubrey shared Hobbes's agnosticism" (154), and then states that, "Like most of his contemporaries, Aubrey believed in witches, supernatural occurrences, and astrology. To dismiss as mere rubbish the first two of these, in the light of the anthropological enquiry and the examination of poltergeist phenomena . . . is no longer so enlightened as might once have been supposed" (66). Even the success of palmistry, Powell adds elsewhere, provides "one of those things extremely difficult for even the most 'rationalistic' to laugh off."[46] Powell has, of course, a lot more to say about extrasensory perception and occult phenomena, but the point to be made is that in only three of his novels are prognosticators given a chance to speak—and in each case their predictions are borne out with uncanny fidelity. Powell, in short, is not "enlightened" as the eighteenth-century Enlightenment knew light. But that "light" in the twentieth century has developed a doctrinaire darkness of its own.

VIII *The Mystique of Marxism*

As esteem shifted in the 1930's from Bloomsbury to Moscow and its fellow-traveling enclaves in London, Powell found a continuity between the two groups of intellectuals. There was a shared discrepancy between their "high-minded ideas about the human race in general"and their conduct, "often . . . malevolent, towards individuals with whom they came in contact."[47] In *The Music of Time,* those who share such a mentality are the liberal spinster Eleanor Walpole-Wilson and her diplomat brother—whose "progressivism" takes the form of trying to get sons of the mercantile class into the Diplomatic Corps—who quarrel bitterly as to which of them is more liberal (2.180-83). Further to the left, Erridge, the fellow traveler, loves mankind in the abstract; but he is cold toward his own sisters (4.131-45).

Among British intellectuals in the 1930's the larger section moved in Erridge's direction, further to the left, in what Cecil Gray calls the "Great Schism" of the decade. This movement is symbolized in *The Music of Time* by the replacement of the liberal esthete Mark Members as secretary to the aging St. John Clarke by the Marxist J. C. Quiggin: "a landmark in the general disintegration of society in its traditional forms" (4.121). Quiggin approves of people only if they have what he calls "all the right ideas" (4.108, 123), and he disapproves of those who refuse to take sides in the struggle between communism and capitalism, or so he informs Nick Jenkins:

> "The Lewis gun may be sounding at the barricades earlier than some of your Laodicean friends think," [Quiggin] had announced in a rasping undertone at the climax of our controversy about Milton—or Meredith.
>
> "I can never remember what the Laodiceans did."
>
> "They were 'neither hot nor cold.' "
>
> "Ah." (4.103)

But the "Ah" of aloofness is part of the deceptively "neutral" mask of Jenkins. When Quiggin looks over the earl's estate and remarks that he would prefer to see an electric power station occupying the lovely countryside—or later when the earl, applying Quiggin's principles of sexual freedom, elopes with Quiggin's own wife—we see that Quiggin has not altogether escaped in the narrator's "aloofness." The esthetic frame of reference in the first instance and the structure of the novel in the second make Quiggin a comic figure—without sullying the novel with rightist satire.

Powell's theory of the novel requires him to be detached, and his habit when speaking in his own person in reviews is to qualify his remarks strongly. But even so, when it comes to the sympathy English intellectuals of the 1930's displayed toward Russian communism, he is firm and clear. He calls it "surely the true 'Treason of the Intellectuals,' who, after, all, had as much opportunity to learn then, as later, of the methods of a Communist regime."[48] Noting in 1954 that "forced-labour camps" now stretch "from Prague to Mukden and from the Tropic of Cancer to the White Sea," Powell adds: "This, surely, is largely the result of liberal-minded intellectuals collaborating in the past to chip away the old Europe for which they now feel such nostalgia."[49]

The 1930's had reechoed with calls to battle against the Fascist hyena; but, when the war finally broke out, it was the Oxford "aesthete" Evelyn Waugh who joined the Commandos and the maligned "neutral" Anthony Powell who volunteered for what he knew to be the most hazardous of wartime jobs, that of an infantry platoon leader. The Goddess of Reason had prevailed again on the Left, or so it seemed to the world at the time: several leading "pink militants" had departed for America. Powell has published few verses, but one appeared in the *New Statesman* in 1940 recording this inconsistency:

> A literary (or left-wing) erstwhile well-wisher would
> Seek vainly now for Auden or for Isherwood;
> The Dog-beneath-the-skin has had the brains
> To save it, Norris-like, by changing trains.[50]

"One of the objections to accepting too seriously the advice of persons holding, in principle, a revolutionary point of view, is the difficulty of keeping up with such persons' constantly changing opinions," Powell observed wryly in 1961. "We have only to think of some of the steady—now almost pompous—literary figures of to-day, who, 25 years ago, were advocating Communism as the only possible answer to everything, to see how let down we should have been (not least those then lively young men), if we had all taken their word for it."[51]

The Labour party victory in 1945 seemed to mark at the same time a liberal wave and a turning of the tide: so an editor of the *New Statesman* observed in 1956—for now "the graying mandarins of office . . . are watching the birth of that rare and terrifying phenomenon—a right-wing anti-rationalist intelligentsia."[52] Leonard Woolf, as editor of the *Political Quarterly*, called a symposium of intellectuals on this conservative trend and labeled it, naturally, "The Revolt Against Reason." Taking Woolf to task, one editor who shared Powell's ideas replied that "What there has been, certainly, is a revolt against the kinds of attitude for which the *Political Quarterly* itself partly stands—a revolt against the mood of the Enlightenment, and against the kind of political radicalism often found in conjunction with that mood, which would like . . . to make society over again from scratch." That the young intellectual now "shocks his elders" by seeing "radical change . . . as more probably dangerous than fruitful" may be due to the fact that "The young intellectual of the 1930's had . . . a vision of the world transformed; the young intellectual of to-day . . . has . . . a nightmare of the world annihilated."[53] For the first time in a century, a Marxist critic notes in some dismay, it is no longer fashionable to be left wing. The culprit has shifted from the aristocrat to "the Common Man . . . the new ruling class," and writers such as John Wain and Kingsley Amis seem to feel it their duty "to come out in a satirical attack on the new master."[54]

From Dylan Thomas to Kingsley Amis the outstanding younger writers since World War II have found Anthony Powell more to their liking because they perceive the subtler web of his mind. Philosophically too, Powell in his conservatism came to seem less out of date in the 1960's than he had in the 1930's.

"Man is the only animal that laughs," William Hazlitt had observed early in the nineteenth century, "for he is the only animal that is struck with the difference between what things are, and what they ought to be."[55] The comic view has drifted back into fashion.

And at the very basis of existential thought is the perception of a deeper though similar discrepancy. As Albert Camus points out in *The Myth of Sisyphus,* the existential Absurd may be defined as an "odd trinity": the Mind perceiving that the divorce between the Ideal and the Real is the basic fact of man's experience. Or, when Man perceives that the discrepancy between his Conception of reality and the Actuality he is trying to discover, which is his intellectual history of the past, must also be his history in the future, we have the Absurd, perceived as man's condition. Periodically Science, like Sisyphus, rolls its boulder up the hill of truth—to frustration again. To perceive the ineradicable nature of the discrepancy that consequently exists between Man's desire for certainty (in the province of logic, rather than revelation) and the blunt denial by his intelligence that the universe is subject to logic at all, as man understands logic—this is what makes the condition of the Absurd. The rationalist is thus, Camus concludes, unintelligent to the point of becoming comic. "That universal reason, practical or ethical, that determinism, those categories that explain everything are enough to make a decent man laugh."[56] No finer theater for observing that "universal reason" in action is to be found than that afforded by the novels of Anthony Powell.

CHAPTER 5

The Early Novels

CRITICS have differed as to the worth of Powell's early novels. Lifting an aged witticism (that the comedies of Somerset Maugham are mere "Wilde and water"), one critic argues that "The five amusing minor novels that he wrote before the war are Firbank and Waugh and water—or perhaps soda water. They do not bear comparison at all with the six volumes so far published in 'The Music of Time' series, upon which Firbank's influence is discernible." John Carter asked in reply if the reviewer had read the early novels recently. "Their elegant, wry flavour and the spare, detached style are individual to Mr. Powell; and . . . they travel, across the decades, remarkably well."[1] Certainly two of these novels, *Afternoon Men* (1931) and *From a View to a Death* (1933), demonstrate that Mr. Carter is essentially right. Although such comparisons with Firbank and Waugh may be inevitable, they are also invidious. Powell experimented with the novel on his own—and both his failures and his accomplishments are unique.

I Afternoon Men

The central character of *Afternoon Men*, Powell's first novel—its "hero," or antihero to be more precise—is a young museum official William Atwater; and the plot that involves him is not, in the Victorian form, an intrigue to be eluded or a mystery to be solved. The plot is that of destiny, which is not so easily evaded; the mystery, that of life, which is not to be solved. Instead of being faced with a sequence of obstacles to be surmounted in the Victorian high-hurdle fashion, Powell's hero is drawn along by time to perceive submerged obstacles all the more formidable because they are buried in the currents of society and his own character. Little could seem more forbidding in its gloom than such a theme; in the hands of a romantic writer, a Gissing or an Orwell, the effect could be depressing; but amused stoicism renders the texture of *Afternoon Men* delightful page by page; and the overall effect is one of a wry melancholy. We might call it "comedy with a tang."

The novel opens with less "stage direction" than a play by either Maugham or Wilde would provide:

> "When do you take it?" said Atwater.
> Pringle said: "You're supposed to take it after every meal, but I only take it after breakfast and dinner. I find that enough."

This conversation of the two young men takes place, we later discover, in the basement bar of a private club in central London. What "it" refers to, the "it" that Pringle takes, we never discover. The conversation drifts away from this vaguely medicinal area without another clue; on the first page of Powell's first novel, the reader's frustration may have begun. But an important fact is clear: Pringle's disregard of sensible rules.

That the novels of Powell differ essentially from those of Waugh in being moved "by sense rather than by outraged sensibility," as V. S. Pritchett puts it,[2] also seems clear from the beginning. Since Pringle the painter continues to disregard "sensible" conventions throughout the novel, any precise definition of the introductory "it" would be superfluous anyway. And to define would be, at least on a symbolic level, undesirable: the essence of Powell's meaning, in the novel as a whole, is the lack of meaning in life, or, as rationally conceived, life's *nonsense*. The conversation does not complete its "sense"; the random fragment of conversation is in turn a fragment of social life; and, with society being in turn a part of nature, the only "sense" one makes of nature is that man's lot is to remain ignorant.

Man does not live by "bread alone," nor does he act by sense alone. "The absurdity of supposing that exact reasons for marriage can ever be assigned had not then struck me," the narrator of *The Music of Time* later concludes (2.197); but in *Afternoon Men* the existential absurdity latent in all human behavior has to be conveyed by the structure, for this novel has no such *raisonneur* or, more exactly, no character groping for the meaning with enough success to have grown articulate about his lack of progress. As the Sisyphus myth represents man's eternal but absurd hope that he has "at last solved," or at least is "just about to solve," the mystery of existence, the structure of Powell's novel is circular. The end finds the two men, Atwater and Pringle, back in the bar, without love again and bored with each other's company; but with another "gay party" —and with all that "gay party" connotes of man's futile hope of finding happiness, sensual or intellectual—looming suicidally ahead (221).

Atwater and Pringle, who are diverse in profession and personality, have the curious love-hate relationship discussed in Chapter 3 which, absurdly, compels them to seek each other's company. Although the secret of this compulsive friendship is never made explicit, they do share a world-view which isolates them from most of the other characters: both are artists whose realizations have not matched their conceptions, and both are destined to wrestle throughout the novel with love for a woman who proves to be unattainable. They are unattainable not in an ordinary but in a comic sense, for the girl worshiped by Pringle has a brief affair with Atwater, to whom she means little; the other woman, loved by Atwater, elopes to America with a cool realist to whom *she* means little. In both cases the nature of the ideal renders its realization impossible and the characters' condition "absurd."

The title, *Afternoon Men,* which comes from Robert Burton's *Anatomy of Melancholy* (1621), seems to imply that Atwater and Pringle, far from being creatures of free will, exist as if under the spell of the "enchanted horn of Astolpho, that English duke in Ariosto, which never sounded but all his auditors were mad, and for fear ready to make away with themselves." Atwater is "a weedy-looking young man with . . . rather long legs, who had failed twice for the Foreign Office. He sometimes wore tortoiseshell . . . spectacles to correct a slight squint, and through influence he had recently got a job in a museum." As a portrait, this is caustically antiromantic; indeed, though Powell is being stringently detached, it may be that he detaches us too far. That a "hero" should be parasitic, lazy, and disinterested in life tends to kill our sympathy; and, from bare tolerance of him, the novel twists us a bit uncomfortably as it unfolds item by item Atwater's store of negative virtues—his stoicism, dry wit, and patience. He gains our sympathy in the end, but the reader approaching *Afternoon Men* for the first time has some wrestling to do.

Atwater, sent to France years before the novel opens to learn the language for the diplomatic career that his quiet parents hope for him, had met an English art student, Raymond Pringle, who "came of a go-ahead family. [Pringle's] father, a business man from Ulster, had bought a Cezanne in 1911. That had been the beginning. Then he had divorced his wife. Later he developed religious mania and jumped off a suspension bridge" (2-3). In this family contrast we see in embryo the relationship between Jenkins and Widmerpool in *The Music of Time*: Pringle, though a painter, is a power-seeker (like Widmerpool), one whose energy leads him into absurdities; Atwater (like Jenkins) is quiescent, a man whose apathy is in itself somewhat absurd.

No doubt Powell puts something of himself into his portrait of Atwater, but his type could be observed widely in the 1920's. For one, the composer William Walton would certainly be labeled a "weed" by any aggressive young debutante. Cecil Gray describes Walton in the 1920's as "a shy, diffident, awkward, inarticulate, rather devitalized young man" and adds that "I was not greatly impressed." His friend Heseltine saw more in the young Oxford graduate—and did well to see it, Gray admits —since musical history was to establish Walton's greatness.[3] No such greatness is prophesied for Atwater, but he spends his spare hours at the museum trying to write a novel, one he is happy to forget on evenings spent with Pringle.

Beauty is a term used in Powell's comic novels only in reference to women.[4] The "sunset touches" that give us pause, as Browning's "Bishop Blougram" would say, in Powell's work come in glimpses of lovely girls; and one is sitting at the bar as the novel opens. Harriet Twining "looked very dazzling," with "fair hair and a darkish skin, so that men often went quite crazy when they saw her, and offered to marry her almost at once." She happens to be with an American publisher named Scheigan ("His Christian name is Marquis. Isn't that sweet?")

discussing her about-to-be-published book ("He likes culture"). Others enter the bar, and she takes them all in a pair of taxis to a party given by a woman whose name they never learn. A second beauty—the one who deflects the trajectory of Atwater's life as sharply as Harriet is to deflect Pringle's—is, however, discussed among fragments of other gossip before they leave the bar:

Harriet said: "Is it true that Undershaft is in America living with a High Yaller?"
Brisket said: "That's one thing. The other is that Susan Nunnery has left Gilbert."
"She's so lovely."
"Very special."
"She's sweet," said Harriet. "I adore her. Don't you think she's sweet, William?"
Atwater said: "I've never met her."
"You must have seen her."
"No, I've never seen her."
"You must have."
"I haven't."
"I say," said Barlow's brother. "Do any of you ever go to the Forty-Three?"
"Aw," said Mr. Scheigan. "Don't gossip. Let's enjoy ourselves. Let's have a good time."
"Tell him about your museum," said Harriet. "He likes culture. We might be going to the party soon." (10-11)

At the party, chaos has already set in. A fat woman says to a man passing Atwater:

"You're host, aren't you? Two girls have fainted in the bathroom and can't get out."
"Nonsense. I don't believe it."
"They can't."
"There's no lock on the door," he said. "I took it off before the party started." (22)

And the American publisher soon finds his "good time" and passes out:

> "He ought to be moved a bit," said Pringle. "People are tripping over his head. He's becoming a nuisance."
> Barlow said: "Nonsense. I like seeing him there. He gives the room a lived-in feeling."
> "He lets down the tone of the party."
> "Not so much as when he's awake." (25)

Through this alcoholic miasma drift the specters of cliché. A young naval officer on leave is asked four or five times if it isn't true that in the Navy he gets his drink cheap, and Atwater has to endure yet another repetitive discussion of Susan (28) before meeting her; but, just as the response "You must have!" starts to become a comic refrain, Susan arrives.

When Atwater sees Susan, no comment is made by the author as to the state of his mind; but her entrance is engineered to produce, amid the babble of the party, a moment of silence: hers is the hyacinth-girl effect of *The Waste Land.* Elsewhere, Powell speculates on the phenomenon of "love at first sight" as being the result of a perception mysteriously "projected out of Time" (2.215). The word too often profaned is not at the moment uttered; but Atwater's own refrain ("I'm a dying man") is stilled. Susan in the doorway looks amused, surprised, and disappointed, as if the party "had been just what she had expected and yet it had come as a shock to her when she saw what human beings were really like."

In contrast to Harriet, Susan is more than physically attractive: her mind is individual, fresh, free from cliché. Powell speaks elsewhere of Henry James as "tortured by the very thought of cliché," and there is a passage in a novel Powell praises, Wyndham Lewis' *Tarr* (1918), that is apropos in that it illustrates the damaging effect of cliché on love, for the painter Tarr grows disgusted with the cliché-mind of his fiancée. In her apartment "there was the plaster-cast of Beethoven (some people who have frequented artistic circles get to dislike the face extremely) [and] a photograph of Mona Lisa (Tarr could not look upon the Mona Lisa without a sinking feeling)" (40).

At the party, a girl had spilled a drink on Pringle—to his fury—and Atwater had met her. But, like everyone else who meets Atwater and learns he works in a museum, the girl says:

"That must be very interesting work, isn't it?" Susan, on the other hand, responds unconventionally: "May I visit you there?" Nowhere does Powell comment on the relative intelligence of the two girls, but the idea that life with Lola would be dull, with Susan bright, is amply conveyed; and, as the *New Yorker's* cliché expert demonstrates, dull as cliché is, the perception of cliché can be in itself a source of comedy.

Lola, met before Susan arrives, has piquant incongruities: an "oafish" expression and "the look of a gnome or prematurely vicious child. But underneath the suggestion of peculiar knowingness an apparent and immense credulity lurked." She has adopted the name Lola. Atwater tells her his name is William: "I was christened it. I'm still called that." Her "liberalism" extends to other "intellectual" areas:

> "When I feel hopeless," she said, "I read Bertrand Russell."
> "My dear."
> "You know, when he talks about mental adventure. Then I feel reinspired."
> "Reinspired to what?"
> "Just reinspired."
> "Do you feel hopeless now?"

Atwater suggests a visit to his flat to talk about "inspiration, and so on" and to take a look at his "interesting first editions." Lola is still wavering when Susan first appears in the doorway; as Lola decides to accompany him, the sight of Susan has changed his attitude. Yet later, when Susan leaves the party with someone else, there is, ostensibly, no reason not to proceed. In the taxi to his flat, Atwater hopes that Lola will not "begin on Bertrand Russell again"; and, when she asks about the first editions, he decides that he cannot "do all the stuff about the books" that night. Pleading fatigue, he rather ill-manneredly allows her to walk home alone (31-33).

Lola telephones him at work a few days later; and, Susan being still unavailable, he proceeds to Lola's apartment and into one of the most amusing representations of boring talk in literature; talk which concludes on the central issue, with all its stale conventions:

"When did you first notice me at that party?" she said.
"Oh, as soon as you came in."
"I think sometimes people do just feel that at once, don't you?"
"I'm sure they do."
"Are you always falling for people?"
"Yes, always."
"You brute."
"I'm sure everybody falls for you," he said.
"No, they don't."
"I'm sure they do."
In her serious voice she said: "Don't you think sexual selection is awfully important?"
"Of course."
"Don't." she said. "You're hurting. You mustn't do that."
Slowly, but very deliberately, the brooding edifice of seduction, creaking and incongruous, came into being, a vast Heath Robinson mechanism, dually controlled by them and lumbering gloomily down vistas of triteness [to] the inevitable anti-climax. . . . Later they dined at a restaurant quite near the flat. (82-83)

It has been well said by Richard Vorhees that "no other novelist has made party-going seem so dreary, and not even Aldous Huxley has made promiscuity seem so depressing."[5]

Powell may have had Ernest Dowson's "Gone with the Wind" poem in mind in these scenes—certainly, he had some similar concept of unfaithful fidelity in mind, some separation of lust and love; for Atwater is faithful to his Cynara, but in his fashion. He succeeds finally in getting a date with Susan, but at the restaurant to which he takes her, hoping to be alone, friends show up and steal his time with discussion of fashionable reducing salons. No one being interested in anyone else, the conversation is a riot of non sequiturs:

"There's a place one can go to just outside Munich. They say it's very good."
"Didn't Mildred go there?"
"It was Mildred's nerves."
"Doesn't he do that too?"
"Mildred went to the man at Versailles. He makes you scrub floors. Mildred said she felt quite different after it."
"Then there are readings from Croce in the evening. It's terrible if you don't understand Italian. You're made to listen just the same." (93)

Only Chekhov and Firbank have done as much to make a comic art of the non sequitur, the zany colloquial irrelevance; and Powell, like Chekhov, finds the non sequitur useful not only to show the indifference of people to each other but also as a kind of structural symbol. Life itself may become a kind of non sequitur, as Atwater discovers when a neatly dressed man named Verelst, who "hardly looked like a Jew at all,"[6] is attracted to Susan's table. "His moustache was arranged so that it made him look as if he might be in the Brigade of Guards, but although it was plausible it was not really convincing" (93). Verelst outpoints Atwater in winemanship and insists on giving him "the address of a quite excellent hotel. . . . Of course the place is always full of international gourmets, if you can stand that." The only clue given to the state of Atwater's mind at this point is his hope "that lots more people would come and talk and drink and sit at the table and make assignations with Susan . . . because then it would become funny and he might feel less angry."

Verelst is seen again as a respectable collector of art at Pringle's private showing. Then Susan telephones the bar where she was to meet Atwater for their second date to say, "So sorry I shan't be able to see you tonight. I'm in the country" (117). An aging man with a well-displayed book called *L'Ersatz d'Amour* is trying to buy Atwater a drink, so he departs for a friend's; and, finding the friend on his way out, he drifts to Lola's, and the following chapter ends with another comic "waste of shame":

> The divan creaked. Lola said:
> "No, dear, no."
> "Yes."
> "No, really, no."
> "Yes."
> "Draw the curtains, then."
> As Atwater drew the curtains he noticed that it was spotting with rain outside and in one of the back rooms opposite a man wearing an overcoat was playing the piano. Lola said:
> "In modern sculpture I think the influence of Archipenko is paramount." (122)

With this fragment of Archipenko pretentiousness, the curtain closes—and the chapter too.

Atwater's third date with Susan is designed to get them away from "arty" friends; he takes her to a second-rate boxing hall in the slums.[7] The boxing is reminiscent of the bullfighting in Ernest Hemingway's *The Sun Also Rises* (1928), not only with its anti-intellectualist turn to violence, but with its use of the combat within the arena to counterpoint the struggle going on among the characters. To Atwater, each of the fights seems symbolic. The first matches a Welshman and a Jew; and the former turns "pink in the face" with effort, while the latter's hair remains neat as he wins. Two fights later, a boxer named Ernie Hyams kisses a girl's coat and a brassiere before his bout:

"Is that his girl's too?"
"I don't know. Perhaps he's got two girls and one wears the coat and the other wears the whatnot."
"I think it's sweet."
"His having two girls?"
"I think it's sweet his kissing the things like that."
"Would you like me more if I did that sort of thing?"
"I like you all right," she said. "What I tell you is that it is no good either of us liking the other." (137)

Although Atwater predicts Hyams' defeat, his opponent Gunner Haskins hits him below the belt, admits his fault, and the fight goes to Hyams. Susan chooses the next break to refer to Lola, exhibiting an "illogical" hint of morality:

"Anyway, if you feel like that, what about your little friend who wears the funny clothes?"
"What about her?"
"Do you still see her?"
"Sometimes."
"Oh, God," she said. "I don't really care."
"I know you don't."
"I mean I understand about all that."
"Yes?"
"Yes," she said. "That's not why."
"Why, then?"
"I don't know. Just I feel like that, I suppose."

"Yes, I see."

She said: "You're rather sweet really."

"Aren't I?"

"Yes. But that's how I feel."

"Anyway, I never see you, so it doesn't make any difference."

"Exactly."

"Don't be like that," she said. (138-39)

This dialogue is like the visible portion of Hemingway's iceberg: strong emotions are hidden below. Two bouts later a Welshman with a straightforward, emotional style is outboxed by an "intellectual faced man from Battersea." There is no underlining of correspondences, but Atwater's defeat in love's arena by the coolly rational Verelst and his panoply of romanticism is foreshadowed, as we see clearly enough in retrospect. Susan is, like the English crowd, for the underdog; for the Jew who was hit below the belt:

"I like Jews."

"I'd noticed it."

"They all behave like that," she said. "Kissing the coat and so on." (137)

As they are leaving the arena, Susan and Atwater encounter an homosexual acquaintance with his "very pale young man." "Why, fancy meeting you here, Walter." "Not at all, I made the place fashionable." "Seeing there was no escape, Atwater said: 'Are we all going in the same taxi?' " His third date with Susan ends with their resubmergence in the sterile crowd.

Discretion, reserve, and failures of communication also mark the denouement. Susan refuses to tell Atwater where she is going when he too leaves the city on his vacation; and, when he returns toward the end of the novel to the apartment house where her pleasantly alcoholic father lives, he finds that Susan has gone to America with Verelst. Atwater controls his emotions carefully until he is back on the street; then he walks unseeing:

They had written each other no letters, but he thought of the inflections of her voice on the telephone, so that all the things she had said lost with the different tones he gave them any meaning

> that they once had had. And so she was gone, ridiculous, lovely creature, absurdly hopeless and impossible love who was and had always been so far away. Absurdly lovely, hopeless creature who was gone away so that he would never see her again and would only remember her as an absurdly hopeless love. . . . What a fool. And yet, as she had said, what would the good have been?

Their friend Undershaft is said to have come back from America, to have taken up Lola, and to have relayed one comment of Lola's on Atwater's suspenders, one clue to the question that Susan would not answer as to why "it" would have been no good: "She told Undershaft she thought it so funny the way you mended your braces with wire" (220).

The weakest aspect of *Afternoon Men* seems to arise from the plurality inherent in its title, the structure-distorting necessity of seeing how the other "afternoon man," Pringle, is brought by thwarted love to the verge of making away with himself. Having accepted Henry James's esthetic of the novel—the novelist's self-imposed limit to a single point of view and having selected the viewpoint of Atwater—Powell must interrupt Atwater's story to bring him to where he can observe the Pringle story. This occasion comes when Pringle invites Atwater to the cottage he has rented for August near the sea.

Atwater is aware that no sentiment is attached, that the invitation came to him only because "Apfelbaum, the picture man, has fallen through"; and, when he arrives, he finds Harriet there, having become Pringle's mistress, though, as she says, "That always sounds such a pompous thing to be." The painter Barlow is there with his bovine, kind, mistress-model Sophy; and so is the elderly art collector Naomi Race, who has been met before as a London hostess and as a candid, generous friend of Susan's.[8] Barlow, on the other hand, is a crass Nietzschean—his copy of *Thus Spake Zarathustra,* as we noted in Chapter 3, is much battered (49, 198)—and he has become a comic bore because of his insistence on discussing potential marriage partners with his friends though none of the possibilities includes good old Sophy. Indeed, none of the girls, among whom the friends are asked to decide, is known to them.

Late the second day Pringle takes a walk with Atwater to discuss his own plans to marry Harriet:

"We like each other a great deal."
Atwater said: "That always makes marriage more satisfactory. . . ."
"I think she's lucky in a way." (172)

As they grope back into the house in the dark, Pringle is thus doubly outraged to discover Harriet rumpled on a sofa with Barlow. He calls Barlow a cad.

"I know. We both are. You said so only yesterday. . . ."
"You've been a bad influence on me ever since I met you. I've felt my painting getting worse and worse."
"In what way?"
"In every way."
"I'm sure you're wrong." (174)

Pringle storms into the kitchen and, in a scene of hilarious farce, catches his coat on the levers of the water faucets above the sink. Atwater tugs and pulls in vain to release him, but Pringle only curses at the suggestion to solicit Barlow's help:

They pulled again a good deal. Then Barlow came in to see what was wrong and why Pringle was making so much noise. He said:
"Can I help?"
Atwater said: "Yes."
Atwater and Barlow lifted Pringle bodily into the air to take the weight off his coat. By pulling again in this position they managed to get it free, but it took several minutes to do. Then they lit the candles . . . and went to bed. Pringle was white in the face. No one said good-night to anyone else. (177)

The next day Harriet asks Atwater to take a walk with her; and high on the cliffs above the sea, with the air "fresh, rather metallic and Scandinavian," they spot Pringle walking on the shore below; they see him stop, undress completely, scratch himself for some time, swim out to sea, and disappear in the glare.[9] Harriet and Atwater, walking on, each discover that the other is in love, Harriet with a man in Spain—" 'but I never see him,' " Harriet says, " 'so what's the good? Do you think that one of these days everything will come out right?' " " 'No.' " " 'Neither do I,' she said. She laughed again" (182).

They move rather mechanically into what might be called a seduction; and, when reality again becomes "more contiguous," Harriet giggles, combs her hair, and they wander home in the cold darkening air, amid the more insistent noise from the sea. At the house, in expectation of the host Pringle, luncheon is delayed for quite a while. When hunger overwhelms them, they move to the sideboard and discover a farewell note from Pringle "on top of the beef." Depressed by the failure of his life, the note says, he wishes his money to be divided between his maid and his sister. Only Sophy cries. "Mrs. Race said: 'I refuse to believe that this is not one of his heavy jokes. If we have lunch, I have no doubt he will turn up'" (188). Though all feel sure the note is no joke, hunger has already been staved off for some hours; Naomi's rationalization is accepted; and they eat in wildly comic solemnity. Later, observing Barlow rehearse his "guilt symptoms"—"But it's absurd that I should have been the cause of it. I mean he always seemed to like me"—while he speculates again about the best marriage partner for himself, Atwater "wanted . . . to leave at once before he followed Pringle into the sea." At this moment, Pringle turns up alive. After surreptitiously and vainly seeking his note on top of the beef, he says, "I decided against suicide on the whole."

When we next see Atwater and Pringle, they are in the London basement bar where we met them. Pringle and Atwater are again "alone," Harriet having picked up another stranger: "I don't know what his name is, but he says a friend of his is giving a party and we can all come." They are all deciding to go as the novel ends—the wheel full circle, the stone of Sisyphus again at the bottom of the hill. We foresee another "Montage" (so Powell subtitled the first part of the novel) as new faces sift into the social frame; another "Perihelion" (the title given to the central third of the novel) in which Atwater dates the girl he loves, high in orbit, warm, blinded by the sun, so that later he cannot even recall what she looked like or even what she sounded like; and a final "Palindrome" (the third section's subtitle) in which things, absurdly, are seen to read the same backward as forward.

One of Powell's most important and least understood technical innovations is his development of a character type who may be called the parody-*raisonneur*. His function is to express the novel's point of view, but comic side out so that we see why others do not express it. In *Afternoon Men* the character who expresses what Atwater feels about the world is Fotheringham, who suffers from a noisy weltschmerz. The subeditor of a spiritualist paper, Fotheringham has tried to get Undershaft to write an article on occult music, although of all people Fotheringham has come to like spiritualists least:

> "Now listen to me for a minute. I may not be as talented as you, Hector, or as beautiful as Sophy, but don't you agree that I'm wasted?"
> "No, I don't think you are in the least."
> Fotheringham laughed. He said: "Now you're joking. Be serious."
> "Not a bit. You're very lucky to have a job at all."
> "You don't mean it?"
> "I mean what I say."
> "No, that's absurd," said Fotheringham. "I don't believe you when you say things like that. . . . You're merely offensive, Hector."
> "I mean to be."
> "You know, you go too far. People who don't know you as well as I do would never guess that you were joking." (56-57)

To balance Fotheringham's inflated concept of his abilities, we have his deflated view of man's destiny, expressed in pure cliché:

> "Where is it all going to lead? I ask you that, Atwater."
> "I don't know."
> "No. You don't know. I don't know. None of us know. We just go on and on and on and on and on."
> "We do."
> "We sit here when we might be doing great things, you and I."
> "Might we?"
> "Do you know what we are doing?"
> "No."
> "Shall I tell you?"
> "Yes."
> "We are wasting our youth."
> "Do you think so?"
> Fotheringham said: "Every minute the precious seconds flit by. The hour strikes. Every moment we get a little nearer to our appointed doom." (60)

Boring talk is conveyed with comedy that almost amounts to grandeur as Fotheringham traps Atwater and Barlow at the bar and grows maudlin on the subject of "friendship." The passage is typical of Powell's greatness as a creator of a world between the lines and needs quoting at length, to establish this ironic tone.

"No, no. Don't repeat it."
"Yes," said Fotheringham. "I shall say it again, and more than once again, how fortunate I count myself to have such friends as I have; and whatever people may say about friendship, and no one knows better than I that it's a quality that in these days is often rated lower than those temporary emotional connections between this or that sex . . . yet it is eventually a thing, in fact it is *the* thing, that in the long run the happiness of men like you and me . . . depend on most of all in this struggle, this mad, chaotic armageddon, this febrile striving which we, you and I, know life to be; and when we come at last to those grey, eerie and terrible waste lands of hopeless despair, unendurable depression and complete absence of humour that drink and debt and women and too much smoking and not taking enough exercise . . . lead us to, when the vast and absolutely impenetrable mists of platitude or, in the case of some, dogma envelop us and cover us up entirely, when we have . . . sunk to those slimy horrible depths of degradation . . . that comes to those who would sell their name, their intellect, their mistress, their old school, their honour itself for the price of a bitter; when love has come to mean the most boring form of lust, when power means the most useless pots of money, when fame means the vulgarest sort of publicity, when we feel ourselves exiled for ever from . . . debonair insouciance (pardon the phrase), which is, I suppose, the one and really only possible mitigation . . . for the unbridled incoherence of this existence of ours, it is then . . . that we shall realise in its entirety, that we shall in short come to know with any degree of accuracy— What was I saying? I seem to have lost the thread."
"Friendship."
"That was it, of course. I'm sorry. That we shall realise what friendship means to each one of us and all of us, and how it was that, and that only, that made it all worth while."
"Made what worth while?" . . .
"Everything," he said.
"As, for instance?"
"I'm not a religious chap. I don't know anything about that sort of thing. But there must be something beyond all this sex business."
"Yes."
"You think so?"

"Oh yes. Quite likely. Why not?" [Atwater says]
"But what?"
"I can't help."
"You can't."
Atwater said: "But what has made you so depressed?"
"Depressed?"
"Yes, depressed."
Fotheringham finished his drink at a gulp. He said:
"I suppose I must have sounded rather depressed. You see I had rather a heavy lunch." (61-63)

Here is the world view of Atwater and Pringle, Susan and Harriet, articulated at last—but in caricature. From "A million barmaids all saying the same thing" and from "Drink . . . so nasty one can hardly get it down," there seems to Fotheringham, in his optimism, one escape: " 'Ah,' said Fotheringham, 'America. But the date isn't actually fixed yet' " (60). Susan too leaves for America, but the structure of the novel denies that last exit; for America's gaiety is represented by Scheigan, the drunken publisher, and America's love by the girl whom Undershaft has left; and Undershaft, the pioneer of their circle, has come full circle back to London and is sleeping with Lola as the novel ends. The year has come full circle, as Atwater turns into the club where we first met him—where another party is beginning its cycle and a homosexual is to have the last acidic word on Susan: "She's very attractive in her way. . . . But too individual to be *chic* really" (221).

II Venusberg

The second novel, *Venusberg* (1932), is both the most satiric and the least successful. Most of the action takes place in an unidentified Baltic capital that resembles Riga (especially in the German *ritter* or Tannhauser tradition that helps give the novel its title); but in its homogeneity it is Ruritanian; and Ruritania (any state imaginary but European), when it came to novel writing, was young Oxford's worst addiction. Graham Greene's second novel, *The Name of Action* (1931), similarly loses power as it moves "abroad" to an area that is unidentifiable, however much the French occupation of the Moselle-Trier region in the 1920's may have been in the back of Greene's mind. When the cable is cut, as Henry James observed, the balloon has a tendency to drift from reality; and Powell's "reality" would have been worth keeping in range.

The satiric object of *Venusberg* is "*modernisme*," but the method is conventional triangulation. In London we find a young journalist (Lushington) in love with a divorcée (Lucy) who in turn is hopelessly in love with the journalist's friend (Da Costa). Da Costa is so shy that, to escape Lucy, he has fallen back on family connections to secure a post as an attaché at a Baltic capital. As the novel opens, Lushington, "who believed implicitly in eventual progress on a scientific basis," is being dispatched to the same Baltic capital by a press lord who shares his faith in progress. Foreign correspondents, his editor says, have "taken the place of the old diplomat. Better educated. Better informed. Better paid. And of course, more reliable. But they carry on the same fine tradition."

The structure of the novel is foreshadowed when Lushington meets an aging German baroness aboard the ship from Copenhagen who tells not only his fortune but that of a professor's wife and of a Russian count whom he has met aboard. Count Scherbatcheff interrupts at sight of the ace of spades: "Ah, yes, I see. You need not explain it. The card of death. My poor grandmother. I knew that it must come sooner or later. But .... In spite of her obstinacy I am quite attached to her" (15). The Count is a comic characterization of some merit (100), but there is perhaps too distinct a touch of Little Lord Tangent as we follow his growing illness (129) to the later scene with its ironic power as the grandmother walks through the slush to the cemetery to bury him (140).

The Baltic capital seems a cross between the world of Beerbohm's *Zuleika Dobson* and that of Eliot's *The Waste Land*, an "unreal city" with a skyline as illusive as "the dreaming spires of Oxford" (82) but of abandoned apartment houses with rusting cranes still perched on their steel skeletons and dreary wastes of petrol cans between them. "The new railway station," a symbol of national pride, is "designed on a substratum of modernismus, with pylons and tumid, angular caryatids . . . in red stone . . . and it stood out uncompromisingly against the sky" (42).

As uncompromisingly modern is a professor of psychology whose "spruce animal" wife Lushington had taken to bed on the boat. Professor Panteleimon Marvin is delighted to demonstrate his advanced views when a stranger asks his wife to tango. "Woman has become her own master," he says to his wife's lover. "And," Lushington replies, "very often someone else's mistress." The professor, delighted, copies down the wit that, at convocation, will "no doubt add in some measure to my popularity" (145). He later comes, in Restoration fashion, to his wife's lover for counsel on love. That encounter ends when the Professor egoistically struggles to establish his theory that his wife must be in love with Da Costa and is thus flirting with Lushington because she subconsciously suspects some sexual attachment between the two Englishmen and is jealously trying to break them up. Although the Professor has "always been a steadfast upholder of advanced thought," as he explains, the intricacies of life occasionally force him to be in this fashion unorthodox. He interprets Lushington's stunned reaction to an Englishman's shock that a married woman could love someone other than her husband, the English being by national reputation naïve. In Restoration mood again, the lover shortly thereafter orders his mistress to show more respect for her husband.

Lushington is a journalist, and Powell's novel could have anticipated Waugh's *Scoop* (1938) in raking journalism over the satiric coals; and there are a few bits in *Venusberg* about sending "long expensive cables to the paper which subsequently appeared in two lines." But the satiric eye focuses on the diplomatic world of Da Costa. The French ambassador's corpulent wife derives her only fun in life from being rude to the German minister. The American minister is seen at a nightclub "energetically lowering his country's prestige": "The tongue of Shakespeare and *The Saturday Evening Post* is good enough for us and you can take it from me, Colonel—and you, Viscount, you bear this in mind too—if people are worth talking to they talk *English*" (155). The American minister has a Texan mannerism of pointing his finger at people and of saying *Bang*! or *Pop!*—habits which embarrass the southern gentleman who assists him.

Curtis Cortney, this quiet American, comes "from the New World, where we still try to retain our homely code of morals."

Like Fotheringham in *Afternoon Men,* Cortney is the parody-*raisonneur* and does a clearer job of caricaturing the traditional values upon which the novel rests than Lushington does of rediscovering them: "Now in America, I hope not too late, we are realising what a sacred institution the home is and how it is threatened by the stress of modern life." Typically, he is the only character in the novel to use the word *aristocrat;* and each time he confounds the real aristocrat with the bogus. But he remains a stock figure based on reading, like his own concept of the English gentleman. "How will it feel when the Recording Angel calls your bluff for the last time?" may be American idiom, but it is not that of a southern gentleman, however fatuous.

That the knight Tannhauser was once held in thrall by Venus, the novel's epigraph from Baedeker reminds us; and the climax of the novel comes on the night of the annual ball at the House of the Knights. All the diplomatic and social world is assembled, all but Professor Panteleimon who is said to be at home with a migraine. Breaking out of enthrallment—but for no very satisfactory reason on the literal level of the novel—Lushington sends the professor's wife home with Da Costa as escort—at about the time General Kuno, the power behind the president of the country and a very unpopular man, leaves the ball. Apparently mistaking the drosky of Da Costa for that of General Kuno, "assailants" open fire and kill Da Costa (as the baroness had foretold)—also the professor's wife. Lushington at last gets his "scoop" and returns victorious to London. But whether the professor was actually home, or whether, among the "Many unprogressive prejudices" he confesses to, revenge for cuckoldry is one—and has made Da Costa the "stand in" for Lushington instead of for General Kuno (as Lushington reports to the world)—the novel does not make clear. A suspicion is aroused, without being laid to rest.

We last see Lushington back in London with Lucy looking over the foggy Thames. The doorman at the News Palace has been eyeing her: "I expect he thinks I'm a tart," Lucy says. And the novel closes with Lushington's acidic reply: "I was just wondering." In view of Lushington's conduct, his last remark seems more priggish than "dis-enthralled." The novel had begun by quoting Baedeker on the Venusberg: "Here according to popular tradition, is situated the grotto of Venus, into which she enticed the knight Tannhäuser; fine view from the top." We end the novel feeling that we have indeed toured a Venusberg, but have not been given a "fine view from the top."

III From a View to a Death

Anthony Powell's third novel, *From a View to a Death* (1933), draws its title from the words to the song "John Peel," the tune of which signals the last dance at hunt balls. Freighted thus with nostalgic sentiment, the periphery of the novel turns toughly contrapuntal when the epigraph quotes two lines from the song about the fox hunter's pursuit of the fox: "From a find to a check, from a check to a view / From a view to a death in the morning." Nowhere in the novel are the human correspondences made overt. But the roles of hunter and hunted in the sporting world can be superimposed with multiple ironies on the "views" and "checks" of Powell's protagonists in the social world.

From a View to a Death opens, like Huxley's *Crome Yellow*, with the arrival of a young man at an English country house; the young man (the fox) is an artist named Arthur Zouch, bearded, and dressed with "conventional unconventionality": "He was ambitious, naturally, and painted bright, lifeless portraits that would have been hung in the Academy if he had sent them there but which he preferred to show in smaller galleries having the reputation for being modern" (11). As a painter, he is second rate: "He had some skill in catching a likeness, and this, combined with a simple colour formula and an instinct for saying the sort of thing that sitters expected of a painter, caused him to be spoken of as promising." What singles out Zouch from the run of mediocre artists is his recent conception of himself as a Nietzschean *Ubermensch.*

One of the last scenes in *Venusberg* had shown Lushington as a captive audience on the ship back to Copenhagen listening to a bogus Russian count's solution to the woman problem: "A good friend of mine, a Brazilian, once told me that the rich men in his country, when they smoke a cigar, take only the first two or three puffs. Then they throw the cigar away. Those puffs are the best and when they want more they can buy another cigar. Sometimes I think that it is good to be with girls as my friend was with his cigars. It is the sentimental who do most harm in this world of ours. You are no doubt familiar with the works of Nietzsche?" (183). That Zouch conceives of himself as a superman ready to use women a few times and then throw them away is so far known only to some women in his life. Others "would learn all in good time; and to their cost. Meanwhile he went on his way, taking but not giving, treating life as a sort of quick-lunch counter where you helped yourself and all the snacks are free" (12). At the moment he is congratulating himself for having looked ahead and charmed a country-house invitation from a young lady (chicken number one) met at the house of a London patron.

Mary Passenger, the young lady, had made her debut some years before; but dancing and hunting have palled, and she has taken, with some unfortunate Madame Bovary side-effects, to art. She likes Zouch "because he talked to her about persons who earned their living by writing or painting, and in this way he represented to her a world with which she had no first-hand contacts. She was not really interested in these subjects, but then for that matter neither was Zouch, and it made a nice change for her." Zouch, who has accepted her invitation for the "weekend" with the picaresque intention of extending his stay, by dint of charm, through the dull London summer, finds Passenger Court, at the end of a drive between gaunt lime trees, lovely. He finds Mary on the croquet lawn above the lake.

The Passengers are better fixed socially than financially. The family money came from Georgian successes, and "*mariages de convenance* of an earlier generation had left them related, even if distantly, to almost everyone of any importance in the world in which they lived." A grandfather had served in Gladstone's cabinet and had turned down a peerage. But "for several generations none of them had had any clear idea of how to manage their business affairs and the family had become accustomed to having less and less money as the years went on." Their townhouse near Belgrave Square (good) is "barely habitable on account of its draughts" (bad). On the other hand, their country house, Passenger Court, is comfortably graced with good food, but is "of no architectural interest." Thus, Powell uses Firbank's technique of placing the family high and then kicking it downstairs. And at Passenger Court is played out the classic comedy of the pretender hoist with his own petard.

When Zouch meets his host Mr. Passenger (the fox hunter), he recognizes at once another "superman," despite the fact that history recorded only the melancholy fact that Mr. Passenger had hitherto been consistently a failure:

> As a young man he had become tired of London society and had gone out to the Boer war as a volunteer, but a few days after his arrival in South Africa he had nearly died of measles. When he came back to England and before he had fully recovered his health he began to edit the works of a seventeenth-century minor poet. But his convalescence had allowed him little time for research and the edition was found on publication to contain so many errors that he withdrew the whole of it at his own expense. This incident had given him a distaste for the life of the mind from which he had never wholly recovered.

Having felt pro-German sympathies at the beginning of World War I, "it was no wonder that he was often morose" (30). Belligerent, he is most happy when he can spend an afternoon "pottering round the town and aggravating some of his *bêtes noires* among the local tradesman." Conflict with his guest Zouch is almost automatic, but is conducted by the rules of "one-upsmanship": "Mr. Passenger took every possible advantage that accrued to him on account of his age, position, and the fact that he was host, while in return Zouch presumed on his own standing as a guest, allowed himself considerable latitude of behaviour on account of his profession, and extracted the utmost from his status as Young Man" (42). Mr. Passenger, as a descendant of Whigs, is a bit given to self-pity. "Mentally he compares himself to King Lear. A Lear without a Cordelia" (178), for his elder daughter Betty has made a disastrous marriage to an Italian duke—Umberto, Duca di Civitacampomoreno, who abandoned her upon learning she was not wealthy, possibly for " 'the lads at the *Boeuf* "—and his younger daughter Mary has taken to art and invited the bearded painter home.

Zouch in the 1930's is beginning to sense that his beard is

growing dated "and that with a newly acquired social consciousness he would soon do better with bare cheeks." And the doing better is what Zouch wants: power, not integrity. What intellectual curiosity he has comes from the aphorism he recalls that knowledge is power (95); and he dislikes the elder Passengers "with their eccentricities and prejudices about ambition, which he himself had always imagined to be a virtue" (131). He even has faith—among this foxhunting crowd, a fatal trust—that "The will to power should teach him how to ride" (142). But he is essentially more philistine than his hosts. Betty Passenger's bohemian language outrages him, for she is of the upper class yet speaks like "any little model of his acquaintance" (36).

Betty is among those who are at home where Mayfair and Bohemia overlap; partaking of both Mary and Zouch, she quickly realizes their incongruity. "You're more like one of my friends," she remarks to Zouch. "I thought Mary only liked young men in the Foreign Service or the Brigade. She's always been terribly shocked by the people I know." She makes a joke of Zouch instead of opposing him, as her father does, with dreams of violence. Her sense of humor, as a matter of fact, is the keenest in the novel; and, despite the strict objectivity of Powell's technique, the author clearly finds her most sympathetic. Stranded with her daughter Bianca under the somewhat hostile wing of her father, she occupies a middle ground between her egoistic elders and her idealistic juniors (a character structuring that anticipates that of Henry Green's *Doting* and *Living*).

When Zouch mentions her father's kindness in furnishing him with a "mount" for the fox hunt to come, Betty replies with frank good humor:

> "Oh, it isn't kindness with father, it's cruelty. Absolutely pathological, I can assure you."
>
> Zouch laughed heartily, thinking that what Betty said was all too true.
>
> "I haven't been on a horse for eighteen months," he said conversationally, and without any reference to actual fact.
>
> Betty said: "I haven't for eighteen years and it will be eighteen centuries before I do again."

"But, dear," said Mrs. Passenger mildly, "you used to like your pony so much when you were a child."

"I know," said Betty, "I know. But look how I've ended up. I'm a warning to all girls who like animals." (170)

The big event of Zouch's visit, as it lengthens into the summer, is a pageant held in commemoration of King Charles II's visit to the town: the "Restoration Restored." Betty appropriately is to play Nell Gwyn. Big-hearted, she invites Joanna Brandon, the daughter of a poor neighbor, to stay at Passenger Court for the festival.

Joanna Brandon (chicken number two for Zouch) is at the bottom end of the social pecking order—the Passengers have a butler, chauffeur, gardener, maids; the Brandons have only a woman of all work—but Joanna is in society, local society; and Zouch has already spotted her at church. When Betty notices his roving eye and he protests that the girl's physical beauty means nothing to him except as a subject for his art, Betty laughs: "Well, you must be different from all the other painters I've ever met" (78). Although Joanna has been courted by the local golfer, she dreams of escaping to the art world of London from her "provincial" mother. The widow of a naval officer, Mrs. Brandon has withdrawn from life and spends her days hypochondriacly reclined on a sofa, "wearing a *negligee* of yellow material edged with fur," rereading "her favourite book, *The Story of San Michele*," and wondering why all books are not beautiful:

"Why don't writers only write about the beautiful things of life? You know, Joanna, there is so much beauty all round us."

"What's happened to the dogs? Why aren't they here?"

"Poor Spot has been sick."

"Again?"

"It was the mutton. . . . It was too stringy."

"I'll take him to the vet on Monday."

"Poor Spot must go see doctor. Give him nasty physic. Hand mother a cigarette, darling."

"I saw the young man staying with the Passengers. He has got a beard. It looks funny. But he seems rather nice."

"When I first met your father . . . he wore a beard. . . . He looked like a Greek god. I remember once saying that to Vernon Passenger and him saying, 'And he used to behave like one too.' Wasn't that a tribute? From someone as critical as Vernon Passenger, too." (54-55)

On his exploratory visit Zouch leads Joanna to the gardenhouse while her mother lies asleep: but he is rejected by the operation of some instinctual mechanism in Joanna which later seems irrational to her: "Her conduct had been of the very kind which in theory she most despised. She thought of her favourite heroine, Marie Bashkirtseff, and also about Madame Bovary. . . . And then there was the whole of D. H. Lawrence's works. Besides she now knew that she was in love with Zouch" (123). Accordingly, she writes him a letter to apologize for her prudish conduct.

Betty Passenger's invitation to Joanna to stay with the Passengers during the Restoration Festival opens the free-lunch counter to Zouch, and Joanna that night welcomes him to her bed. The next day, Mary Passenger, convinced that her "unreal" dream "about a tall husband with a country house" has been adequately replaced now with a realistic concept of herself as "a fashionable painter's wife," presses Zouch into proposing to her. Consequently, upon her return home, Joanna learns of Zouch's engagement to Mary and wonders "whether this was called having your heart broken." She mounts to her room and cries. Later she remembers that "it was early closing day so that she had to go out and do the shopping after all."

The Restoration Festival at which Zouch seduces Joanna enlists a third neighboring family, the Fosdicks—defined socially as having a cook and a handyman; and the second of the three social events around which the novel is organized is a cocktail party at the local *Fox and Hounds* given by Torquil Fosdick. Torquil has been sent down from Oxford for a term, having failed an examination; but he gained a reputation at his small college, someone having entered his room and smelled incense. "Torquil will be a great success in life," his mother says to Zouch. "We thought he would probably do well in the Diplomatic. . . . and then they say that they are getting a very nice type of young man in the B.B.C. now, and besides there's no examination for that" (132). Torquil enjoys knowing Betty is a duchess, "even thought it might be only a Neapolitan one," and her talk baffles and excites him, while his bungling ineptitude brings out her maternal streak:

"Oh, but, Betty, you can't say that. You've lived. You've had adventures. Known famous people! I'm still at Oxford."

"That doesn't matter," Betty said. "It doesn't depend on what you've done. Look at Mary. She's never had any experience but she knows how to look after herself far better than I do. Look at Jasper. He's had plenty of experience and look what he is, even though he is your brother, my pet."

Torquil felt that he was getting into deep water. He said: "Anyway, I want to live too."

"You shall," said Betty. "One of these days I'll take you out and show you people and then you'll be able to judge for yourself. You can choose what you like from the whole cockeyed world."

This sort of talk made Torquil quite breathless. (62)

When later she proposes to Torquil to cheer him up, she does so with no serious conviction that matrimony will ensue. Their fathers have had a long-standing grudge. It began when Major Fosdick secured a lease on the North Copse of the Passenger estate, and since then Vernon Passenger has been convinced the Major is ruining the area:

"He shoots all my game, his wife is for ever bothering me about the thousand and one committees that she sits on, his eldest son does nothing but ride on my hounds, and as for that boy Torquil—"

Mr. Passenger stopped . . . trying to find words strong enough. . . .

Mrs. Passenger folded up the piece of work she had in her hand and looked across, a little hopelessly, at her husband. . . . Betty said:

"Now, father, you mustn't say anything against Torquil. I like him very much."

"You like him?"

"Of course I do."

Mr. Passenger said: "He's the worst of the lot."

When Betty blurts out that she is engaged to Torquil, "Even Zouch was outraged." In a splendidly comic bit of slow motion, Mr. Passenger shakes out his newspaper, folds it up carefully, tucks it with controlled fury under his arm, and walks out, pausing only long enough to say: "It is unbelievable" (172).

The articulation of the novel is subtle. Passenger has been hackled for years by the very appearance of Major Fosdick, who has "the air of a legendary creature of the woods, Herne the Hunter almost, with a touch of the romantic gamekeeper, some Lady Chatterley's superannuated lover, and yet at the same time he looked more of a country gentleman than perhaps any country gentleman could ever hope to look" (15). Passenger drives in a fury to Fosdick's to demand that the Major assist him in breaking off the engagement; and, as he waits for the door to be opened, he conjures up a vision of the Major in jodhpurs, carrying a crop, "dressed like the Old Squire in a melodrama" (177). At the pageant the Major had stuffily objected to any changing of dress in public, even to portray General Monk: "It's absurd at my age. Dressing me up like this. I feel a regular figure of fun" (135). He is truculent about the North Copse largely because of class pride: "Just because they happen to have made a few good business deals in land at the time of George III I don't see why I should kowtow to them" (51).

But the Major treads the hairline of sanity: he exists for the afternoons he can lock himself in his room and compose himself for writing poetry by donning a sequin dress and by "singing and muttering a little to himself. Lately he had become very careless about the rest of his household finding out about his eccentricities" (155). At times he worries about this carelessness: "The more disciplined side of his nature told him that he would soon be going too far but there was also something in him which made him enjoy these risks of discovery" (156).

Alone in the house on the day Mr. Passenger learns of the engagement of the Major's son and his daughter, the Major feels cold and, wrapping "round his shoulders the antimacassar from the top of one of the drawing room chairs," begins to write verse in his exercise book. He has stopped to seek a book on the breeding of retrievers from the hallway when Mr. Passenger impatiently opens the door (174). Passenger had called the Major insane for some years, yet he is surprised at discovering him in feminine attire. With dignity, as they face each other in the hall, the Major opens talk by mentioning the North Copse: "I have been thinking it over, Passenger, and I have decided that you have a just cause of complaint about North

Copse." They complete the transaction like gentlemen, and Passenger leaves "overcome by a sense of failure. He had not risen to the situation. As a superman he had let himself down. In this moment of emergency he had been thrown back on the old props of tradition and education and when he might have enjoyed a substantial revenge he had behaved with all the restraint in the world." He drives home slowly. "It had been a bad day" (181).

The next we hear of the Major he has been taken to a sanitarium; Passenger's involuntary, gentlemanly reprieve has been to no avail. We revert to our first view of the Major as to a better fate: "Major Fosdick, followed by his plebian spaniel . . . debouched . . . from the green lane on the main road, both narrowly escaping death from a Brobdingnagian bus, lumbering towards the town at fifty miles an hour on the wrong side of the road" (17).

Mary has hopes that a return to Passenger in the autumn by a Zouch clean-shaven and pink-coated for the fox hunts will change her father's attitude toward their engagement. As destiny has it, she comes down with a cold the week of the hunts. Although Zouch repeatedly postpones riding in hopes of making his debut backed up by Mary, he is "aware that every time he refused, it scored a point to Mr. Passenger's hand"; and, with several equestrian lessons behind him, he finally agrees to ride. The following day, stoked with enough whiskey to steady his nerves, he mounts Creditor. "Ah, 'e's a playful little rogue, 'e is," the diabolical-looking groom says. The cold air makes Zouch "feel all at once a little muzzy." The "leathers look to me a trifle short for you," Mr. Passenger says to give him fair warning. The road has a coating of light frost; and a large bus comes suddenly out of the haze:

> "These things are the curse of the roads," said Mr. Passenger.
> "There seem to be a great many of them round here."
> "Far too many. Keep an eye on Creditor. He hates buses."
> They drew in a little to the side of the road, Zouch in front. The bus came rolling past. A cluster of putty-coloured faces looked out at them from behind glass. Zouch felt Creditor quivering under his weight. He tightened his hold on the reins. Creditor gave several quiet snorts. The bus passed on and Zouch relaxed his hold again.

They walked on along the road. And then, quite suddenly, without any warning, Creditor was off. (195)

Though Passenger now shows up Zouch's pretensions to horsemanship, all might yet have gone fairly well had not the horse slipped on the frost: "Zouch came off, landing on his head. . . . At the beginning of the next chapter, the crowd at the Fox and Hounds is discussing the death of Zouch—"one of those shapeless entities torn out of the abyss of time."

At the Brandon's, Joanna's mother is lamenting, as usual, the state of her health, blaming inconsiderate doctors who tell her that except for her heart trouble, there is nothing wrong with her:

"To-day I feel very weak. I shan't last much longer. I shall be gone soon. I don't expect I shall see another summer."

Mrs. Dadds said: "We're none of us getting any younger. What's more there's a great deal of sickness about . . . and there's Miss Joanna looking as white as chalk . . . and my pains have been something terrible. . . . I've had to stop sometimes and sit down in a chair. . . ."

The maid-of-all-work keeps talking for a while, wandering on to the subject of her own husband, in her opinion a "sex-maniac," and his funeral: "*Day of Wrath! O day of mourning! See fulfilled the prophet's warning!* they played that and I shan't forget it if I live to be a thousand. I thought, You're getting your deserts by now, my man." After some time she starts to get back to her work:

She was an unobservant woman and did not notice that her mistress was dead. She made a few more remarks about human nature, illustrating them from incidents from her late husband's career, and, as these called forth no response from Mrs. Brandon, she concluded that . . . Mrs. Brandon preferred sleep that afternoon to conversation. . . . Talking to someone who was asleep . . . cheapened her. She went back to the kitchen in a rebellious mood. (203)

At Passenger Court Betty's father is expressing relief at getting control of North Copse again:

"It was annoying to have old Fosdick shooting at my birds. It was more than annoying. It was maddening."

"It drove him mad anyway," Betty says.

"You should not joke about that sort of thing, Betty. That is one of the sides of you which I can never understand. You never seem to be serious."

More evidence that her father disapproves of her continued sojourn at home with her daughter comes after he leaves the room. Asked by Betty why the cigarette box is empty, the butler replies that her father has given orders that no more cigarettes are to be put out. Before the butler withdraws, she recalls a last relic of Zouch and asks him to "take the picture of Miss Mary off the easel in the old school room and hide it somewhere. I see that Miss Bianca has painted a moustache on the face." The novel ends as Betty, left alone, goes "to her father's desk to look for the cigar-box."

Comic to the end, pure in tone, beautifully written, acute in its depiction of society, and wise in its understanding of man, *From a View to a Death* is a small masterpiece.

IV Agents and Patients

T. S. Eliot argues in his essay "Tradition and the Individual Talent" that, since "no poet, no artist of any art, has his complete meaning alone," the historical sense is "nearly indispensable to any one who would continue to be a poet beyond his twenty-fifth year." In Powell's fourth novel, *Agents and Patients* (1936), he seems to be taking Eliot's advice and to be looking back into tradition for "private admirations" to bring freshness of form to his materials. The branch of the English comic tradition next essayed at any rate is the Jonsonian one of coney-catching comedy. Powell brings the essential plot of the gull and coney-catchers up to date by substituting psychiatry for the alchemy that was the popular pseudo-science in the seventeenth century. Yet he carries the gulling operation into the smart capitals of Europe; and with this deracination the novel gains an additional measure of unreality and seems to mark a negative oscillation in his development.

Powell has always had a weakness for dividing the population of the world into those who act, and those acted upon; and he finds in John Wesley's sermons an operative line to serve as the novel's epigraph: "So in every possible case; He that is not free is not an *Agent,* but a *Patient.*" At first glance, the chief patient, or gull, seems to be a young man just down from Oxford named Blore-Smith. But, from the first, he is not a "patient" simple enough to reduce the plot to farce. He has dignity; caution is mingled with his impulses toward rash action; and, like "Erridge" later in *The Music of Time,* he is aware of his gullibility in a general way and, like an educated bunny, tries to avoid coney-catchers. He has started "reading for the Bar, but he was not much interested in law and did it to have something to tell people when they questioned him about himself" (6). He has taken rooms in Ebury Street—a section of Belgravia steeped in art tradition; he has mounted his Medici prints and a reproduction of Van Gogh's *Sunflower*; and he spends "enjoyable" evenings there reading Roger Fry's *Vision and Design.* But he feels constricted by life and longs for "freedom."

The novel opens with the coffee house talk of the coney-catchers (the "agents" of the title), picaros of some education and social standing, in the modern manner; and the novel closes with a poker player's demand to see the winner's openers. Thereupon, one of these young men—with at least a touch of symbolism—flicks two knaves across the table. Oliver Chipchase, knave number one, is a bachelor engaged nocturnally (as his surname suggests) in the pursuit of low women; he is engaged by day as an art critic and amateur psychiatrist. He has even "published a short book on psychoanalysis in relation to automatic writing, but its sales had not been large."

Knave number two, Peter Maltravers, has also dabbled in journalism—it "left both of them with its attendant paranoiac leanings"—but at present he is a scenarist for an English film company with a contract to work in Berlin, an intrigue to get himself to Hollywood, and a scheme to produce a revolutionary documentary film of his own. The documentary trend is the latest in the cinema world, he explains to Chipchase: "Russian peasants acting Russian peasants. Chinese looking oriental.... My extension of it is to collect a cast of... intellectuals...

and watch them behave intellectually. All I need is a little backing" (3-4).[10]

The three young men—Blore-Smith, Chipchase, and Maltravers—meet after Chipchase wheels his car around a corner and knocks Blore-Smith down. Finding Blore-Smith uninjured, Chipchase takes him along to a picture gallery, and there he discovers Blore-Smith is wealthy when he nervously blurts out acceptance of the first price quoted for a painting. Encouraged by Chipchase, Blore-Smith reveals his secret desires:

> "London is such a disappointment," Blore-Smith said. . . . "One doesn't seem to get any of the things one expected."
> "What sort of things?"
> "Well, I mean life and so on."
> "But you seem to get plenty of excitement. For instance, I've just knocked you down in my car."
> "Oh, I don't mean things like that," Blore-Smith said. He hesitated. "Women," he said, and then he felt that he had gone too far. (32)

With this clue, Maltravers drives him to a flower shop called *la cattleya* (in the Firbank-Proust vein) that is managed by "the most beautiful woman you have ever seen." The beautiful Mrs. Mendoza, however, is threatening to move to Basra: "I shouldn't have everybody nagging at me there, living on my vitality, telling me all about themselves and their beastly affairs, and . . . never giving me a moment's peace. Nor should I have to look after this wretched shop. . . . Why, Peter, she said, how are you, darling? I heard the bell and thought it must be a customer." Her backer in the flower shop has begun to tire her, a Commodore Hugo Venables; he is portly and cheerful but exasperatingly unable to pick out a cigarette lighter of modern design. Mrs. Mendoza is attractive intellectually ("You always want everybody's individuality taken away from them," she says to Chipchase), but Chipchase recognizes trouble in her fatigue and spirits Blore-Smith away to Maltravers' flat. Maltravers' wife is out with a racing motorist named Nipper, with her husband's tacit consent, theirs being a "modern" menage; but Maltravers, to make room for Blore-Smith, reveals his irritation by throwing the manuscript of a novel she is writing on the floor.

Blore-Smith is entranced upon meeting Sarah Maltravers; and, when she later visits his flat and sighs "Isn't life awful," he blurts out a proposition: "Will you be my mistress?" (115). Sarah laughs and reports him to her husband and Chipchase.

"But, I say," said Chipchase. "What frightful cheek! Did he really now?"

"I believe you put him up to it," Sarah said.

"My dear, don't be so absurd. . . . He must have gone off his head."

"What do you mean?" said Maltravers. "I hope you aren't trying to suggest that Sarah isn't attractive."

"This isn't a moment for your habitual bad taste," Chipchase said. "It's a preposterous thing to have happened."

"But I like my wife to have successes. It gives me confidence in myself."

"Is that really all you have to say?" Sarah said.

"What else do you expect me to say, darling? What did you do anyway?"

"I didn't do anything. I was laughing too much."

"There you are. You treat the thing as a joke yourself and then expect me to be furious." (118-19)

This is not a comedy about marital infidelity, as the Noel Coward tone might suggest, but about the absurd discrepancy between the characters' feelings and their principles, their "primitive" instincts and "up-to-date" rationalisms. In the course of a minute, the values have been reversed. Maltravers grows indignant at the thought of Blore-Smith's income and his wife's callous neglect: "You only laughed at him! You stand there discussing a man who is admittedly such a mass of nerves that he had to get Oliver here to put him right psychologically and . . . you only laughed at him. . . . You've probably done irreparable damage" (120).

Chipchase induces Blore-Smith to be his "patient" by alluding to ominous symptoms and allowing time to prey upon his worries. The psychoanalysis stays upon the surface of Blore-Smith's mind, so far as the novel is concerned, couch sessions beginning as chapters end ("Have you had any more dreams about the Prime Minister. . . ?"). Persuading Blore-Smith that he needs "psychic release," Chipchase gets him to underwrite an expedition to Paris, where Chipchase hopes to regain a lost girlfriend. American artists discussing their conquests loudly at the Dôme, drunken Continental aristocrats *A la Vache enragée,*[11] frescoes "conceived in a spirit of complete moral detachment" Chez Zouzou, various homosexuals, and a girl named Yoyo lead Blore-Smith into the life that Torquil Fosdick had longed for in *From a View to a Death.* That Yoyo makes off with Blore-Smith's wallet can be chalked up to "buying experience," Chipchase assures him as they return to London with a new secretary (the girl Chipchase sought) who has been hired to take notes on Blore-Smith's "case."

Maltravers, on the other hand, begins his assault on Blore-Smith's money by maneuvering Blore-Smith into admitting that he believes the cinema to be "the most living of the arts":

> "Once decided you will not be able to turn back," Maltravers said. "Think it over. Do you want to spend your money in the cause of Beauty? Wouldn't you rather invest in something more gilt-edged?"
>
> Blore-Smith made an effort to control himself. He muttered: "Is there anything more gilt-edged?"
>
> Maltravers banged on the table so that the group of waiters posed near him all jumped at the same time like a perfectly trained *corps de ballet.*
>
> "Excellent," Maltravers said. "Excellent."
>
> Blore-Smith knew that for once he had said something worth saying. For perhaps the first time in his life he had come up to scratch. (50-51)

The Berlin which they visit as the focus of the cinema art form is the one of Christopher Isherwood, but it is seen through a different camera.[12] From the name of their hotel, the Sans Souci Palast, to the mostly transvestite clientele at the Eden Bar, an ironic eye surveys Germany of the early 1930's—where, as Stephen Spender said, urging a friend to join him there, "youth had started to live again, free of the shackles of the past and ossifying bourgeois conventions."[13]

At the Eden Bar the beautiful Mrs. Mendoza overtakes Chipchase and Maltravers and charms Blore-Smith away from the epicene crowd. On a café terrace in the heart of this city of ultimate pagan "freedom," they sit together "for some time in silence watching a child prostitute with a face like a white mask, passing and repassing along the pavement below them":

"Do you know . . . why I should most like to have been born a man? . . . I could have learnt Greek," Mrs. Mendoza said.
Blore-Smith caught his breath with surprise. . . .
"Is it too late to take lessons?" he said.
"Don't be absurd," Mrs. Mendoza said, so crossly that in order to cover his mistake as quickly as possible Blore-Smith added:
"Some of Herodotus was very amusing, I remember."
But Mrs. Mendoza was not listening.
"The Greeks knew how to live," she said. "If they heard music they danced; if they saw a stretch of golden sand they raced along it. . . . They were natural, beautiful, free. They didn't live horrible constricted fussy little lives like us."
Mrs. Mendoza clenched together her hands and held out her arms stiffly on either side of her, looking, Blore-Smith thought, . . . like Artemis carved on the prow of a ship.
"Don't you like Berlin, then?" he said.
"Like it? I hate it. Every minute I stay here is sheer hell." (144-45)

The final action takes place at Broadacres, an English country house lent to Maltravers' film company by an art collector who hopes to keep a French aristocrat (called Gaston, Marquis de la Tour d'Espagne) amused with film making while he dickers with him for the sale of his chateau full of ancestral art treasures. Maltravers has arranged "pictorially" a sizable number of intellectuals on the lawn of the estate with camera poised waiting for something "psychological" to develop—in order to begin his documentary film on the intellectuals—when a hoodless two-seater grumbles up the long curved drive. The Commodore—abandoned by Mrs. Mendoza, drunk on the champagne he has brought to her cottage as a peace offering, and, accompanied by the dismal medical student she had left watching the cottage for days with nothing to eat but caviar—comes stumbling angrily across the field toward Mrs. Mendoza and the intellectuals just as an airplane swoops down to land in the polo field. The plane contains an agent for a rival collector who persuades the French aristocrat to sell; he in turn quickly persuades Mrs. Mendoza to elope; he then wheels to meet the pursuing Commodore, charges him like a goat, butts him in the stomach, and takes off with

Mrs. Mendoza in the chauffeured plane for Paris. "Cut!" shouts Maltravers to Chipchase, who has been working the camera.

The intellectuals have behaved like—intellectuals, or human beings; and Blore-Smith disappears. In the first unscrupulous act of his life, he commandeers a car and is driven back to his rooms in Ebury Street. When Chipchase and Maltravers call upon him later with their final bills for the film and for their psychiatric service, they assure him that he has had his money's worth: "You don't suggest . . . you would have had the courage to talk to me like this when we first met?"

But, though the novel ends with this cool detachment, the French aristocrat has stolen its emotional focus[14]; the attractive Sarah Maltravers as a character has been lost to view, and the symbol of the chains Blore-Smith was to break is lost. And classic aloofness is lost by Powell in what seems to be a catering to public taste. When Sarah (in her job as motoring correspondent for *Mode*) says, "I'm writing an article on French bodies," the author informs us that "Blore-Smith could hardly believe his ears" (112-13). Such underlined humor is at some remove from that which depends upon recognition of clichés. Descents in style and structuring run counter to what now seems to be Powell's natural development; and *Agents and Patients* remains an interesting exhibit, but not a fine work of art.

V What's Become of Waring

Three years elapsed before Anthony Powell's next novel appeared, and *What's Become of Waring* (1939) broke step with Powell's esthetic past in even more radical ways than had *Agents and Patients* and is a better novel for it. Two differences are fundamental, however: it has the comic incidents of the earlier novels but not the comic tone; the ironic denouements of a comic novel, but not the structure. As the title suggests, the novel, built upon a question, is structured like a detective story to answer that query. A better analogy is A. J. A. Symons' book *The Quest for Corvo,* the fascination of which grows upon the reader as Symons interviews people who knew the mysterious Corvo, reads letters from him, visits the scenes of his activity, and tries to fit the pieces together, only to unveil new puzzles.

The central figure of *What's Become of Waring*, so far as the theme is concerned, is a writer who appears in only one brief scene and then is revealed to have half a dozen aliases. But the central figure structurally is the narrator, a publisher's reader who manages, somehow gracefully, to exist throughout the novel without a name. Were any of the characters to address him by name, they would probably call him Nick Jenkins; for *What's Become of Waring* is technically, as well as thematically, closely allied to *The Music of Time*. The theme of the tentative nature of most of what passes for human "knowledge" is here, though not yet generalized; and the mode is conversational and social ("Your father said he was married—twice." "We thought so at first. Now it seems uncertain. It may be someone else with a similar name.")

As the narrator picks up bits of fact and pseudo-fact, he reveals only enough about himself to become a plausible character: he has moved from the advertising to the publishing business in order to have more time to work on his literary study, *Stendhal: And Some Thoughts on Violence* ("After three years the second chapter, 'Laughter Is Power,' remained uncompleted"). Two brothers head the publishing firm, and the narrator is the "hired [manuscript] assassin" for the younger, Hugh Judkins, a man of Nonconformist background who is absurdly torn between the two alien strains of that tradition: the fundamentalist and the rationalist. Hugh seeks spiritualists, for instance, and then tries to "expose" them (96, 224). His favorite author is a writer of inspirational travel books named T. T. Waring, whose style has the "woolly" quality "that appeals irresistibly to uncritical palates . . . tinny echoes of a biblical style." The novel opens when Hugh takes the narrator to a séance during which a medium called "Mimi" ("Don't forget that Mimi is George Eliot. We only call her Mimi becouse she asked us to") seems uncooperative. She says only "tee-tee" during the course of the evening—but prophetically, it appears, when news headlines announce the death abroad of T. T. Waring.

As Waring's publishers, the brothers must decide who shall write Waring's biography, and the narrator breaks their stalemate by introducing an admirer of the life of action that Waring apparently has led, a Captain Hudson, who is writing his own regiment's history in a cliché-free style. Captain Hudson's motive in undertaking the biography is financial and amatory: to speed his marriage to the girl Beryl Pimley. The skeleton in the Pimley closet is her vanished brother Alec, a remittance man whose escapades have annoyed his father Major-General Pimley, Ret., and delighted his grandfather Captain Pimley, Ret., who, outranked at home by his own son, supports underdogs wherever they can be found.

Hudson's first discovery is that his idol Waring has cleverly plagiarized much of his material from books "unlikely to be translated." When he makes this report to the narrator at a café in southern France, the arm of coincidence that later is a hallmark of *The Music of Time* begins to arrange events: in a neighboring harbor-town, Hudson and the narrator discover the missing brother, Alec Pimley. Under the name of Mason, he has married a rich American widow and is living on her yacht. As he attempts to conceal his change of identity, he reveals that he is also T.T. Waring, alias Robinson; and to escape his creditors he has announced his "death" as an author, after marrying the rich widow, by sending a cable to a New York newspaper. Although he promises to pay a minor debt the next day, when they look back on the road to Toulon, they see his yacht moving out to sea. Additional revelations come when we learn, after the death of Alec's grandfather, that the grandfather has all along concealed with delight the first act of plagiarism—Waring's purloining of Captain Pimley's own *Memoirs of Ceylon*—and with it the identity of Waring.

The novel ends with further comic twists in the plot. The younger publisher, Hugh, in a rationalist mood takes a young lady on a Scandinavian cruise and, when she holds him at bay, reverts to his fundamentalism and orders that the plates for a "hopelessly sprawling" American novel called *Lot's Hometown* be destroyed on the grounds that it is "muck." The yacht bearing Pimley-alias-Waring sinks in a storm as he flees, bearing him to his death; thereby he not only "gives the world the slip" but also confirms the New York newspaper report that he drowned.[15]

But *What's Become of Waring* as a whole lacks the humorous ambiance of the earlier novels. Powell at this point in his career seemed in danger of following Aldous Huxley from the comic into comic theory, from amusing the reader into boring him with descriptions of situations or people alleged to be amusing. He describes Hudson in Toulon, for instance, as looking "like an Englishman in a French caricature." Hudson brings comic joy to the reader, however, only structurally, when he departs at the end for "a camel" in Iraq and the life of action—action in the tradition of Richard Burton and Charles Doughty—that his "idol" T. T. Waring had lived only vicariously.

In *Afternoon Men* the Nietzschean painter Barlow had enjoyed manipulating Pringle; and the Nietzschean painter Zouch had pursued his hopes of power through matrimony to the grave in *From a View to a Death.* But, at the end of Powell's interwar novels, the narrator converts the question about Waring to one as to whether everyone seeks power, as he drifts off to sleep—a question that points ahead to *The Music of Time*: "His schooldays. The masters had been a funny crowd. French. . . . It was power Hugh wanted too. Everybody wanted power. Bernard . . . Roberta. . . ." He wonders if even the gayest of his friends had also wanted power: "It was an interesting question. . . . Was money power? . . . But. . . . T. T. Waring wanted power more than any of them. . . . The milk arrived in the street, making a great clatter. . . . Sleep, like a long drink, came at last."

CHAPTER 6

A Prelude to The Music of Time

THE narrator of *The Music of Time* admits the ability of other artists to shift gears in wartime and to return sporadically to creative activity; but he feels himself "incapable of writing a line of a novel . . . however long released from duty" (7.113). Whether or not an autobiographical note is to be detected in this remark, World War II came and went without another novel by Anthony Powell.

I *Biographer, Critic, and Parodist*

It could be argued that Powell's silence was due to his desire to try his hand at something new. In June, 1939, a letter appeared in the *Spectator* asking the readers of that journal for help in locating certain lost manuscripts by John Aubrey and made it obvious that Anthony Powell contemplated writing a biography. War was in the air even then, Powell seems to have felt (as Nick Jenkins does as early as 1938); and the letter seems to have been a way of preparing a wartime avocation. Less demanding than creative work, biography can be written during interludes. Indeed, the Aubrey biography suffered errors in the first edition, Powell was to admit, due to forced composition far from his notes. Another letter in the *Spectator* early in 1946 announced a more concentrated effort on the biography with the end of the war, and *John Aubrey and His Friends* was published two years later.[1]

Powell is certainly at least half right in complaining about "the appalling, genial verbosity of American scholars who write of great men as if writing the script of a Hollywood film."[2] *John Aubrey* as a biography suffers from the opposite fault, an over-scrupulous avoidance of the dramatic. When the English novelists of Powell's generation turn their hands to biography, they seem to suffer from a similar malady: theirs is such a rigid adherence to fact and so stark a refusal to speculate that only the dry bones show through. Perhaps bones are better than the flabby gush of their predecessors, but the dryness makes their biographical studies easy to lay down. It would be best, perhaps, to consider *John Aubrey* a readable, scholarly, and therefore useful act of homage.

Work on the book must have contributed to the genesis of *The Music of Time,* however. John Aubrey had a character similar to that of Nick Jenkins, Powell's narrator in *The Music of Time*; and the curiosity which led that seventeenth-century Welsh antiquarian to peer into the lives of contemporaries and predecessors is matched by the humility which led him to record conflicting anecdotes without attempting to force a reconciliation by means of theory or rationalization. Aubrey's social ties were of interest to Powell, too, not only in his connecting the worlds of art and aristocracy, as we have noted, but in his strange friendship with Anthony à Wood, a rival antiquarian whom Aubrey knew to be malicious, stingy, and bad-tempered. Powell found in their relationship "yet another instance in the strange annals of friendship of the unlikely human beings who can inspire deep affection."[3] Wood and Aubrey had in common a mutual lack of interest in material things, which may have been the key to their friendship; and in the novels ahead Nick Jenkins ponders the absurdities and profundities of several such human entanglements, including his own with Widmerpool.

The first public appearance of Powell after the war was as a literary critic. Powell had long been what he calls a "memoir addict," and in 1945 his long article analyzing the *Journal Intime* of Henri Frederic Amiel was published in the *Cornhill* magazine. Reviews began to appear in the *Spectator* in 1946, and for some years Powell contributed anonymously to the *Times Literary Supplement.* In 1953, when Malcolm Muggeridge was appointed editor of *Punch,* a brilliant five-year epoch opened in Powell's life; for Muggeridge invited Powell to join the circle of senior editors of *Punch*—or to become "a member of the Table," as the editors put it. Neither Powell nor Waugh, Graham Greene, nor John Betjeman ("the most original of the lucid poets between the wars") had contributed to *Punch* before 1953; but, with Powell installed as chief of the Booking Office, many of his talented Oxford contemporaries began to contribute. Powell shared Muggeridge's joy in the "comedy of the fight for power, and the humour of personal idiosyncrasy," as well as his Tory politics. But with Muggeridge dismissing all style as illusion and disapproving of subtlety in satire (a cartoon he liked, for instance, and Powell did not, depicted the aging Churchill as a corpse-in-office), there was friction enough for stimulation.

Unlike Waugh and Greene, Powell has not published much "small stuff"—story, verse, or essay; but these years with *Punch* encouraged him to write articles that the historian of the periodical calls "brilliant."[4] The best are wry, ironic skits (relating the Greek shipping magnate Onassis to Moby Dick, for instance) or parodies (those of Graham Greene's plays and of Edmund Wilson's literary criticism being the most memorable). At best, these works seem too ephemeral to merit rank with those of, say, Beerbohm's collection *Seven Men* (1919). Perhaps Beerbohm sets too high a standard of delight, but Powell's ephemera seem on the whole, like Chekhov's, more ephemeral than those of most great writers. The cause should probably be traced to the circumstances of his association with *Punch*. By tradition, like the staff of the *New Yorker*, the staff of *Punch* meets but three times a week; and Powell must have accepted the position in London with his heart on the work he was creating on the alternate days back in Somerset.

II *Marcel Proust*

When a note informed the world in 1951 that *A Question of Upbringing* was but the prelude to a sequence of novels to be called *The Music of Time*, the overall title, the first-person narrator, and the *roman fleuve* structure put critics in mind of Marcel Proust's *In Remembrance of Things Past*. More than one concluded that Powell must have devoted his wartime nights to the pages of Proust. After the appearance of the fifth volume, Edmund Wilson remarked a bit tartly that "If Evelyn Waugh is the Shakespeare of the School, Powell is the Middleton or the Day. It's a pity he ever dipped into Proust. . . ."[5] But Powell had not "dipped into Proust"—he had absorbed him; and those who casually refer to Powell as "the English Proust" do justice to neither writer—and befuddle their own thinking.

Proust's seven volumes (1913-27) and Powell's eleven to date (1951-73) derive as composite structures from a reactionary tendency in the novel: a return to something like the massive Victorian triple-decker, but they return with greater esthetic control. The *roman fleuve*—no equivalent term is available in English—may be defined as a multiple-volume work having a unity of design. It is distinguished from the "sequence novel" (such as *Little Women* and *Little Men,* or *A Portrait of the Artist as a Young Man* and *Ulysses*) in which characters recur, but in new and unrelated plots, and from the "serial novel" (such as those which feature James Bond or Tom Swift) in which characters recur with no integral carryover in scene, plot, or theme. The difference is fundamentally in the unity of impact, the singleness of effect that can make the collectivity of the *roman fleuve* a work of art rather than a string of possibly attractive but mismatched stones.

Of course, if the only similarity were that of flowing and spacious form, the question of Proustian dominance would not have arisen. The role assigned to the memory is also central to the long novels of both Powell and Proust. To Nick Jenkins a painting brings back "memories of childhood," and "the sight of Widmerpool called up in a similar manner . . . all kind of recollections of days at school. I remembered the interest once aroused in me by Widmerpool's determination to become a success in life, and the brilliance with which Stringham used to mimic his movements and manner of speech" (2.30). As with Marcel, Nick's memories explode with emotion "like wounds, unknown and quiescent, that suddenly break out to give pain, or at least irritation, at a later season" (2.143). Finally, what one critic calls "the mnemonic episodes" in *A la recherche du temps perdu* and what another terms "discontinuous memories . . . in homogeneous blocks"[6] are akin to Powell's unit mode of structuring, as we see, for instance, when an almost forgotten popular song, "Pale Hands I Loved Beside the Shalimar," brings into focus by way of the memory the sequence of five distinct but related episodes in *Casanova's Chinese Restaurant.*

But there are differences of importance. Proust lingers over the process by which imagination and memory translate the evanescent odor or image into a concrete evocation; for Proust's final point, the miracle of the process is important. For Powell, the process of evocation is not, and the details are left to be assumed. Proust, moreover, emphasizes the exquisite, emotional pleasure that springs from "remembrance of things past"; Powell emphasizes the drier intellectual pleasure that comes to the understanding as the memory suddenly throws into juxtaposition two areas of time, either of which may be in itself only painful. The only intellectual tools of the critic are analysis and comparison, T. S. Eliot has remarked; and what may be called the "Proustian memory" is used by Powell as an agent in the criticism of life: it is the ugly sight of a bombed-out pub which evokes the lovely song "Pale Hands" which in turn evokes the pleasurable agony of life in the 1920's in *Casanova's Chinese Restaurant.* Furthermore, Proust emphasizes the involuntary act of memory; in Powell, the recollection is as often deliberate, as when he parallels the narrator's recognitions of the onset of two world wars in *The Kindly Ones.*

Also, Proust's explorations of time are typically impelled by fleeting images—a rain-swept street, steeples seen from a moving train, or an odor insinuated in the wind. The inexorableness of the loss of these images induces the will to "fix" the memory—a process which leads to the narrator's discovery of his vocation: to fix all the memories as an artist. Powell's images are more often static—though they too may take Jenkins by surprise, as a painting by Mr. Deacon does when he enters the home of the Walpole-Wilsons (2.14). That "Truth comes, not to those who seek her, but by surprise to the relaxed will" is an adage that might apply to either novelist, but Powell's images are less urgent, are less often evanescent. The tension is more relaxed; the pace, more casual.

As a consequence, it seems unlikely that Powell is aiming at the erection of a thesis of permanence-in-art upon "piles" of memory. He has not emphasized, after all, the memory as a factor beyond the ordinary in the elucidation of life, and he has dwelt on other theses of his own. He merely uses a device brought to perfection by Proust, much as subsequent novelists have used the epistolary technique of Richardson or the baptism-into-life plot of Fielding; and it seems likely that this link between Proust and Powell, which seems major now, will slowly cease to be thought important.

That the Proustian "I" cannot choose what is to be remembered and cannot by will transpose that into art makes the imagination a central index to life's mystery to Proust's narrator Marcel. Powell's narrator is less romantic in several ways. Proust's almost Freudian emphasis on the memories of childhood, for one thing, is not to be found; when we do retreat toward the childhood of Nick Jenkins, we find a surprising mental health. Objects of nature, too, such as Marcel's hawthorn hedge at Tansonville, have played no role yet in Nick's memories; and, on the other hand, his memories are more clearly fixed in the frame of history, as if Powell thought less of the inner flux than the outer, or less of the personal ambiance than the social. The hunger marchers of 1932 and Templer's loss of Mona, the Abdication Crisis of 1937 and Widmerpool's social deflation, history and personality are inextricably linked in Powell's work; personal events in Proust tend to float more in time.[7]

In subject, theme, and style other resemblances between Powell and Proust do exist, but most are less profound than appears to be the case at first sight. Both artists deal with a "decaying aristocracy," but Powell more than Proust deals also with lower strata of society. Despite the fact that the aristocracy as an idea (like that of Christian knighthood) began its decay on the day of its birth, making the phrase somewhat tautological, let us note that the novelists' views of the "decay" are significantly different. To Proust, the decline and fall seem irreversible; to Powell, the movement is cyclic. When a critic points out that, unlike Proust's narrator, "Nick has no nostalgia for a fading aristocracy,"[8] we must admit that he is partly right—but largely because Powell does not agree that it is fading. Stringham, for instance, is not unlike Sir Winston Churchill: when the mercantile class—Templer, Widmerpool, or Neville Chamberlain—is in the ascendancy between the wars, Stringham languishes, only to come into his own again as World War II begins, as a health-wracked but happy warrior.[9]

On a more abstract level *A la recherche du temps perdu* and *The Music of Time* do deal with time's ineluctable strangeness, and the idea of time does much to control the form of both novels. "It is only upon Anthony Powell that Proust has exerted a direct influence," C. P. Snow argues. "The rest of us, faced with our individual problems of form, have tried other kinds of solution."[10] Still, there is a deep, fundamental difference in the ways in which time influences form in their novels: Proust emphasizes its recoverability; Powell, the revelations of its flow. Bellini's statue *Truth Unveiled by Time* in the Villa Borghese, a reproduction of which haunts *Casanova's Chinese Restaurant*, indicates that Powell values time for the revelation it can give to the present, rather than for the permanency it may give to the past.

III *The Patterns of Time*

When lives cross in time, when we meet a stranger on the Munich express who turns out to be the uncle of a neighbor in Ohio, we feel a kind of unseen power at large in the world. The probabilities are against such encounters, but all people seem to experience them, and repeatedly. A typical case of this sort is noted by Powell in the unlikely encounter between a French critic, whom Proust despised, and a Russian novelist, whom Powell admired: "For those who enjoy literary coincidences, there is a good one in Sainte-Beuve's life. He was returning from Italy to Marseilles in 1838 . . . and . . . had economised by not taking a cabin. Trying to catch some sleep on deck, he made friends with a Russian who spoke bad French, but was evidently a man of remarkable intelligence and distinction. It was Gogol." And we should note Powell's conclusion—"In such patterns is life arranged"[11]—for in such patterns *The Music of Time* is arranged.

Even matter-of-fact men take note of the strangeness of such patterns. After Lloyd George during the Boer War offered R. C. Lehmann the editorship of the *Daily News*, his son John Lehmann observes that, "curiously enough, he had as his assistant editor Harold Spender . . . father of Stephen Spender, with whom I myself was to become so closely associated in the literary world. When one remembers that my father . . . was following in the footsteps of his great-uncle W. H. Wills, who had been sub-editor to Dickens . . . one cannot help being struck by the way in which patterns of family activity and the family friendships that arise from them persist."[12] An English woman novelist G. B. Stern admits to being startled by those moments when the "tiny filaments that invisibly bind the world and time together, suddenly became visible and iridescent." The sight of a woman yawning on the balcony of a chalet in the Tyrol suddenly and bafflingly reminds her of Massine's dance "and a remark from Mr. H. G. Wells . . . at Monte Carlo"—until she recalls that the date on the lintel and that on a fan at the ballet were the same. "An invisible pattern which links everything to everything, and suddenly, in one place, for one moment, it comes up clear like a bit of a message written invisibly in lemon. . . . This was pattern, not coincidence. . . . Coincidence is a much more arbitrary matter than association. And though coincidences do strangely happen in life, they have always an air of clever fiction about them."[13]

Although examples could be multiplied almost indefinitely, the experimental patterns in the life of a man Powell knew well, Cecil Gray, run thematically through Gray's memoirs: "How oddly things and people link up, making a pattern!" "I am not more superstitious than the majority of people," Gray writes, "but I have always had a deep unalterable conviction of the existence of what is vaguely called 'destiny,' a belief in a design, purpose, and pattern underlying the outwardly confused and incoherent surface of one's life, a kind of hidden meaning." Typical of the many substantiating incidents that Gray cites to show patterning in life is the occasion when "Jacob Epstein . . . suggested that we might be interested to meet a musician of his acquaintance. . . . To my astonishment he proved to be none other than the mysterious, enigmatic personality whom I had encountered at the Berlioz concert . . . and who had since haunted my imagination." Gray continued to be amazed. "In the writing of this book I have been struck . . . by the number of coincidences that have occurred in the process; how, when I was thinking . . . of such and such a person, I would receive a letter from him or her, or encounter them in the street, after a lapse of perhaps twenty years or more." In another analogue to a time-structuring principle in *The Music of Time,* certain acquaintances of Gray's, though rarely met, would, when met, "provide a kind of thematic link connecting all the various aspects and phases and movements of the symphony which is my life."[14]

In *The Music of Time* these patterns are, however, only slowly perceived by the narrator:

> Widmerpool's advent in Eaton Square that night did not strike me at the time as anything more than a matter of chance. He had cropped up in my life before, and, if I considered him at all as a recurrent factor, I should have been prepared to admit that he might crop up again. I did not, however, as yet see him as one of those symbolic figures . . . round whom the past and the future have a way of assembling. (2.29)

Powell is not only intrigued by "that inexplicable magic throughout life that makes us suddenly think of someone before turning a street corner and meeting him" (4.11-12), but he organizes the novel to demonstrate its existence.

Powell likewise seems to reject the notion of mere chance. Widmerpool's later appearance at Lady Molly's "helped to prove somehow rather consolingly, that life continued its mysterious, patterned way" (4.44). The narrator is receptive to patterns of all sorts, apparently because he is hoping at this time or that, out of the memory that gives birth to the idea of coincidence, "to construct one of those formal designs in human behaviour which for some reason afford an obscure satisfaction to the mind: making the more apparent inconsistencies of life easier to bear" (4.66). The novel as a whole may be leading to some grand resolution such as *A la recherche du temps perdu* affords, perhaps in the consolation that perception of design in the universe provides. In the end, will all the pieces click into place in the puzzle? "Son of man, You cannot say, or guess, for you know only a heap of broken images. . . ." But, if the images swirl into patterns, the riddles may not be eternal. Man's lot may not be terminally absurd.

That Powell has such a conclusion in mind is, of course, merely speculative. The ground is prepared, in volumes one through eleven, for such a conclusion—prepared at least as well as it is for Proust's terminal relation of memory and art to the recoverability of time and thus to the discovery on his part of the meaning of existence. However, Powell's friends have not pointed to such a terminus; indeed, Evelyn Waugh in a fashion scolded Powell for his use of coincidence: "In reading his brilliant series of novels I have sometimes thought . . . that the recurring seemingly haphazard conjunctions of human life, which comprise his theme, pass beyond plausibility. . . . After I had written [in a review my] doubts of the authenticity of so many coincidences, I began to reflect on my own acquaintance with him and understood that his was genuine social realism." Waugh then lists half a dozen bizarre criss-crossings of his life and Powell's and concludes that Powell's emphasis on such coincidences is merely a result of his desire to portray a peculiarity of British society: "I suppose that in the looser society of the United States or in the tighter society of, say, France such fortuitous connections would be barely possible. It is one of Tony's achievements to record this interplay which, I think, is essentially English."[15]

That Powell may be aiming no higher than "local color" is certainly possible; perhaps Waugh should know; but there is reason to suspect Powell has a more universal theme in view. His selection of a French painting from the eighteenth century as his opening image—a pattern of men and women dancing in measured beat, with unexpected interchanges and connections—and his superimposition of this image upon the antithetical image of twentieth-century British laborers repairing a street in winter, but moving in a pattern suddenly perceived to be similar, leads to another inference: the movements of people in time and with apparent chaos will probably be seen in retrospect as patterned by the half-heard music of life, for which the initiatory image is not mere English documentary but the universe of man in microcosm.

IV *A Question of Style*

Finally, the style of *The Music of Time* is in some way close to that of *A la recherche du temps perdu.* The clipped, telegraphic style of Powell's earlier novels, even the astringent narrative commentary in *What's Become of Waring,* is replaced in *The Music of Time* by a convoluting style in which passages of speculation turn into labyrinths of words. Such verbal high-texturing, beautifully cadenced, is a hallmark of Proust's final style. Powell's new style being similar in texture to Proust's, if less sensuous in its details, it is one easily made to sound pompous in extracts; and, without sympathy for what Powell is trying to do, a reader may find it irritating. "Powell's method of getting on with the story," one American concludes, "must be the most ponderously inefficient of all time."[16] Since Powell's earlier style was brisk to the point of losing readers in the opposite direction, it seems obvious that he made himself anew in middle age because he had something he wanted to do besides "getting on with the story." The new style is an admirable vehicle for conveying complexity and uncertainty, and it was forged by Powell, as consciously as the novel's structure, to convey what he had to say.

The narrator of *The Music of Time* drops a clue as to how a novelist might decide to refashion his style. Nick Jenkins, the author of novels in the 1930's, begins "to brood on the complexity of writing a novel about English life." It is, he finds, "a subject difficult enough to handle with authenticity even of a crudely naturalistic sort, even more to convey the inner truth of the things observed." Especially as a novelist, he is forced to regret that the "Intricacies of social life make English habits unyielding to simplification, while understatement and irony—in which all classes of this island converse—upset the normal emphasis of reported speech" (3.32). Given an almost infinite complexity of life (2.159), and the desire to give a major dimension to the scope of that complexity, the dialogue style of the early novels seemed an inadequate instrument.

The character of the narrator, the ostensible "creator" of this style, is that of a quiet man who is much given to analysis, as even his schoolmaster Le Bas complains: "You know, Jenkins, do always try to remember one thing: it takes all sorts to make a world." And, even as the schoolmaster admonishes him, the narrator wonders "whether Le Bas had himself truly accepted his own last proposition. Nothing in his behaviour had ever suggested that his chosen principles were built up on a deep appreciation of the diversity of human character. On the contrary, he had always demanded of his pupils certain easily recognisable conventions of conduct though, at the same time, it occurred to me that the habit of making just such analysis of motive as this was precisely what Le Bas had a moment before so delicately deprecated in myself" (1.224-25).

As the narrator gropes toward an understanding of such individuals as Le Bas and toward that self-knowledge his "teacher" lacks, and through these to a knowledge of human nature, and perhaps of life, his mind moves tentatively from apperception to apparent conclusion. He notes, typically, that a restless quality in a certain girl disquiets him—a restlessness "of that deceptive kind that usually indicates a fundamental deficiency, rather than surplus of energy, though I cannot claim . . . to have speculated on this diagnosis until many years later" (2.17). Convolutions of style appear, that is, when variant strands are traced through time toward knowledge; and the effect is often as if a philosopher were digesting years of tea-table and public-house gossip, seeking in that an answer to the riddle of life.

The style is apt for conveying uncertainty of judgment as well. That "pressure from above" may have caused one diplomat's resignation is "a point upon which opinion varied" (2.19), and opinion varies about every character in *The Music of Time.* At moments the very theme seems to be our ignorance of others —"how inadequate, as a rule, is one's own grasp of another's assessment of his particular role in life" (2.78); and the narrator —almost as if he personified a history of modern science, with mind and ears open to a fault, with a curiosity that is never tempered by boredom—is forever, like science itself, making errors of assessment, supplanting one assessment with another more tenable, and having to supplant that one.[17]

"Who can be said to know. All men are mysteries," says Dr. Trelawney (6.191); and Dr. Trelawney might be called a keynote speaker were he not in his dogmatic simplicity a parody-*raisonneur*, like Fotheringham and Cortney of the earlier novels. To raise the idea of complexity that Dr. Trelawney expresses above the level of platitude, we have several of the more intellectual characters, however, such as General Conyers and Moreland, who, in addition to the narrator, wonder even about close friends:

"One passes through the world knowing few, if any, of the important things about even the people with whom one has been from time to time in the closest intimacy" (6.217). As *raisonneur,* Moreland provides us with aphorisms rather than speculations; and in his own metaphoric style: " 'Valéry asks why one has been summoned to this carnival,' Moreland once said [speaking of life itself], 'but it's more like blind man's bluff. One reels through the carnival in question, blundering into persons one can't see, and, without much success, trying to keep hold of a few of them' " (6.217). If the style of *The Music of Time* on occasion seems to reel, it may be trying to keep pace with a new and dizzying perception of life's rhythms. And if the more speculative passages remind us of Proust, the more dramatic passages remind us of the older Powell; and his later volumes have tended to be more dramatic.

Actually Powell's style in *The Music of Time* seems indebted as much to the novels of Wyndham Lewis as to Proust. Powell has ranked Lewis among the outstanding comic talents of the century,[18] and the subtlety of the social comment in a novel such as Lewis's *Tarr* (1918) is achieved in large means by way of style. In this novel the English painter in Paris named Tarr brings lunch to the studio of his plump German girlfriend, for instance, and they quarrel. "Aren't these strawberries good?" Tarr says. "Have some more cream?" Bertha replies " 'Thank you.' She should have said no. But being greedy in the matter she accepted it with a heavy air of some subtle advantage gained."[19] Deft human commentary such as the last sentence manages to convey is also a characteristic of *The Music of Time,* and the style is often similar; but it remains Powell's own, the implement he had forged between 1939 and 1951.

CHAPTER 7

The Music of Time

THE major work of Powell's life began to appear with *A Question of Upbringing* in 1951, and the next volume *A Buyer's Market* followed rapidly in 1952. Subsequent volumes have appeared at a more leisurely pace: *The Acceptance World* (1954), *At Lady Molly's* (1957), *Casanova's Chinese Restaurant* (1960), *The Kindly Ones* (1962), *The Valley of Bones* (1964), *The Soldier's Art* (1966), *The Military Philosophers* (1968), *Books Do Furnish a Room* (1971), and *Temporary Kings* (1973).

How many volumes are yet to appear in *The Music of Time* sequence of novels is uncertain. The publishers have announced that there will be one more, or twelve in all; but they had announced at one time that the series would comprise but six volumes. The major problem in judging the work as a whole is, therefore, that its ultimate form has not yet been determined. Instead, we must look at the volumes one at a time.

I A Question of Upbringing

The first volume of *The Music of Time* introduces four boys at an English public school much like Eton in the early 1920's. The narrator Nicholas Jenkins is having tea in the room of his aristocratic friend Charles Stringham when Peter Templer, the son of a rich but middle-class businessman, returns from a dental appointment. Together from a window they observe the fourth boy, Kenneth Widmerpool, running doggedly and alone, and are interrupted by the arrival of the narrator's Uncle Giles. After leaving school their paths began to interweave as Jenkins visits Templer's home and is intrigued by his sister Jean and then finds Widmerpool staying with a French family to whom he has been sent to improve his French. Finally an episode at Oxford in the mid-1920's brings the three friends together again and introduces a new set of characters, an Oxford don and his literary protégés.

The opening image of *A Question of Upbringing* (1951) must have been selected only after much cogitation, for it serves as an objective correlative of the central theme of *The Music of Time* as a whole. One major device of the modern novelist (Joyce, Woolf, Proust) is that of the musical composer: he states in some manner the central theme in a "prelude" and then begins the elaboration. In this tradition Powell's opening image is of red lanterns and workmen in a fog, and narrator Nick Jenkins watches the workmen move "with large, pantomimic gestures: like comedians giving formal expression to the concept of extreme cold." Suddenly life breaks into the scene when one workman, "with a jocular demeanor and long, pointed nose like that of a Shakespearean clown," throws something, perhaps the remains of some kippers, onto the coals of the fire. The narrator remains forever ignorant of that part of the mechanism; but as flames shoot up, the scene revolves in an instant from Romantic to Classic, from individuality to order: "the physical attitudes of the men . . . as they turned from the fire, suddenly suggested Poussin's scene in which the Seasons, hand in hand, . . . tread in rhythm to the notes of the lyre that the . . . naked graybeard plays." This music controls the pattern of the dance and is the key to the novel: "The image of Time brought thoughts of mortality: of human beings facing outward like the Seasons, moving hand in hand in intricate measure."

Life is a sort of dance like a quadrille (or like a country barn dance without a "caller") in which "certain people . . . seem inextricably linked . . . so that meeting one acquaintance in the street means that a letter, without fail, will arrive in a day or two from an associate involuntarily harnessed to him, or her, in time" (1.225). The formal movements of this dance of life are jarred by awkward movements of one partner and, temporarily, by "seemingly meaningless gyrations" of another, although the reappearance of "partners" as in a quadrille, restores, fortuitously for the mind, "pattern to the spectacle." Insofar as the dancers are unable to control the tempo or the melody, they are subject to chance and verge upon being creatures of a Bergsonian machine, comic in that they seem deprived of free will—"unable, perhaps, to control the steps of the dance." Inflexibility provokes laughter. But, as the activities of human life return to some control of the will, they lead to other comic discrepancies in which even the narrator shares—discrepancies in form which lead to absurd efforts to adjust the will to the form in some cases; in others, to ridiculous failures of the will to influence the form.

The first violation of good form evoked by the fire image is that of a public-school boy named Widmerpool, who is trotting through the fog to discipline himself by pure effort of the will to an athletic eminence he is destined never to achieve. Widmerpool is seen from a warm room where his antics are being mimicked by the narrator's friend Stringham. At opposite poles socially, Widmerpool and Stringham are both within the social limits of a rich school; but Widmerpool bears with him (like Margot Asquith) the threatening onus of his father's reputation as a manufacturer of artificial manure; and Stringham is the heir of that social group which looked with condescension on the low buffooneries of the Hanoverian Court. Stringham's mimicry of Widmerpool thus seems to represent, on a symbolic level, the residual supremacy in the early 1920's of the aristocracy; and it leads forward, on the plane of immediate action, to the first comic episode.

The initiatory comic episode occurs one afternoon a short time later when Jenkins, Stringham, and a third friend Templer leave the school grounds for a walk. Stringham reverts to his mimicry of Widmerpool's grotesque trot as they saunter along. They notice a "Wanted" poster: the police are seeking the embezzler Braddock-alias-Thorne, who in the photograph looks like Woodrow Wilson or, Stringham suggests, like their housemaster Le Bas. They later jump over a bank and nearly land on Le Bas, who is reading classical verse in a field. Moments later Stringham conceives a joke that he implements by phoning the police, using Le Bas's voice, to report the presence of Braddock-alias-Thorne in the field where they have left Le Bas. Of the four students mentioned, only Widmerpool actually witnesses the arrest of Le Bas, and only Widmerpool is unaware of the joke. The narrator's attitudes toward him, and toward Stringham and Templer, crystallize around this first comic event.

The Music of Time is to a large degree structured upon such comic events, each making a plateau of a separate day in a separate chapter, with reminiscences and speculations to bridge the chasms of time. *A Question of Upbringing*, the first volume, erects four such episodes. The second episode might be called the Stripling-Farebrother Chamberpot Reversal. Spending part of his vacation at Templer's home, "an enormously swollen villa, red and gabled, facing the sea," the narrator sees another side of the adult world in the struggle between Templer's brother-in-law Stripling, a racing motorist noted for his horseplay and practical jokes ("none of which, in retrospect, sounded strikingly amusing" [1.93]), and Sunny Farebrother, a business associate of Templer's father. Stripling becomes the comic figure, when his jokes on Farebrother embarrass him more than they do Farebrother. Farebrother's absurd "collar-turner" ruins his shirts, and Farebrother's innocent appearance in the hall as Stripling is about to substitute in his hatbox a chamberpot for Farebrother's top hat, deflates him further (1.98). And the next day Farebrother steps out of Jenkins' life "for twenty years."

The third episode concerns the first major coincidence in the novel, as Widmerpool and the narrator, having gone their separate ways after school, become boarders with the same French family in Touraine. Farce dominates the action as Widmerpool, with his usual egocentric oblivion, intrudes upon the narrator's absurdly romantic love scene. Finding Nick with a French girl named Suzette in the summer house, Widmerpool "sat down between us and began to talk of *Les Miserables*" (1.151).

The final episode brings the first volume full circle with the imbroglio of an auto accident outside Oxford which leads to the estrangement of two of the three friends—Templer and Stringham—who were assembling for tea as the book opened. The car ditched in the rain and the absurd consequences did not make Stringham dislike Templer for having gotten them into it: "On the contrary, he used to refer to Peter as frequently as he had done in the past; and the story of the drive . . . was embroidered by him until it became an epic of discomfort and embarrassment; and at the same time, something immensely funny. . . ." Nonetheless, intimacy between them ended (1.200). A pattern is broken as the novel ends.

Each of the four scenes, that is, embodies one of the great clichés of comedy. At the root of each, giving it form, is some familiar pattern of slapstick, farce, or burlesque. Although Powell had achieved in earlier novels some originality, in *The Music of Time* he seems deliberately to eschew novelty and to stick firmly and consciously to the traditional. Thus he constructs a Classical comedy by employing only time-honored comic myths. Farce has patterns which do recur in life. The grotesque and the absurd are parts of the human condition, and "Even in the quietest forms of life," as the narrator observes, "the untoward is rarely far from the surface" (2.114). In this context to employ hoary comic situations is to follow tradition back to its roots in the primary comic symbols of the race, and to treat them as if the function of the comic were to reconcile man to the absurd elements of his condition.

The hackneyed sequences, moreover, are treated with such care and precision that they are rejuvenated. For instance, in the narrator's account of the train ride that links his visit with Templer and his stay in central France, we should note the slow, almost pedantic accumulation of detail, every item in itself realistic, until by surprise we are sent skating down the edge of laughter. The young narrator has returned from the dining car to find his seat taken by a Frenchman:

> I decided that it would be less trouble, and perhaps cooler to stand for a time in the corridor. . . . After a while the corridor became fuller than might have been thought possible. I was gradually forced away from the door of the compartment, and found myself unstrategically placed with a leg on either side of a wicker trunk, secured by a strap, the buckle of which ran into my ankle, as the train jolted its way along the line. All around were an immense number of old women in black, one of whom was carrying a feather mattress as part of her luggage.
>
> At first the wine had a stimulating effect; but this sense of exhilaration began to change. . . . At last the throbbings in my head became so intense that I made up my mind to eject the man with the beard. After a short preliminary argument in which I pointed out that the seat was a reserved one, and, in general, put my case

> as well as circumstances and my command of the language would allow, he said briefly: "*Monsieur, vous avez gagné,*" and accepted dislodgment with resignation and some dignity. In the corridor, he moved skillfully past the priest and his boys; and, with uncommon agility for his age and size, climbed onto the wicker trunk, which he reduced almost immediately to a state of complete dissolution: squatting on its ruins reading *Le Figaro*. He seemed to know the girl, perhaps his daughter, because once he leaned across and pinched the back of her leg and made some remark to her; but she continued to gaze irritably out at the passing landscape, amongst the trees of which an occasional white chateau stood glittering like a huge birthday cake left out in the woods after a picnic. (1.107-8)

The situation is hackneyed; the style is the preservative.

Waiting for Jenkins at the station in southern France is a time-worn taxi out of *opéra bouffe,* driven by an ancient whose mustache and peaked cap give him the air of a Napoleonic grenadier: "Even when stationary, his taxi was afflicted with a kind of vehicular counterpart of St. Vitus's dance, and its quaverings and seismic disturbances must have threatened nausea to its occupants at the best of times." Ancient joke though the collapsing taxi is, it is not more antique than the story of the narrator's repeated attempts to declare his romantic attachment to the French girl Suzette. The last of these involves the classic mistaken-identity routine, which begins when Jenkins finds the girl's sunbonnet missing from the hat rack and presumes she will be in the garden. In the summer house he sees the sunbonnet, seizes the hand of the woman wearing it as he approaches her from behind, begins to declare his affection, discovers he is addressing a middle-aged woman, and blunders on, using up the platonic "phrases that I had rehearsed so often for Suzette." There is probably no older joke in the history of romantic comedy, and yet, somehow, by virtue of the style, the incident is made immortally amusing.

In a similar fashion, many of the characters in the classic mode represent banal types who yet have unique identities. In Jenkins' own family we find a descendant of T. T. Waring, the remittance man long a feature of English comedy, in the person of his Uncle Giles. First appearing as a seedy relative to embarrass the schoolboy among his friends—and to spark Le Bas's anger when he detects a lingering tobacco odor in Stringham's room, and thus to spark Stringham's practical joke on Le Bas—Uncle Giles

> had been relegated by most of the people who knew him at all well to that limbo where nothing is expected of a person, and where more than usually outrageous actions are approached, at least conversationally, as if they constituted a series of practical jokes, more or less enjoyable, according to where responsibility for clearing up matters might fall. The curious thing about persons regarding whom society has taken this largely self-defensive measure is that the existence of the individual himself reaches a pitch when nothing he does can ever be accepted as serious. If he commits suicide, or murder, only the grotesque aspects of the event dominate the circumstances. (1.16)

And with a typical Uncle Giles joke, a quiet one, the first volume ends. Uncle Giles, who has mailed his nephew Nick Jenkins an invitation to dine with him, blandly assumes a student at Oxford will find dining in London no difficulty. As it happens, Stringham has invited Jenkins down only to drop him for a more attractive social engagement. Jenkins recalls the first invitation almost with surprise and decides to drop by the restaurant. "You're a bit late," Uncle Giles said. "So I started" (1.230).

The most original of Powell's creations in *A Question of Upbringing* is, however, the character of Widmerpool. At the same time Widmerpool can be seen as belonging to a rather hackneyed type. On the literary side he descends from the fussy tutors Thwackem and Square in Henry Fielding's novel *Tom Jones* (1749) or the greedy schoolmaster in Washington Irving's "The Legend of Sleepy Hollow" (1820)—all of whom have, like Widmerpool, a yearning for power coupled with physical qualities so grotesque that the eye and the imagination are captured involuntarily. And Widmerpool is seen as a type. Even as a schoolboy he is noted for an overcoat so odd that schoolboys recognize it "immediately as a traditionally ludicrous aspect of everyday life" (1.16). Yet Powell adds freshness to the type by meticulous observation. Some critics will argue that that observation started as early as his own schooldays at Eton, for among his contemporaries there, and later with him at the same Oxford college, was a young man who bears certain resemblances to Widmerpool, a young man named Frank Pakenham.

Readers of Frank Pakenham's autobiography *Born to Believe* may be impressed by the fact that, like Widmerpool, Pakenham was a fanatic about exercise and sports, and too clumsy to be successful. However, quite unlike Widmerpool, Frank Pakenham confesses as much quite frankly. A wry humor underlies his memories of his own youthful absurdities. As late as his thirties he felt undaunted: "I made a fetish of physical exercise and... was always annoyed at any suggestion that anyone of my age was fitter than I was." Later in the army he was to have a "fanatical desire to be a good officer" but no ability to keep in step.[1] Also like Widmerpool, at Eton and later, Pakenham managed to become thoroughly unpopular. His own report is that after a football game, at which he played badly and his best friend Roger Chetwode played well, he was hissed for his presumption in leading the team off the field. An index better than most is the fact that he was the first captain of Oppidans (a ranking honor in Etonian athletics) to miss getting elected to "Pop" (the top Etonian social club) because, so a friend told him, he was "the most unpopular boy in the school." Typically, Pakenham disputes both aspersions but—unlike Widmerpool—records them frankly.[2]

Later Pakenham was to be elected at Oxford to the most desirable club, the Bullingdon, due to the efforts of his friend Chetwode, the Field Marshall's son (Chetwode's sister Pamela a few years later was to marry John Betjeman, "the only true poet among my friends," Pakenham reports). Moreover, at Charlton, the Earl of Birkenhead's country house near Oxford, Pakenham "was initiated into Conservative politics at their most romantic: at the point, that is, where they made contact with the more intellectual side of London society." Freddy Furneaux (the future second Earl of Birkenhead) took Pakenham out to meet his sisters, and there is a touch of Widmerpool perhaps in their meeting: "Eleanor, without turning her head, stretched her hand and arm over the back of the sofa, and Pam, after a furtive glance sideways, copied her sister precisely. Totally nonplussed, I grasped Eleanor's hand in one of mine and Pam's in the other and stood there gaping while Margaret Birkenhead burst into laughter."[3] Freddy was later to be best man at Pakenham's wedding, however, and his wild, gypsy-like elder sister

Lady Eleanor Smith in the interim became socially "news" as a symbol of the flaming 1920's; one of the half dozen original Bright Young People.

Pakenham describes himself as being at one time "a kind of fellow-traveller of the Bright Young People. But I soon saw, as did others, that my future did not lie in those regions." On his forehead, above dark-rimmed glasses, the Widmerpool brand may seem to glow again, as he describes two fancy-dress pageants. At one of these he excited ridicule by appearing in "a child's sailor suit . . . the first cyclist in the Park," while "Lady Lavery (as Lady Hamilton) . . . Eddie Marsh (as Joshua Reynolds) and Hugh Walpole (as Thackeray)" added more quietly to the merriment of nations. At the second party, he even more absurdly appeared "as Bacchus with vine leaves in my hair." Pageants of this sort, with all their potential for ironic comedy, Powell re-creates not only in *From a View to a Death* but even more powerfully in *The Kindly Ones* (6.123ff.).

A mood at Eton that had been congenial to Powell was the one that the Duchess of Westminster called "Edwardian" in 1964. "What a completely forgotten age that is! Any form of publicity was vulgar. Even being good at anything was slightly vulgar, as it might attract attention."[4] With such an atmosphere lingering at Eton in 1920, Frank Pakenham must have seemed particular *outré*; for, like Widmerpool, he can be viewed as an embodiment of the will to excell, or of sheer will. The irony that attracts the imagination of Anthony Powell to people of this type is that, unpopular as displays of ambition make such a character and absurd as are the imbroglios into which his will may drive him—as when Widmerpool, in the courtyard of a financier he is trying to impress, backs his car into a gigantic vase (2.218)—the character is perhaps more likely than not to succeed—if sometimes in ways ultimately found to be undesirable. Frank Pakenham was to become one of those who succeeded: he was, unlike Widmerpool, a solid winner of First Class Honors when he graduated from Oxford in 1927; later, one of the "107 directors of London's top financial houses"; even the Chairman of the Committee for London Government. "Lord Longford (the old Frank Pakenham is still splendidly at large behind the still unfamiliar new style) is the least professional of Londoners," one commentator noted; but that only "makes him infinitely more useful as chairman."[5] Exercise of the will lends its possessor resilence, bounce, success.

But Pakenham must not be identified with Widmerpool in any simple manner. His father was a peer, not a manufacturer of a liquid manure; and he succeeded in ways where Widmerpool fails. Nor should any simple identification be made politically. Widmerpool's will for power in *The Music of Time* leads him to approve of Fascism in the 1930's (4.64); Pakenham's led him in almost the opposite direction, to the left. And more than one reviewer has named other figures prominent in current English political life as their candidate for Widmerpool's original. In all likelihood, he had many. As importantly, Frank Pakenham differs from Widmerpool in the areas in which his will to succeed operates. Widmerpool attempts to climb socially by marrying a "daughter of King Edward's friend, Lord Vowchurch" (4.4). Frank Pakenham is more like the amiable Lady Molly Ardglass who marries a middle-class automobile salesman (4.16). He married a middle-class commoner, Elizabeth Harman, only to succeed again.

Elizabeth Harman (now the Countess of Longford) showed herself to be a peer intellectually. Mother of eight children (several of whom have now begun to publish books of their own), she has written several books to aid in the rearing of children, such as *The Pakenham Party Book* (1960) and *Points for Parents* (1954); and she has also written in her "spare time" historical studies—*Jameson's Raid* (1960), for one, dedicated "To Frank"—and biographies, such as *Queen Victoria* (1965), a best seller on both side of the Atlantic. More important than good reviews, she made good friends: obviously a favorite among Powell's friends, she became in December, 1939, the godmother of Evelyn Waugh's first son Auberon and five months later the godmother of Powell's first son Tristram.[6] And if Lady Longford contributes her bit to characterization in *The Music of Time*, it is probably to the amiable portrait of Lady Warminster, who writes books and broods over ten stepchildren, the Tollands we meet in *At Lady Molly's*.

II A Buyer's Market

In *A Buyer's Market* (1952), the second volume of *The Music of Time,* the scene is London in the spring of 1928 and the contemporaries of Nick Jenkins are, so to speak, in the marketplace, on the auction block. But it is not a seller's market. As the novel begins, none of them is doing well. Nick Jenkins works for a publisher of art books, and Stringham has gone to work for an industrialist named Sir Magnus Donners. Widmerpool also joins Donners' staff; and, despite the forecast of their school life together, Widmerpool is the success in the end as he ousts the "coming young man" who had brought Stringham into the firm. And the power of love grows as pervasive as that of business: Stringham is being pursued by a socialite some years his senior; Jenkins finds himself oddly attracted by the same debutante who has attracted Widmerpool; and in the end the girlfriend of a leftist painter named Mr. Deacon euchres Widmerpool into paying for an abortion.

Stringham and Widmerpool together work in what is called by Londoners "the City." The term conveys roughly what New Yorkers mean by "the Street," taking Wall Street to be the symbol of the universe of banks and bonds. That part of London within the old walls has become the financial bastion of the empire, and in *A Buyer's Market* and in *The Acceptance World* Powell skirts the area as he begins the general study of power hinted at on the last page of *What's Become of Waring.* The City has rarely been described in print, Powell remarks in a review: "some literary critics seem to have no idea that, for the last fifty years at least, to 'go in to the City'—and work very hard there—has been a characteristic 'upper-class' vocation."[7] He cites as an example Lord Salisbury; but he might have cited as well his wife's uncle Arthur Child-Villiers, a son of the Earl of Jersey and a director of Baring Brothers.

A City marriage that sheds light also on Powell's conception of his fictional magnate Sir Magnus Donners may be seen in the 1963 wedding of Angus Ogilvy, a son of the Earl of Airlie, to Princess Alexandra of Kent. Along with a photograph of the pre-wedding ball at Windsor Castle, one journal headlined a story "Mr. Ogilvy's Chief Tells How Angus Made the Grade."

The princess is to enter the "robust new world of big business" and "tycoon-studded parties," the interviewer assumes, for "Mr. Ogilvy is a protégé of Mr. Harold Drayton, the City magnate, who tells me that he is hoping that Ogilvy will not feel inhibited by his new social position. 'Damn it. I've trained him.'" Though Drayton himself had started as a cigar-counter clerk at a few shillings a week, he started Ogilvy at six hundred pounds a year "and told him he had two years to make good. With Angus the bell rang straight away and he remained." Asked how many companies he was now directing, Drayton replied he did not know: "There are so many new ones, y'see. Angus and the other little devils are always up to something."[8] It is this drive that Sir Magnus Donners looks for in his bright young men, half a dozen of whom figure in *The Music of Time*.

Sir Magnus deals vaguely in metals, possibly with munitions as well in the Sir Basil Zaharoff manner, though Powell rightly leaves the "field" vague to retain about Donners an inky octopal impression. The portrait of Sir Magnus may owe something to such press barons as Lord Beaverbrook, too, but his significance is more universal. Financially, Sir Magnus' power is international; but we suspect behind all his parade of "kept women" and the wildly conflicting rumors about his odd sexual predilections that he will turn out to be impotent, that the beautiful women are bric-a-brac around his castle, or "conversation pieces" to conceal his area of failure. For Powell's thesis is already clear: as power corrupts, the absolute pursuit of power corrupts the sensual life. "Like many persons more interested in power than sensual enjoyment, Sillery touched no strong drink" (1.212), and it is Sillery, the don, who manipulates Stringham out of the university (without a degree) into the Donners-Brebner power structure.

Power is seen in a multitude of facets—from the familiar raw physical power as Widmerpool wrestles Stringham and from the military power that stands in opposition to the artistic life—to unexpected varieties of it, some of them reminding us of the narrator of *What's Become of Waring* and of the chapter he is unable to complete on Stendhal, "Laughter Is Power." The legendary Lord Vowchurch who got power in Edwardian days by his practical jokes (such as clockwork mice and monkeys released at a ball [4.4; 6.10]) may be seen as a variant of the least power hungry of them all. Nicholas Jenkins prepares "ribald jokes about Widmerpool's honeymoon for friends who knew him" (4.65), and his repeated musings on the absurd to please friends may be leading the reader—and Jenkins—to a discovery of the self. We have yet to hear him tell one of the stories that he prepares with a leavening of malice, but it seems likely that he is to discover that he does so, unconsciously, to gain social power—status and authority among friends—through comic anecdote. Similarly, the young Stringham's greatest pleasure is the enjoyment of private jokes (2.202); and, perhaps significantly, in *A Buyer's Market*, when he no longer needs the audience Nick Jenkins provided at school, they see less of each other.

Structurally *A Buyer's Market* is quite similar to *A Question of Upbringing* in that it also focuses upon four exquisite comic moments. The first occurs at a society ball that we view in slow motion as Powell perfects a technique which seems almost to freeze the comic action into symbol. To Jenkins' shock, he has found Widmerpool attracted by the same debutante that has attracted him, and the three are together at the buffet table when Widmerpool attempts to restrain the girl from joining a third man across the room. Widmerpool's pressure on her wrist is only momentary, but she turns to snap "You need some sweetening." The passage that follows, describing her lifting the sugar bowl, tilting it over Widmerpool's head, the sticking lid, the total inversion of the bowl, the lid suddenly giving, the sugar cascading has been often quoted:

> More from surprise than because she wished additionally to torment him, Barbara did not remove her hand before the whole contents of the vessel . . . had descended. . . . Widmerpool's rather sparse hair had been liberally greased with a dressing—the sweetish smell of which I remembered as somewhat disagreeable when applied in France—this lubricant retaining the grains of sugar, which, as they adhered thickly to his skull, gave him the appearance of having turned white from shock at a single stroke. . . . He had writhed sideways to avoid the downpour, and a cataract of sugar had entered the space between neck and collar; yet another jet streaming between eyes and spectacles. (2.70-71)

But the episode is not farce for farce's sake. The detailed registry of the horror brings a revelation about the character of the girl which ends the narrator's infatuation.

The second episode, which has similar qualities of slapstick and dignity, takes place near dawn the next morning and involves a painter named Mr. Deacon. First seen in Paris in 1919 when Jenkins' father was working in vain for a just peace with Germany, Mr. Deacon in the cocoon of his art and ego had been indifferent to the fate of the world. When the paths of Deacon and Nick Jenkins again cross at a Hyde Park coffee stall in the early 1930's, when a time for militant toughness might be thought to have come, Deacon is passionately distributing pacifist leaflets. At this moment of intersection Stringham also appears and invites them to a party given by Mrs. Andriadis, the woman who has been pursuing him. At the party a quarrel breaks out between Deacon, who has his own sexual peculiarities, and a Noel Coward-like pianist, Max Pilgrim, who loves to sing his own songs (and Powell composes an appropriately fay song for the occasion):

> Even the fairies
> Say how sweet my hair is;
> They mess my mascara and pinch the peroxide.
> I know a coward
> Would be overpowered,
> When they all offer to be orthodox, I'd
> Like to be kind, but say: "Some other day, dears;
> Pansies for thoughts remains the best way, dears." (2.118)

Outraged at the flagrantly homosexual implications of the song, Deacon furiously opens battle: "There are always leering eyes on the look-out. Besides, your song puts a weapon in the hands of the puritans." Eventually, Deacon storms away, pausing in the foyer below to gather up his bundle of peace pamphlets. Mrs. Andriadis in pursuit of Stringham, who has left unexpectedly, reaches the door at the moment Deacon—still furiously bellicose, pamphlets crammed under one arm—is trying to break the jammed catch: "All at once there was a sound as of the rending of silk, and the papers, like a waterfall . . . began to tumble, one after another, to the ground from under Mr. Deacon's arm. He made a violent effort to check their descent, contriving only to increase the area over which they were freely shed; an unexpected current of air blowing through the open door . . . helped to scatter sheets of *War Never Pays!* far and wide . . . even up to the threshold of the room beyond" (2.150).

The third episode, equally farcical and equally symbolic, involves Widmerpool again. In the courtyard of the restored castle of Sir Magnus Donners, the industrialist he is trying to impress, Widmerpool concludes his business in apparent triumph and, going to depart, he starts up his car in reverse gear, shoots backward, and knocks a tremendous urn into a sunken garden (2.217-23).

With the fourth section the focus returns to Mr. Deacon as his birthday party adjourns to a nightclub. Offended by the odors in the men's room, Mr. Deacon dies for his ideals, protesting the inexorable nature of things. He is climbing the rickety stairs to the manager's office to complain of the odor when his fatal slip occurs (2.229). This section has two epilogues, however, that diffuse this tragicomic effect: one deals with Deacon's slatternly pacifist girl-companion; the other, with the homelife of Widmerpool who met the girl at Deacon's party. Jenkins, in the meantime, has been amazed to learn that Widmerpool had succeeded in his attempt to impress Donners, and has ousted Stringham's champion from the firm. The terminal joke involves Widmerpool, however, when he, without having had carnal relations with Deacon's companion, Gypsy Jones, is pressured by her into paying for her abortion (2.232). The failures of Widmerpool's sexual life have begun—as he triumphs in the buyer's market.

Mr. Deacon has been publicly identified already as modeled upon the London bookseller and bibliographer Christopher Millard, a "grey-haired, disreputable, handsome . . . bibliophile."[9] Perhaps such an identification is oversimple. The "wheeler-dealer in the antique world" aspect of him seems to derive from another bibliophile, T. J. Wise, exposed in 1934 as a creator of faked first editions. "Pushing and vain"—so Powell describes Wise—"he ingratiated himself with most of the prominent men of letters of his period; and, to be just to him, his qualities as a collector, bibliographer and editor were very high. There is a particular kind of unctuousness and pretension to modesty in some of his letters . . . which must have put shrewd people on their guard. Even so, it would hardly have prepared them for the truth."[10] But less in accord with Millard or Wise is the early Mr. Deacon; for, when we first meet him in *The Music of Time*, he is touring the Louvre and is still active as a painter of gigantic canvases; and a candidate for this aspect has yet to suggest itself.

III The Acceptance World

Groans were heard when *The Acceptance World* (1955) appeared. Some reviewers were led by it to doubt Powell's ability to sustain the literary edifice the first volumes had projected. The title suggests that the volume will continue the investigation of power in the City and it must be admitted that it does not, though in these early years of the Depression (1930-34) a further look at the community of business and finance might seem apropos. Moreover, initially only one new character is introduced: a fortuneteller named Mrs. Erdleigh who at first does not make a strong impression even upon the narrator. Most troublesome at first reading, *The Acceptance World* seems vagrant. We wander from one episode to another, as if no one were at the wheel, or we seem to; and this episodic effect tends to cast doubt on the promise of order given by Powell's esthetic.

In actuality the title acts as a bridge between the business community of *A Buyer's Market* and the wider cultural and political community; for it links that part of the financial world that deals in futures with the rest of the world equally anxious about the future; it links strangely Widmerpool and seekers of power for self with Mrs. Erdleigh who "tells fortunes" for others. Who will be the future secretary of the novelist St. John Clarke is of concern to two of Sillery's young men, Mark Members and J. G. Quiggin, and what the future will hold for love becomes Jenkins' concern as he enters an affair with Peter Templer's sister. Further changes of partner occur when the painter Barnby loses his girlfriend to Dicky Umfraville, and Quiggin, having ousted Members as Clarke's secretary, is ousted in his turn. Perhaps Powell makes a tactical error in allowing the title to focus imaginative attention upon Widmerpool who is less central here. This focus comes when the narrator, Jenkins, meets Templer and passes on news of old acquaintances. One item of news is that Widmerpool is in the City with Donners-Brebner. Jenkins' news is out of date, Templer suggests: "Widmerpool is joining the Acceptance World." He explains that Widmerpool is going to become a bill-broker and engage in the financial activity that in America is called "dealing in futures"—in this case, making present payment on expectation of future delivery. "If you have goods you want to sell a firm in Bolivia" Templer says—as an insider explaining "the nefarious ways of the City"—"you probably do not touch your money in the ordinary way until the stuff arrives there. Certain houses, therefore, are prepared to 'accept' the debt. They will advance you the money on the strength of your reputation" (3.45). This is the "world" Widmerpool is joining, but we see almost nothing of Widmerpool until the last chapter (3.178).

Indeed, we see less of big business itself in *The Acceptance World* than we did in *A Buyer's Market,* and only toward the end does the relevance of the title become thematic. At this point, Jenkins admits that he had been struck by the phrase:

> Even as a technical definition, it seemed to suggest what we are all doing; not only in business, but in love, art, religion, philosophy, politics, in fact all human activities. The Acceptance World was the world in which the essential element—happiness, for example—is drawn, as it were, from an engagement to meet a bill. Sometimes the goods are delivered . . . sometimes . . . not . . . and disaster follows; sometimes the goods are delivered, but the value of the currency [has] changed. Besides, in another sense, the whole world is the Acceptance World as one approaches thirty; at least some illusions discarded. The mere fact of still existing as a human being proved that. (3.170)

The primary extension of the term is from the business community to the world of love, and it is here that *The Acceptance World* receives its focus. The first scene introduces us to Mrs. Erdleigh under the wing of Uncle Giles, who renders even this relatively sober scene comic; and Mrs. Erdleigh, we might say, "deals in futures." She retails the "commonplaces of fortune telling," dealing cards for Nick Jenkins: "You live between two worlds. . . . You are thought cold, but possess deep affections, sometimes for people worthless in themselves. . . . You must make a greater effort in life." Quite casually speaking to Jenkins she refers to love, both past and future: "a fair woman was not very pleased with me; and a dark one almost equally vexed!" Jenkins finds the applicability of this past history to Suzette and Barbara too facile to take Mrs. Erdleigh's "futures" seriously, and the chapter ends with the painter Barnby, always the *raisonneur* in the field of love, who wonders why literary artists had never portrayed woman as she really is, and who ignores the suggestion of Jenkins that painters had not done much better. Both conversations are so casual as to seem lackadaisical, but we see in retrospect that the groundwork for the volume has been soundly laid.

Barnby on a train has met a new woman. "Like Valmont in *Les Liaisons Dangereuses,* he set store 'upon what terms' he possessed a woman, seeking a relationship in which sensuality merged with power, rather than engaging in their habitual conflict" (3.24). The mystery woman has posed for him, but has refused to identify herself; and the narrator is able to assist Barnby's "futures" by identifying her. For Jenkins, Mrs. Erdleigh has indicated three "futures"; and Barnby in turn supplies a clue that could have aided Jenkins in the resolution of one of them, the business "inconvenience" that "has to do with an elderly man—and two young ones connected with him" (3.16). The major business problem Jenkins faces in the publishing world is getting St. John Clarke to supply an introduction to the works of his aged friend Isbister. Supposing that Clarke's secretary Mark Members is the only young man associated with his problem, Jenkins concludes that Mrs. Erdleigh has simply misstaken the proportions of young men and old. In this he errs. With Clarke being converted to "modernism," Barnby suggests, he is not likely to supply the introduction to the work of a dated painter, even a friend: "He fell in love with himself at first sight and it is a passion to which he has always remained faithful" (3.28).

The next chapters take place on successive days a year later. As one by one all three of Mrs. Erdleigh's predictions begin to come true, the structure of *The Acceptance World* turns out to be pivoted upon the matter of "futures." First, the death of Isbister renders St. John Clarke's continued failure to supply an introduction even more "inconvenient"; at the same time, its being written at all becomes less likely with the arrival of the predicted second young man in Clarke's life. The rival secretary is J. G. Quiggin whose hostile friendship with Mark Members had been noted in *A Question of Upbringing.* His Communist party line proves to be more fashionable in 1931 than the psychiatric jargon of Members. "When I first came to [Clarke] he thought Matisse was a *plage*—no, I mean it," Members says. "Then one morning at breakfast he said Cezanne was 'bourgeois' " (3.123-26). "Bourgeois" is the first clue that Quiggin is to supplant him.

As Jenkins awaits Members in the lobby of the Ritz, however, his dance in time again intersects that of Peter Templer, and another of Mrs. Erdleigh's predictions begins to resolve itself into actuality. Templer had been the authority at school in matters of the opposite sex and had bragged of picking up a woman of the streets while in London to visit his dentist (1.33). Moreover at the very time Jenkins desired Templer's sister Jean and found himself to his chagrin too shy to break through the veil of her aloofness, he was forced to see that Templer had spent the night with a visiting divorcée (1.100). Further proof of the ineptitude of Jenkins in love came with the farce of his courtship of Suzette in France; and, in *A Buyer's Market,* the "dark woman," the debutante Barbara Goring, had been courted only platonically. Now the suppressed theme of love becomes dominant, as, under Templer's aegis, *The Acceptance World* centers upon the first of Mrs. Erdleigh's predictions, that of "a much more important lady . . . and I think you have run across her once or twice before, though not recently. But there seems to be another man interested, too. He might even be a husband. . . . In business. Often goes abroad" (3.15).

Peter Templer is at the Ritz to meet his wife and his sister Jean, who is currently estranged from her husband, a businessman who is at the moment abroad. The occasion is Templer's first wedding anniversary, and he invites Jenkins to join them: "Afterwards, that dinner in the Grill seemed to partake of the nature of . . . a rite from which the four of us emerged to take up new positions in the formal dance with which human life is concerned. . . . But in a sense, nothing in life is planned—or everything is—because in the dance every step is ultimately the corollary of the step before; the consequence of being the kind of person one chances to be" (3.63). Jenkins had planned to dine with Members (in connection with the Isbister introduction), but the "well known critic" J. G. Quiggin shows up instead. Amid the opulent decor of the Ritz, Quiggin's red tie and his black-leather coat make his reluctance to explain his presence both ominous and ludicrous, but Templer's ridicule of him later infuriates Templer's wife Mona: "Is he one of those fascinating people you sometimes tell me about, who wear beards and sandals and have such curious sexual habits?" In Quiggin Mona glimpses the bohemia she had left behind without regret as her face began to appear on toothpaste billboards, and her interest in Quiggin starts Templer's marriage toward the rocks.

As in a quadrille, the severing of one couple is usually accompanied by the joining of another. That evening in the back of the car as they drive through the snow to Templer's country house, Jenkins embraces Jean, the first girl he had desired; and love comes to him for the first time in a plurality of senses—and in as sensuous a passage as Powell had yet published: "her body felt at the same time hard and yielding, giving a kind of glow as if live current issued from it. I used to wonder afterwards whether, in the last resort, of all the time we spent together, however ecstatic, the first moments on the Great West Road were not the best" (3.65). That night (repeating the pattern Peter Templer had initiated with the divorcée a decade before) Jenkins visits Jean's room; and his affair is begun in a house where "Isbister's huge portrait of Mr. Templer still hung in the hall, a reminder of everyday life and unsolved business problems" (3.66).

The conduct of Jenkins and Jean is as discreet as Powell's handling of the details; and, though the affair lasts into the spring, Jean's brother Peter Templer remains unaware of it—partly because of the breakup of his own marriage. Bored by the business world, Mona had insisted the next day that Jenkins invite J. G. Quiggin to the country. "To regard Quiggin as a competitor with Templer for a woman—far less his own wife —was ludicrous even to consider," Jenkins thinks (3.133). When Quiggin's arrival is followed by the startling arrival of Mrs. Erdleigh, and when the revelations she makes with a Planchette board so prey on the nerves of Quiggin that he flees back to London, in fear of losing his job as Clarke's secretary, we would suppose Templer remained in control. But Quiggin's departure is interpreted by Mona as indifference to her flirtation, and she is intrigued; one of the laws of love has operated. Impossible as it seems, in the end the suave stockbroker loses the beauty on whom he dotes to an uncouth leftist critic.

Though life with Jean brings to an end Jenkins' inexperience, it does not end the mystery of love. Shock number one comes when Jean remarks almost casually that she has had an affair with her ex-brother-in-law, the stolid type who had brought Mrs. Erdleigh to Templer's. Her statement is a flick of verbal sadism, and Jenkins is left to ponder the ways of love. But there are shocks to come in successive volumes, and pondering about the mystery of love is to grow more profound.

Mrs. Erdleigh's third prediction had been that she would see Jenkins again but not before a year had passed; and she has. But her supervision of the Planchette board is just as eerie. "Force is the midwife," the board writes, and Quiggin testily identifies the source as Marx. "I suspect it was Nick," he adds angrily, "as he is the only one who knows I'm a practising Marxist—and he persuaded me to come here." Quiggin refuses to accept Jenkins' denial of any such knowledge; but, when the Planchette board suggests that St. John Clarke is ill in "The House of Books," he is superstitious enough to rush back to allay his doubts. Clarke is indeed ill and, in the absence of Quiggin, has called in the "psychoanalytic" or rival poet Mark Members. Quiggin's return is just in time to prevent his own displacement. Yet in the fourth chapter we discover that Quiggin has in turn been displaced by one yet more "modern," the Trotskyite Guggenbühl.

The central event in the chapter is a multiple meeting at Foppa's Restaurant where Jenkins and Jean meet Barnby and his new "discovery," Lady Anne Stepney. There they all encounter a stray personification of the spirit of the 1920's, Dicky

Umfraville, who has just arrived from Kenya. The time is the 1930's, and Umfraville is shocked to find all his old friends "become so damned serious, what?" He is sure of Milly Andriadis—although, as he confesses later in the lift to her flat, their telephone contact has not been sentimental: "She said, 'Oh, God, you again, Dicky. Somebody told me you had died of drink in 1929.' I said, 'Milly, I'm coming straight round with a few friends to give you that kiss I forgot when we were in Havana together.' She said, 'Well, I hope you'll bring along that pony you owe me, too, which you forgot at the same time.' So saying, she snapped the receiver down" (3.161).

However, Mrs. Andriadis has also lost her frivolity; she has metamorphosed backward from butterfly to serious grub, or is trying to. She has picked up a new set of attitudes for the 1930's, and a smattering of dialect from Guggenbühl, St. John Clarke's new secretary. "I can't think why we don't have a revolution here," she says. Guggenbühl arrives a bit later that evening, to pile coincidence upon coincidence. He is a German dramatist:

> "I think it would not interest you," he said. "We have done with old theatre of bourgeoisie and capitalists. Here is *Volksbühnen*—for actor that is worker like industrial worker—actor that is machine of machines."
>
> "Isn't it too thrilling?" said Mrs. Andriadis. "You know the October revolution was the real turning point in the history of the Theatre." (3.166)

The episode furthers the dialogue on love, for it leads to Barnby's loss of Lady Anne Stepney to the courteous, father figure Umfraville; and, by the end of *The Acceptance World,* both of the men whom Jenkins has looked upon as experts in love have lost the women they desire.

Umfraville has suggested to Jenkins that they attend an Old Boys dinner at the Ritz in honor of Le Bas, and Jenkins is surprised to find Templer there. "I've really come here tonight to see Widmerpool," Templer says, and refers to his sister Jean's husband, ignorant of the fact that Jean and Jenkins are having a love affair. "Bob Duport is in England again. . . . I am rather hopeful things will be patched up with Jean, if Bob's business gets into running order again.... The whole family can't be in a permanent state of being deserted by their husbands and wives" (3.176). Jenkins sees an ironic layer of Jean's life below that seen by her brother—and yet he fails for the time being to see a layer below that.

In this final chapter, the comic focus is upon Widmerpool, who gives a speech of such deadly tedium, it is implied, that Le Bas has a mild stroke. The sight of Widmerpool, oblivious to Le Bas's illness, droning on with his speech so infuriates Stringham that he consumes a greater quantity of champagne than even his lush quota permits; and the evening ends with Widmerpool's marshaling a taxi to take him home. At home, Stringham recovers consciousness in horror. Widmerpool with his usual cliché insists they are putting him to bed for his own good:

> "I haven't got my own good at heart."
> "We will get you anything you want."
> "Curse your charity."
> Once more Stringham attempted to get out of the bed.
> Widmerpool threw himself on top of him....
> "So these are the famous Widmerpool good manners, are they?" Stringham shouted. "This is the celebrated Widmerpool courtesy.... Here is the man who posed as another Lord Chesterfield. Let me go, you whited sepulchre...."
> The scene was so grotesque that I began to laugh.... He must have been quite powerful, for Stringham was struggling like a maniac.... And then, quite suddenly, Stringham began laughing too. He laughed and laughed, until he could struggle no more. (3.208)

The new order has conquered the old; and Widmerpool, who is to be the agent who effects the separation of Jean from Jenkins, emerges again in apparent triumph.

The authority on love who loses the girl he loves at the end of the novel, the painter Barnby—who also introduces Nick Jenkins to bohemian London (5.15)—seems to be a composite of several painters that Powell had come to know in London in the 1920's. Of these, figuring importantly in Barnby's mentor aspects, is the painter Henry Lamb. Twenty years older than Powell, Lamb had spent an apprenticeship in Paris before the war and in London he held exhibitions of his paintings every second year. By 1926 he was well established in bohemian society. He had higher social connections as well, being considered, with his fellow painter Augustus John, among Lady Ottoline Morrell's closest friends.[11] Lamb did not share John's fondness for Bloomsbury, however, or Lady Ottoline's respect for it. For him, Bloomsbury art represented a kind of "aesthetic puritanism" (3.118) for which he had little taste, and his portrait of Bloomsbury's great debunking biographer Lytton Strachey has itself been called a "debunking in oils."[12]

From the mid-1920's Lamb was close to the Oxford esthetes, although the only "university" he had attended was the Manchester Medical School. In 1928 he married Lady Pansy Pakenham only a few months after she had served as "bridesmaid" at Evelyn Waugh's quiet wedding to her apartment-mate (the Honourable Evelyn Gardner). Eight years later, when Powell married Lady Pansy's younger sister, Powell and Lamb became brothers-in-law. During World War II, Lamb–like Barnby (7.110)–was appointed an official war artist. Not a great painter but widely respected, he was made a trustee of the National Gallery in 1942 and of the Tate gallery in 1944.[13]

But the character Barnby in his social aspects has the more violent energy Powell seems to have associated with an older painter whom he respected intellectually, Walter Sickert; and Barnby in his gay and philandering aspects seems to contain at least a trace of Augustus John. Note too that in the castle of Sir Magnus Donners paintings by Sickert, John, and Barnby hang side by side (6.109) as if Powell were dropping a clue as to Barnby's composition.

The novelist St. John Clarke is also based upon Powell's years in London's literary world; and one of the principal contributors to Clarke's portrait may be a rich American expatriate, Logan Pearsall Smith of Philadelphia. Smith was attempting in the 1920's to follow in the footsteps of Henry James, and Smith was armed with an acidic distaste for America. His main effort was to penetrate English society at a high level, either esthetic or social; and his writings seem to have been conceived as a means of attaining that end. Like the novelist St. John Clarke in *The Music of Time,* to whom publications are also implements of social power, Smith disapproved of marriage—"My idea of a happy ending to a love story is to begin at the engagement, where the hack writer ends, and show how they escape from the storms and the wild beasts back into the safe harbour of celibacy"—but Smith himself traded on his marital connections. "To the piety of Frank Costelloe, the first husband of his sister Mary, he owed his admission to Balliol; in her second husband, Mr. Bernard Berenson, he found an incomparable director of Italian studies; and when his sister Alys married Bertrand Russell he found himself allied . . . to a family whose grandeurs and bizarreries he never tired of deciphering."[14] Bloomsbury attracted Smith, only to mock him. But, since Smith had accepted Bloomsbury's opinion of itself, its rejection of him was a matter of life-long pain.

About the time of Anthony Powell's arrival in London, Smith hired as secretary a man whose sense of humor Powell recalls affectionately in his memoir of Eton, Robert Gathorne-Hardy. As a younger son of the Earl of Cranford and as a promising poet, Gathorne-Hardy had an entrée that his richer employer could only covet. Yet from such a secretary, Smith "at once exacted and despised an absolute compliance with his wishes." Although Gathorne-Hardy steered Smith to his only good book buys and strove to overcome his fundamental lack of interest in the pictorial arts, the relationship could not endure. Smith thought of himself as a "man of letters" until 1930 when another "friend and disciple," Mr. Cyril Connolly, went so far as to celebrate the "doom of the men of letters!"

Smith changed with the times, and this quality of being swayed by younger men, each more "in the know" than his predecessor, Powell borrowed in creating his portrait of St. John Clarke. The three secretaries who follow one another in *The Music of Time*—as Clarke turns from the estheticism of Mark Members, to the Communism of J. C. Quiggin, to the Trotskyism of Guggenbühl—are paralleled to some degree by the successive "secretaries" of Logan Pearsall Smith—Gathorne-Hardy, Cyril Connolly, and John Russell, all of whom have left memorials of the man they so painfully served. Russell reports that George Orwell's *Critical Essays*, which might be described roughly as Trotskyite, at least in their rejection of Stalinist communism, were Logan's "enthusiastic discovery" the day before he died.[15]

But novelist St. John Clarke is not simply Logan Pearsall Smith (who, for one thing, was not a novelist). He bears quite a few attributes of a novelist who was more sociable, more "clubbable": George Moore of Ebury Street—whose cook Anthony Powell and his wife "inherited."[16] Moore possessed a fine appreciation of art, as Powell admits; but he also shared a characteristic pettiness of spirit with Logan Smith: when he "had trouble with his waterworks he took it out on his secretary."[17] A young museum official of the 1930's remembers Moore, when his reputation faded, as growing "obsessed with 'Style'" and as "quite intolerable. . . . Perhaps he will survive as a character. Miss Hogarth told me that when he saw the portrait Sickert had painted of him, he was much annoyed. 'You have made me look like a booby,' he said. 'But you are a booby,' was Sickert's answer."[18] Powell's novelist St. John Clarke is a booby of similar petulance. Troubled by the difficulty of keeping intellectually à la mode, he is poised as a kind of literary touchstone above succeeding volumes of *The Music of Time*.

IV At Lady Molly's

Newcomers to Powell were troubled by *At Lady Molly's* (1959), the fourth volume of *The Music of Time*. The novel so overwhelmed them with new characters and with allusions to old ones that cries for an index were heard, and one British weekly obliged.[19] But those who had freshly read the early volumes were delighted, for *At Lady Molly's*, unlike *The Acceptance World*, is from the opening lines tremendously entertaining.

The year is 1935, and Jenkins is working on a scenario for an English movie when he is taken by a fellow scriptwriter to Lady Molly's house. There he begins meeting Lady Molly's nieces and nephews; by the end of the volume he has met all ten of them, the whole Tolland clan, from Erridge, the Earl of Warminster, the eldest and most radical son, to Lady Isobel, with whom he falls in love and whom he is later to marry. In *A Buyer's Market* Widmerpool had surprised Jenkins by being attracted to the same girl; now he surprises Jenkins by contemplating marriage

—for a time—to a raffish aristocrat some years his senior. Life grows more serious for them both.

Among the dozen new characters, Lady Molly Jeavons and her husband Ted are two of the most attractive. Lady Molly is a true aristocrat, so confident of her position that she does unconventional things without a second thought; she is like an amalgam of Rosa Lewis of the Cavendish Hotel, famous for her love of dukes and Americans, and of Lady Ottoline Morrell of Garsington, hostess to Britain's literati, though Powell had models closer to his own family tree, if less widely known.

Lady Molly's house is a shelter for all, irrespective of class, as long as they display good manners. When, for instance, "Lord Amesbury looked in on his way to a Court ball . . . she was giving the vet a meal she had cooked herself." The title *At Lady Molly's* refers, however to two domiciles; for, before her unconventional marriage to a car salesman, Lady Molly had been the wife of the Earl of Sleaford and mistress of one of England's great houses, Dogdene. Ugly and meaningless as the word *Dogdene* is—in the way of the names of great English houses—it connotes to those in the know centuries of cultivated taste, luxury, and art. When St. John Clarke in self-pity catalogues the real accomplishments of his career, for instance, he recalls bitterly as its zenith "One week-end at Dogdene twenty years ago" (5.191).

The network of historical associations of the house goes back into history; Henry James had spent a weekend there; and Powell has fun contriving a bit of what might be called "pseudo-Pepys" since that seventeenth-century diarist had recorded many a flirtation and affair. Powell invents a visit to Dogdene and Pepys' meeting there with "a great black maid" who "toyed wantonly" with him, and who "would not have denied me *que je voudray,* yet was I afeared and time was lacking. At which afterwards I was troubled, lest she should speak of what I had done, and her fellows make game of me when we were gone on the road" (4.11). Pepys' account of his failure to seduce the wench is counterpointed at the end of the novel with Powell's replay, also at Dogdene, of that classic of folk comedy: the man of power who proves to be sexually impotent—and tries to conceal the fact.

Attempting a climb in society, to match a climb to power in

the City, Widmerpool has become engaged to a socialite named Mildred Blaides. Some years younger than she, Widmerpool is appalled at her "modern" suggestion that it would be wise for them to spend a weekend together before marriage. As the youngest daughter of Edward VII's friend Lord Vowchurch (and the sister-in-law of General Conyers), she awes Widmerpool. Indeed Jenkins, when he had met her as a boy, was struck by her flashy slang, glamorous ways, and raffish attitudes. Jenkins is as shocked by the idea of Widmerpool's engagement to such a woman as Widmerpool is by her aggressive sexuality. In anxiety Widmerpool invites Jenkins to his club, hoping for advice, even as to how he should register for a clandestine weekend. As "Mr. and the Honourable Mrs. Smith?" Jenkins drily suggests (4.61). In the end, Mildred arranges the "trial marriage" by getting them invited together to a weekend at Dogdene and by suggesting that Widmerpool visit her room the first night. The next morning she breaks the engagement. Widmerpool has failed again in the field of love. Apprised of the story, Jenkins is amused later at Lady Molly's to hear Widmerpool evasively allude to the prudential reasons he has decided, after all, against matrimony (4.214).

During World War I, Dogdene had been turned into a hospital for wounded officers; and there the lowest of them, a car salesman in civil life named Ted Jeavons, had met both Molly, the Countess of Sleaford, whom he was to marry after she became a widow, and Widmerpool's fiancée, Mildred Blaides, then a nurse. But Dogdene is more than a locus for temporal intersections: it is a symbol of the great English family and its roots. The geometric leap in density of character that baffles the reader who begins with *At Lady Molly's* is accompanied by the introduction of a nephew of the first Lord Sleaford, Chips Lovell, who is a colleague at the film studio where Jenkins now works as a scriptwriter. A gossip columnist by inclination, Chips Lovell is given the encyclopedic knowledge of genealogy (5.59) that Evelyn Waugh suggests Powell himself had at Oxford;[20] and Lovell appears in the nick of time, for rarely has a novel so needed an expert in family entanglements.

At Lady Molly's might be called *The Book of the Tollands,* for the most numerous and important of its new characters are the twelve members of the Tolland clan. This family may turn out to be the greatest, as it now seems to be the largest, family in English literary history. All twelve are acutely characterized, from the "baby" Priscilla (who has not yet made her debut, but who has already attracted the matrimonial eye of Chips Lovell) to her stepmother, the family *doyen* who presides over the family in its townhouse while writing volume after volume of biography.[21] "Lady Warminster, eccentric herself, showed a decent respect for eccentricity . . . so that the Tollands were left largely to their own devices. Life at Hyde Park Gardens might be ruthless, but it was played out on a reasonably practical basis, in which every man was for himself and no quarter given; while at the same time a curtain of relatively good humour was usually allowed to cloak an inexorable recognition of life's inevitable severities" (4.208). Since Lady Warminster is the sister of Lady Molly, the Tollands frequently visit Lady Molly; and, indeed, Jenkins first finds hospitality at Lady Molly's when Chips Lovell, after a day at the studio, takes him along on his own quest for Priscilla.

The door is opened by a butler who has been loaned to Lady Molly by Erridge, the titular head of the Tolland family. The butler is on loan because Erridge has closed the vast family country house, Thrubworth, to become a tramp and see how the other half lives. George Orwell went "down and out in Paris and London" for similar motives, his guilt at being a member of a privileged class figuring among them; and Erridge shares Orwell's reaction to social ills. But with Erridge we come to yet another problem.

Usually the English novel is easier to read than the Russian, the reader not having the problem of contending with four or five names for each character; Widmerpool is always either Widmerpool or Kenneth. But English novels about the aristocracy can grow complicated. The name Erridge comes from the baronial title he was given at birth, and the nickname Erry is natural enough, for members of his family. But he can also be called Alfred Tolland, joining christian and family names, or Alf Warminster, since he became the Earl of Warminster upon the death of his father. Powell is aware of the danger of confusing the reader, and the narrator always calls him Erridge;

but social realism demands that the family call him by the title under which he grew up; that friends who disapprove of that "pompous" practice, Lady Molly for one, call him Alfred, that strangers call him Lord Warminster; and those between these categories, such as Chips Lovell, call him Erry Warminster on one page (5.195) and Alf on the next. With Erridge, such realism is worth the effort of following; for he joins Widmerpool as one of the novel's great characters; and we may console ourselves by reflecting that each name used also defines the speaker's relationship to him.

Jenkins comes to meet Erridge through the miscalculation of J. G. Quiggin. Quiggin is open about disliking people who do not have "all the right ideas," and Jenkins is one who does not; but Templer's former wife has grown bored again, this time with Quiggin; and they have invited Jenkins, as a scriptwriter, to the country to discuss securing Mona a role in a movie. They are residing in a cottage in Thrubworth Park, and Quiggin is annoyed when Erridge drops by to invite them up to the house the next day. Quiggin says Jenkins has to leave. When Jenkins replies that he does not, that the studio is closed by a strike, Erridge gets the mistaken impression that Jenkins, being out on strike, must have "all the right ideas." Since Quiggin is maneuvering to get Erridge to underwrite a left-wing magazine of the arts that he wants to edit, he can express his irritation only obliquely. And the visit to Thrubworth precipitates two new changes of partner in the dance to the music of time.

At Lady Molly's focuses on the family as Jenkins—gathering "scraps of information" about the Tollands (4.31) as one does in life—meets them one by one. At Thrubworth he first meets Lady Isobel when she and her sister Lady Susan breeze in to announce Susan's engagement to Roddy Cutts, a Tory member of parliament. "Much as I hate the Tories," Quiggin says, "I've heard that Cutts is one of their few promising young men" (4.140). The sight of Isobel marks a change in the rhythm of time for Jenkins: "Would it be too explicit, too exaggerated, to say that when I set eyes on Isobel Tolland, I knew at once that I should marry her? Something like that is the truth; certainly nearer the truth than merely to record those . . . inchoate sentiments of interest of which I was so immediately conscious"

(4.136). At almost the same time Jenkins becomes imperfectly aware of another shift when Erridge sends his surly butler for champagne and Mona seems delighted. Though at the time it seems to Jenkins absurd to suspect that Templer's ex-wife would see in so taciturn a hermit as Erridge hope of relief from boredom, by the end of the volume she and Erridge have gone off to China together, leaving Quiggin behind.

Among the crystallizing scenes in *At Lady Molly's* is an apotheosis of those amiable drunk-comedy scenes that stretch back in literature as far as Plato's Symposium. Thought to be a milktoast by some, scored for his ignorance by intellectuals such as Mark Members, Ted Jeavons is revealed to Jenkins during a pub crawl to be an amiable, modest, and amusing chap. Over the table in a nightclub recently opened by Umfraville, he sings "If You Were the Only Girl in the World":

> "People don't think the same way any longer," he bawled across the table. "The war blew the whole bloody thing up, . . . Always feel rather sorry for your generation as a matter of fact, not but what we haven't lost our—what do you call 'em. . . ."
>
> "Illusions?"
>
> "Illusions! That's the one. We've lost all our bloody illusions. Put 'em all in the League of Nations, or somewhere like that. Illusions, my God. I had a few of 'em when I started. You wouldn't believe it. Of course, I've been lucky. Lucky isn't the word, as a matter of fact. Still people always talk as if marriage was one long roll in the hay. You can take it from me, my boy, it isn't. . . . Molly and I are very fond of each other in our own way. Between you and me, she's not a great one for bed. . . . Still, you have to step out once in a way. Go melancholy mad, otherwise. Life's a rum business, however you look at it, and—as I was saying—not having been born to this high life, and so on, I can't exactly complain." (4.179)

The story Jeavons is leading up to is that of an affair he had had during the war with a once glamorous girl, whom he discreetly does not name; nevertheless, Jenkins is able to identify her as the woman to whom Widmerpool is now engaged, Mildred Blaides. As Jeavons finishes the tale, Widmerpool enters with his fiancée.

Powell does not allow coincidence to rest there. The party to celebrate Jenkins' engagement to Isobel brings out the eldest of the Tollands, Uncle Alfred, Erridge's namesake, who is an Old Boy from Le Bas's house. Indeed, it was after sitting beside Uncle Alfred at one Old Boy dinner that Jenkins had resolved, he now recalls, to attend no more reunion dinners. Coincidence might be said to swirl through the social no-man's-land that is Lady Molly's house: here Widmerpool first meets his own fiancée, and here Erridge meets the novelist St. John Clarke (4.124) with fatal effect for Quiggin. Quiggin had hoped to be Clarke's heir, but Clarke leaves his money to Erridge as one more likely to use it for the Left. Ironically, Erridge, disillusioned with the Left after his return from the Civil War in Spain (5.197), uses the money instead to repair Thrubworth (5.227).

That Erridge resembles George Orwell in certain details, as several critics have remarked, is true, but there is one caution: the radical peer—the aristocrat by birth who adopts the viewpoint of the peasant or worker—is a familiar English type; and the rest of the English have always found the type amusing. Sir James Barrie in his play *The Admirable Crichton* (1902), for instance, draws the portrait of a radical peer in the character of Lord Loam who forces the servants to eat "upstairs"—sitting down with the family—once a year to show his egalitarian spirit, much to the disapproval of his butler, Crichton. "Can't you see, Crichton, that our divisions into classes are artificial, that if we were to return to Nature, which is the aspiration of my life, all would be equal?" That Lord Loam is wrong, that nature ordains a class system, the play then sets out to "prove." And Erridge moves in that direction.

V Casanova's Chinese Restaurant

Considered as a separable novel, *Casanova's Chinese Restaurant* (1960) is one of the more successful. As the word *Casanova* in the title might suggest, its theme is love—love comic and tragic (5.157), but married love. Jenkins' marriage to Lady Isobel Tolland takes place, but between chapters: the focus is on the marriages of a music critic named Maclintick, who commits suicide when his wife deserts him, and a musical composer named Hugh Moreland, who has married the former mistress of Sir Magnus Donners, but is at the point of leaving her for the sister of Lady Isobel when the suicide occurs. Love partnerships are broken and re-formed, in the cosmic flux, as husbands and wives dance to the music of time, "in seemingly meaningless gyrations, while partners disappear only to reappear again, once more giving pattern to the spectacle." And the Chinese Restaurant of the title points to the spot in London where, in 1926, Jenkins came to know the two husbands, Maclintick and Moreland.

Only the first volume of *The Music of Time* has a more Proustian envelopment of theme. Jenkins sights a bombed-out pub—between 1947 and 1950 we assume since he feels "glad the place had not yet been rebuilt"—with only the word *Ladies* still decipherable on the lintel of a "gateway to some unknown, forbidden domain, the lair of sorcerers." The doorway to the ladies' room leads now into an abyss of rubble. Suddenly "there came from this unexplored country the song . . . of the blonde woman on crutches . . . whose voice I had not heard since the day . . . Moreland and I had listened . . . the afternoon he had talked of getting married." That talk had occurred in the early 1930's, at a period when Jenkins still loved Jean. A more voluntary effort of the memory carries him back to the mid-1920's where the story began. (As a technique new to *The Music of Time*, after four volumes of simple chronological sequence, this use of the time shift opened new possibilities of form; later *The Kindly Ones* takes us back to 1914.)

An index to *Casanova's Chinese Restaurant* is the song "Pale Hands I Loved Beside the Shalimar," which poses a melancholy but appropriate question, "Where are you now?" Moreover, the song moves from the implication of the loss of love to the thought of love's infidelity, "Who lies beneath your spell?" In 1926 or 1927, in the pub, Jenkins had met not only the music critic Maclintick, but the violinist Carolo, a former child prodigy (of North Midlands origin despite the Italianate name). As the novel ends, Carolo lies "beneath the spell" of Maclintick's errant wife, Maclintick lies dead, and Moreland has returned to his wife Matilda after being for a time "beneath the spell" of Jenkins' new sister-in-law Priscilla.

A reproduction of Bernini's statue "Truth Unveiled by Time" is also introduced in the first scene, and it too tends to preside over the novel. Why Quiggin can be irritated despite being praised (5.196) becomes apparent when we learn to whom Clarke has left his money. Why Maclintick's suicide should make Moreland's wife happier becomes apparent when we learn of the breakup of his supposed affair with Priscilla: "What Matilda thought, what Priscilla thought remained a mystery. All sides of such a situation are seldom shown at once, even if they are shown at all" (5.221). And what is to become of these marriages in difficulty because time has already unveiled too much truth, the time flow also reveals.

Jenkins' marriage to Erridge's sister Lady Isobel Tolland seems to have been a society wedding to which at least Templer (6.102), Widmerpool (6.233), and General Conyers (6.208) were invited. In the previous volume, General Conyers had taken time out from playing "Ave Maria" on the cello and reading Freud to comment on marriage, as Widmerpool was released from its threat and as Jenkins moved toward it: "What was it Foch said? War not an exact science, but a terrible and passionate drama? Something like that. Fact is, marriage is rather like that too" (4.234). Since the marriage of General and Mrs. Conyers seems as happy as any Jenkins knows, the words instill some apprehension. His own marriage is less the center of attention in *Casanova's Chinese Restaurant*, however, than the marriages of Moreland and Maclintick.

All of the marriages are puzzling in one way or another. The Maclinticks seem to be engaged in an unending quarrel (5.188, 209)—"To be married to either of the Maclinticks can not be much fun" (5.157)—but, instead of being relieved to be rid of his wife, time reveals that Maclintick's dependence on her is so acute he cannot survive her loss. The first odd feature of Moreland's marriage is that it links a rather conservative young man to a notorious young lady, for gossip has identified actress Matilda as the former kept woman of Sir Magnus Donners. Meeting her, Jenkins discovers a candor and realism that make her character seem to be what Moreland needs in a wife; and it is, after all, only the prospective husband whose pride might object to "damaged goods." Three or four years of apparently happy matrimony elapse; then Jenkins and his wife discover at Moreland's concert that all is not well with the Morelands.

"Is it fun to be married to anyone?" Matilda asks. The shock of Maclintick's suicide induces Moreland to end his incipient affair with Priscilla and return to his wife, Matilda. What adds to the dimension of coincidence is Matilda's revelation that, before consorting with Donners, she had been married to Carolo, who has now in a sense saved her marriage by breaking up Maclintick's.

On the night at the Mortimer in 1926 that Barnby introduced Nick Jenkins to bohemian society, the relationship of the composer Hugh Moreland to the music critic Maclintick puzzled Jenkins the most. Maclintick revered Moreland's genius and was attempting to "better" his character. But Moreland was attractive to Jenkins (who then knew nothing of his genius) because of his character. Having a well-balanced view of life and a profound wit, Moreland becomes one of Nick's closest friends, as later volumes demonstrate. And the chief figure behind the arras of Moreland would seem to be, at least in his friendly bohemian aspects, the composer Constant Lambert (as we noted in chapter three).

Moreland conceives himself to be "the plain Englishman with a pipe in his hand" (5.133, 202), and this conservative side appeals to Nick, but does not deceive him as to Moreland's actual complexity. The characteristic of a man trying to be more simple and more conservative than he is in actuality was to be seen in Lambert. According to his friend Cecil Gray, Lambert exhibited "in himself a disconcerting blend of the most opposite extremes imaginable—a *fin de siècle* Frenchman with morbid *faisandes* tastes, and a bluff and hearty roast-beef-and-Yorkshire Englishman: Baudelaire and Henry Fielding combined... Ronald Firbank and Winston Churchill (to whom he bears an uncanny physical resemblance)...."[26] As Powell's art matured, he dared to be more accurate in giving Moreland the very Churchillian physiognomy that Gray defines—"a massive, Beethoven-shaped head, high forehead, temples swelling outwards, eyes and nose somehow bunched together in a way to make him glare at times.... On the other hand, his short, dark, curly hair recalled a dissipated cherub...." (5.16)—perhaps because the overall pattern of character and action has been more deeply cracked and reformed.

The book is about Moreland's marriage—Lambert was married twice—and also about Maclintick's marriage; and certainly among the ingredients of Maclintick is Philip Heseltine, who never married. Both Heseltine and Maclintick seem to thrive upon quarrels, and both end their lives in a gas-filled room when the quarreling stops. Heseltine's suicide took place in the Christmas season of 1930;[27] Maclintick's occurs in 1937 (5.216). That two people so dissimilar and so antipathetic, even over their evaluation of Casanova (5.31), should consider themselves friends ("Moreland was probably the only human being Maclintick had whole-heartedly liked. In return Moreland had liked Maclintick; liked his intelligence; liked talking and drinking with him" [5.221]) is a matter that puzzles Nick Jenkins (who apparently finds Maclintick unsympathetic) much as it might those who saw Lambert and Heseltine together. Yet "by comparison and contrast" some understanding could be reached.

Their temperaments may have been widely divergent, but Lambert and Heseltine had common features unusual to musicians; and among them was a talent for composing limericks. Gray tells us that Lambert's "series of fifty devoted to double bishops (bishops with two or more dioceses, like Bath and Wells) is undoubtedly one of the most monumental achievements in this difficult and exacting form."[28] Though both were highbrow composers, they had a taste for lowbrow music. The painter Augustus John—who had singled Heseltine out at the Café Royal before meeting him, a "tall blond young man, with a strange derisive smile for ever about his pale handsome features"—recalled setting out from Heseltine's "communal" cottage in Kent by motor-car to visit "the Windmill Inn . . . at Stalham in Norfolk," a hundred miles away, "where of a Saturday evening several local folk-singers were known to gather."[29] And in the same way Nick Jenkins is struck upon meeting Moreland: the brilliant young composer is working on the musical accompaniment for a film and also on an opera, but he frequents the Mortimer because of its mechanical piano 'into which, periodically, Moreland would feed a penny to invoke one of those fortissimo tunes" from the period of "Pale Hands I Loved Beside the Shalimar" (5.2).

Not only character but geography is simultaneously preserved and transformed. The Mortimer public house in London, for instance, seems a blend of the Fitzroy Tavern and The Portland. Gray in his memoirs recalls last seeing a novelist friend "when I was standing outside a public house called 'The George,' at the corner of Mortimer Street and Great Portland Street. . . . I thought he looked ill, and two or three days later he was dead. And then I remembered suddenly that the last time I had seen Robert Nichols before his death a couple of years earlier was in precisely the same place—a strange coincidence. And the last time I saw Philip Heseltine before he died was in 'The Portland,' about twenty yards away. That neighborhood is, for me, thickly populated with ghosts. . . ."[30] As for Casanova's Chinese Restaurant, a name which delights Jenkins with its "unequivocal blendings of disparate elements" which "linked not only the East with the West but the present with the past" (5.29), one element of its composition may be the famed Eiffel Tower restaurant which, despite its French name, came into its glory under the management of Rudolf Stulik, who came from Vienna and spoke with a thick German accent.

Historical counterpoint is supplied to *Casanova's Chinese Restaurant* by Edward VIII's marriage to the American divorcée Wallis Simpson, who is an appropriate totem since she is a double divorcée about to take on her third partner. Widmerpool, appropriately "in" with the Wallis Simpson crowd of American businessmen, anticipates a bit smugly entering court circles after the marriage (5.127). The king's sudden abdication as the volume ends—"to marry the woman I love"—strikes Widmerpool as almost a personal betrayal (5.195).

VI The Kindly Ones

The Kindly Ones (1962) opens on the day of the assassination of Archduke Francis Ferdinand at Sarajevo (June 28, 1914) and closes twenty-five years later, some weeks after the signing of the Russo-German Non-Aggression Pact (August 24, 1939). The narrative begins with the news that Jenkins' father must go to war and closes when Jenkins in turn finds a way to go to war himself. Or, it opens with a demonstration of the leadership ability of General Conyers and his confrontation with the sect leader Dr. Trelawney; resumes the quadrille when Jenkins and his wife, Moreland and his wife, and Templer and his wife act out a pageant in the castle of Sir Magnus Donners; and comes to a close with the death of Uncle Giles—and surprising revelations about the nature of love, from Uncle Giles and from Jean Templer.

Like many memoirs of upper-class childhood, the chapter dealing with Nick Jenkins' "discovery" of World War I is focused on the servants. Among the principals in the household of Captain Jenkins are the cook Albert and the parlormaid Billson; and again the theme is love, in this case Billson's unrequited love for Albert. Albert, stolidly averse to love, direly likens the Suffragettes to the Amazons; and, when he announces that he has decided to retire, Billson's frustration comes to a climax. Stonehurst, the house the Jenkins rent, is haunted, some tales have it; and although such evidences as exist "might have been disregarded in a more rationalistic family; in one less metaphysically flexible, they could have caused agitation" (6.5). The Jenkinses and most of their servants take calmly the stories of the ghosts. When General and Mrs. Conyers arrive for dinner and Billson is expected to serve the *mousse,* her nerves have been wracked by sighting ghosts. When she arrives at the dinner table to announce her own resignation, she is nude.

No book in *The Music of Time* gives more attention to Jenkins' own family. The mother remains a shadowy figure, but Captain Jenkins is brilliantly characterized, with General Conyers as his foil. Captain Jenkins "hid in his heart a hatred of constituted authority. He did his best to conceal this antipathy, because the one thing he hated, more than constituted authority itself, was to hear constituted authority questioned by anyone but himself" (6.38). On the other hand, twice on the afternoon which informs this chapter General Conyers "earns" his position of authority by showing himself a man of action. The first is on the occasion of Billson's nudity: "No one afterwards was ever very well able to describe how he transported her along the passage . . . the shawl always decently draped round Billson like a robe. The point . . . was that action had been taken, willpower brought into play" (6.61). The other occasion involves Dr. Trelawney. "There was something decidedly unpleasant about him, sinister, at the same time absurd, that combination of the ludicrous and alarming soon to be widely experienced by contact with those set in authority in wartime," Jenkins recalls of Dr. Trelawney (6.190). He trots into view across the hills near Aldershot in 1914 followed by his nature-boy disciples in long white robes, only to be stopped by the sight of General Conyers. "The Essence of the All is the Godhead of the True," Trelawney exclaims; and the enlightened general surprisingly replies in kind: "The Vision of Visions heals the Blindness of Sight" (6.64).

Looking back over history, Nicholas Jenkins sees Dr. Trelawney, for all his "religious, philosophical—some said magical—tenets . . . of which he was high priest, if not actually messiah," as the emblem of a confused era: "one of those fairly common strongholds of unsorted ideas that played such a part in the decade ended by the war. Simple-lifers, utopian socialists, spiritualists, occultists, theosophists, quietists, pacifists, futurists, cubists, zealots of all sorts . . . were then thought of by the unenlightened as scarcely distinguishable one from another: a collection of visionaries who hoped to build a New Heaven and a New Earth through the agency of their particular crackpot activities, sinister or comic, according to the way you looked at things" (6.28). The intellectual sickness of a society, and the loneliness of its sentinels whose tradition was slipping away, are telescoped pictorially as Nick recalls seeing as a child, in the sunset, "Dr. Trelawney and his flock roaming through the scrub at the same moment as the Military Policeman on his patrol was riding back in the opposite direction. . . . This meeting and merging of two elements—two ways of life—made a striking contrast in physical appearance, moral ideas and visual tone-values" (6.29). Powell, it is obvious, shares General Conyers' interest in both the ideas and the tones.

Although Trelawney's idiom is that of Aleister Crowley,[31] we should also note that elements of Arthur Machen (1863-1947) probably go into his composition; for Machen—a Welsh-born student of the occult and a member (with W. B. Yeats) of the Rosicrucian Order of the Golden Dawn—was either a neighbor or a family acquaintance of the Powells. "I saw him often when I was a boy," Powell recalls,[32] and it is as a boy that

Nick Jenkins first sees Dr. Trelawney. Decades later, Moreland reveals that he too had been fascinated as a boy by the figure of Dr. Trelawney (6.83). And perhaps the physical culturist disciples of Dr. Trelawney may owe something to those of Georgi Gurdjieff (that "eccentric, filthy, funny, phoney, tender, wise . . . and charismatic" magician of lost souls in the 1920's.[33]

Whatever the ingredients of Dr. Trelawney, his mystic or pseudo-scientific lore—countered by General Conyers—helps demonstrate that general's ability to cope with an esoteric problem. Perhaps Powell aims here at an ironic commentary on the scandalous failures of politically appointed British generals in World War I; for the passage concludes with Uncle Giles's arrival and the news of the assassination at Sarajevo—which Uncle Giles typically and absurdly ascribes to the hazards of automotive transport.

The title *The Kindly Ones* takes us back to Greek myths that Powell sees as powerful yet, because of the patterns of human experience to which they give shape and symbol. The three avenging sisters The Erinyes, or the Furies—who are appeased by being addressed as the Eumenides, or the Kindly Ones—are first encountered by Jenkins in Miss Orchard's class for officers' children near Aldershot. Young Jenkins identifies them with the Suffragettes that have so alarmed Albert: "They inflicted the vengeance of the gods by bringing in their train war, pestilence, dissension on earth; torturing, too, by the stings of conscience. . . . So feared were they, Miss Orchard said, that no man . . . fixed his eyes upon their temples. In that respect, at least, the Furies differed from the suffragettes" (6.2-3). They symbolize the emancipated women in the novel who turn the end of the novel into another torturous round of musical beds. But, so far as the lives of the children and their parents are concerned, Uncle Giles with his news of the assassination at Sarajevo is the first "harbinger of the Furies" (6.70). Evelyn Waugh claims the title "is self-explanatory: the Eumenides accomplish their task of vengeance, begun in 1914, completed in 1939, by the destruction of English civilisation."[34] But it is not certain that Powell has so grim a thesis in mind; it would be more like him to play upon the ambiguity, as in the first association of "the kindly ones" with women.

The second chapter introduces Moreland in a conversation as brilliant ideologically as any in Aldous Huxley. From an antithetical background, one devoted to music, Moreland has had experiences similar to those of Nick Jenkins—even to encounters with Dr. Trelawney. Powell then advances the clock ten years to the period of Hitler's victory at Munich. Jenkins and his wife, not having seen the Morelands since their involvement with Priscilla, visit them in the country, and the four are invited by Sir Magnus Donners to his castle nearby. The "driver" he sends for them turns out to be Peter Templer, and the evening is highlighted by their decision to pose in tableaux of the Seven Deadly Sins for Donners' camera. Jenkins is appropriately cast as Sloth, but the highlight is Lady Isobel's depiction of Pride with Lady Ann Umfraville. "Here, before us, in these two was displayed the nursery and playroom life of generations of 'great houses': the abounding physical vitality of big aristocratic families, their absolute disregard for personal dignity . . . that passionate return to childhood, never released so fully in any other country, or . . . class" (6.128-29).

The dramatic climax comes when Templer, portraying senile Lust with Anne, drives his new wife Betty into jealous hysteria. At this moment Widmerpool arrives in his own new costume, that of an officer of the territorials. After what seems a rather stilted chat about finance with Sir Magnus (6.137), he drives the Morelands and the Jenkins home. Time is to unveil that the artificial talk had another role, to get Templer to gossip about certain financial details (6.174). Time also unveils another consequence of Templer's play for Anne; and by the end of *The Kindly Ones* Anne has left Sir Magnus—and Matilda has left Moreland.

In the third section of the novel, six paths that have crossed before again intersect near the sea where the Jenkins' family chef has become the proprietor of a small hotel. Jenkins goes upon receiving a telegram that his Uncle Giles has died in the hotel. As Jenkins sorts through Uncle Giles's possessions, the revelations of time come as to who is to be Uncle Giles's heir (it is Mrs. Erdleigh, the fortuneteller, who is living nearby), as to Uncle Giles's status (contrary to gossip, he had received a bona fide military commission), and as to his secret life (in the bottom of his trunk is a copy of *The Perfumed Garden, or the Arab Art of Love*). More surprising is the presence of Dr. Trelawney in the same hotel, who between shots of heroin and brandy, gets stuck in a wildly farcical scene in the hall bathroom (6.183).[35] Most surprising is the discovery in the dining room of Bob Duport, not seen for fifteen years, who is here by the sea to avoid his creditors. Unaware that Jenkins had had an affair with his wife, Duport tells him that Jean had returned to him only in order to get a free trip to South America and another man. Jenkins is crushed by the revelation that, when he thought Jean was only betraying her husband, she was also betraying him, and with the most repulsive of Duport's associates, Jimmy Brent. Recalling a chapter in *The Perfumed Garden,* "On the Deceits and Treacheries of Women," Jenkins quietly gives Duport the book as a token from Uncle Giles, who died a bachelor.

The final section leads us to the outbreak of World War II and to the efforts of Jenkins to activate his reserve commission and enter the army. Neither General Conyers nor Widmerpool can help him, although Widmerpool is less than frank about his limitations: " 'You come and ask me for advice about getting into the army, Nicholas,' he said, 'and because I spare the time to talk of such things . . . you think I have nothing more serious to occupy me than your own trivial problems. That is not the case. The General Staff of the Wehrmacht would be only too happy to possess even a tithe of the information I locked away before we quitted the Orderly Room' " (6.230). At Lady Molly's, however, Jenkins meets Ted Jeavons' modest brother who promises him action in a week or two and keeps his promise. The Seven Deadly Sins of Society have invoked the Furies of purgation; and, like Orestes, Jenkins accepts their chastisements as "part of a required pattern the fulfillment of which was in some way a relief" (7.2).

VII The Valley of Bones

The Valley of Bones (1964), the seventh volume of *The Music of Time*, begins with Jenkins' introduction to his regiment in the autumn of 1939, and closes with his departure from the regiment as the German armies near Paris in June, 1940. Except for a brief leave when Jenkins visits his wife and gets briefed on the Tolland family gossip, the cast of characters is completely new and totally Welsh. The focus is upon the drama of life within an infantry company, and the captain and his officers, the sergeant and their men form a miniature society of their own. Here, nevertheless, the old pressures of love and power continue to exact their toll.

The day after Jenkins arrives in Wales is Sunday, and the whole regiment is marched to church where the Welsh chaplain takes his text from Ezekiel (and gives the volume its title):

> The hand of the Lord was upon me, and carried me out in the spirit of the Lord, and set me down in the midst of the valley which was full of bones, and . . . behold there were very many in the open valley: and, lo, they were very dry. And he said unto me, Son of man, can these bones live? And I answered, O Lord God thou knowest. . . . Come from the four winds, O breath, and breathe upon these slain that they may live. So I prophesied as he commanded me, and the breath came unto them and they lived, and stood up upon their feet, an exceeding great army. . . .

The chaplain is from the mining valleys of Wales, not the urban "waste land" of T. S. Eliot: "Oh, my brethren, think on that open valley . . . a valley, do I picture it, by the shaft of a shut-down mine, where, under the dark mountain side, the slag heaps lift their heads to the sky. . . . They are our bones, my brethren, the bones of you and of me, bones that await the noise and shaking" (37-38).

The mighty army has come together; the question is whether it will live. The officers of Jenkins' unit, most of them Welsh bankers, had in peace been as dead men; the question is whether they will come collectively alive. At the end of the volume, it is obvious that they have; forerunners have met the enemy at Dunkirk and taken his measure—but not without price. A man from Jenkins' platoon has been killed; Jenkins' brother-in-law Robert Tolland has also been killed; and Isobel has given birth to a son. War has accelerated the rhythm of life, but the rhythm remains.

Removal from the social matrix of the earlier volumes has several effects upon *The Valley of Bones*. One surprising effect is that, presumably in the name of military realism, Powell for the first time "listens in" as soldiers tell an off-color joke (7.55) and talk obscenely (7.178). As surprising to readers accustomed to the earlier society is the isolation of Jenkins during the first chapters from anyone with whom we are familiar. Among the new characters is Jenkins' platoon sergeant, Pendry, a man who withers away inarticulately for love and ends an apparent suicide. Lieutenant Bithel of Jenkins' company is an engagingly unsuccessful con artist whose reaction to a joke played on him by fellow officers is forever memorable. More important in Jenkins' life, however, is his company commander, Captain Gwatkin (who turns out to be very distantly related to the debutante Barbara Goring [7.187]). The captain is determined to be a good officer, and he has a number of virtues: he is sensible, humane, conscientious, and reasonably intelligent. But he blunders from mishap to catastrophe, alienating the well-disposed and conciliating the inherently vicious. He is handicapped fatally by his very determination and by his ignorance of human nature. In the end, he is relieved of the command of his company, and he finds no comfort in love. Infatuated with a barmaid in Northern Ireland, he overlooks Jenkins' suggestion that her character might not be of the best—and in the gardens of Castle Mallock, commemorated by Byron and Thackeray, he finds her in the arms of a soldier.

In the third of the four chapters—a quadrille structure is maintained in seven of the eleven volumes—Jenkins is posted to Aldershot for a two-week training course and finds himself back on the fringes of the society we know. Marching beside Jimmy Brent, Jenkins painfully learns more about Jean Templer's perfidies (7.30). His single weekend away from camp is spent in the country where Isobel is awaiting the birth of their child, and there the novel resumes its web of marital interweaving. The ultra-dignified Lady Frederica is now engaged, he discovers, to the infra-raffish Umfraville, one of those bizarre "human relationships easier to accept than to rationalize or disentangle" (7.145). Umfraville tells Jenkins the story of how his first wife Dolly had eloped with Buster Foxe (7.153), Stringham's stepfather, just as Commander Foxe himself arrives, looking "immensely distinguished . . . in naval uniform." Robert Tolland has married Stringham's sister Flavia; and Buster has come to implore Flavia's assistance in stopping Flavia's mother from divorcing him to marry the actor Norman Chandler (who had discovered the statuette "Truth Unveiled by Time"). But Buster arrives at the moment Robert receives an urgent call to report back to duty—unknown to them that evening, the German army is set to invade Holland—and Lt. Odo Stevens, a narcissistic salesman of costume jewelry in civilian life, arrives with a brooch for Priscilla, whose husband has been at sea for some time. The threat is there, in her strange encouragement of Odo, of another ruptured marriage.

Serial polygamy, as a sociologist has called the new pattern of marital living, is to be perceived as much in British upper-class circles as in Hollywood, and its floating lovers are seen to be no happier—at least as observed by Jenkins from the vantage point of his own apparently solid marriage. Certainly the changing of partners is seen as a characteristic of modern life, however, if not of life itself. Changes may not be made quite as casually as in a quadrille, yet the fact that the choice of mate so often remains inexplicable—Jean's choice of the fat Brent, Frederica's of the wild Umfraville, Conyers' of the astringent Tuffy Weedon, and Priscilla's of the obscene Odo—makes human lives seem like electrons, whose quanta leaps cannot be predicted. *The Music of Time* probes the unknown quantity, as if Powell would analyze the character of the Wife of Bath by seeking the common denominator of the five husbands she survived.

When the fourth part of *The Valley of Bones* brings us back to North Ireland, we witness the dispersal of the infantry company Jenkins knew. He himself is posted to division headquarters, where he discovers that he has become Widmerpool's underling. "I had no reason to suppose you would be the most efficient," Widmerpool says with his usual crass pomposity, "but since none of the others had any more legal training . . . I allowed the ties of old acquaintance to prevail . . . subject to your giving satisfaction, of course." The volume ends rather ominously—"I saw that I was now in Widmerpool's power"—though not bleakly, since the general to whom Widmerpool is in turn subordinate seems hardly a man to admire the Widmerpools of the world.

VIII The Soldier's Art

The second volume of the war-novel trilogy within *The Music of Time* covers the years 1940-42 when Nicholas Jenkins is a lieutenant attached to the headquarters of a British infantry division. By coincidence, Widmerpool and Stringham are also attached to the headquarters unit, and the focus is upon the struggles for power up and down the echelons of command. The situation is congenial to neither Jenkins nor Stringham, and they eventually escape, Jenkins after a visit to London on a quiet day of the Blitz—which leaves three of his friends killed by bombs.

The title *The Soldier's Art* (1968) is of distinguished literary provenance. We can trace it back at least to Shakespeare's *King Lear.* King Lear, half mad, is followed into a storm by a friend who, in order to approach him, has to feign madness. The scene of their meeting is ended, as they enter a hut, with Edgar's enigmatic and ominous words: "Child Rowland to the dark tower came;/ His word was still/ "Fie, Foh, and fum!/ I smell the blood of a British man'" (3.4.173). In 1852 Robert Browning, after reading the play, was inspired to write one of his better poems, the enigmatic "Childe Roland to the Dark Tower Came." In that dramatic monologue a knight is depicted crossing a grisly landscape to a mortal but otherwise uncertain combat. The only living thing he comes upon is a "stiff, blind horse, his every bone a-stare":

> Seldom went such grotesqueness with such woe;
> I never saw a brute I hated so;
> He must be wicked to deserve such pain.
>
> I shut my eyes and turned them on my heart.
> As a man calls for wine before he fights,
> I asked one draught of earlier, happier sights,
> Ere fitly I could hope to play my part.
> Think first, fight afterwards—the soldier's art;
> One taste of the old time sets all to rights.

But the effort of the memory to retaste past time is in vain. "Not it!" the knight exclaims, as recollection brings only the faces of friends disgraced or hanged as traitors.

"Better this present than a past like that," the knight reflects as he resumes his journey into desolation. The sentiment he expresses is that of Stringham, who reads the passage from Browning aloud to Jenkins as they stand on a street corner just before the climax of World War II (8.221). Stringham is the happy warrior, but his years of dissipation have left him so wasted physically that he has been denied entrance into glamorous fighting units such as the commandos and the paratroops. When remet by Jenkins, he is serving as a waiter in an officers' mess.

The former governess who cured Stringham of his alcoholism had also introduced him to the poems of Browning. When Jenkins protests that he personally is "never sure what I feel about Browning"—presumably because of the glibness of some of Browning's moralizing—Stringham insists that "there's a lot in what he says." Moreover, Stringham identifies with Browning's knight. Jenkins tentatively follows Stringham's reading with a query: *"Childe Roland to the Dark Tower Came*?" "Childe Stringham—in this case," Stringham replies.

Of Jenkins' acquaintance during this dark period of the war, the period of the Blitz, many turn back to the great Victorian writers as to wells of moral surety from a world where, as Yeats puts it, "the best lack all conviction." Victorianism reborn might almost be considered a minor theme of the volume. It is General Liddament's shock that Lieutenant Jenkins does not share his enthusiasm for the novels of Anthony Trollope and his discovery that Jenkins reads Balzac in French instead (8.47) that leads to Jenkins' salvation. The general recommends him to the Free French as an interpreter; and, although Jenkins fails his examination with a Major Finn (a character much like Stringham in that he resists escalation of his own rank), in Major Finn's office Jenkins meets Pennistone who tacitly promises to rescue him from the Infantry Officers Replacement Pool to which Widmerpool would have consigned him upon his own departure to higher things (8.106).

Widmerpool had reproached Nick earlier for trying to get

Stringham a better position. "'I have always been told,' said Widmerpool, '—and rightly told—that it is a great mistake in the army, or indeed elsewhere, to allow personal feelings about individuals to affect my conduct towards them professionally.... Why should Stringham have some sort of preferential treatment just because you and I happen to have been at school with him?... War is a great opportunity for everyone to find his level. I am a major—you are a second-lieutenant—he is a private'" (8.72-3). But Stringham in battle, where a soldier is tested, may turn out to be the better soldier. Certainly, Powell hints as much. During Jenkins' absence on leave, Widmerpool has Stringham transferred to Lieutenant Bithel's Mobile Laundry Unit; and we learn that Stringham has the loyalty to his superiors that is another part of the knightly tradition. When he finds his commanding officer drunk on the street, he telephones Jenkins for aid in getting Lieutenant Bithel, who loves the army and drinks because he knows his position in it to be insecure, back to the officers' quarters before the police spot him.

Ironically, the three of them in the blackout bump into Major Widmerpool. Widmerpool dismisses Jenkins as the air-raid alert sounds: "Stringham and I will get this sot back to bed. I'll see this is the last time the army's troubled with him." The sight of Widmerpool by flashlight sets Stringham to musing. "'It's interesting to recall, sir,' he said, 'the last time we met. I myself was the inert frame. It was you and Mr. Jenkins who so kindly put me to bed. It shows that improvement is possible, that roles can be reversed. I've turned over a new leaf. Stringham is enrolled in the ranks of the sober, as well as the brave'" (8.185). The volume closes as Stringham cheerfully sets forth, carrying his volume of Browning, apparently destined for service in North Africa where a rear-echelon laundry, in the fluidity of desert war, may easily find itself on the front line.

A possible model for this phase of Stringham's life can be seen in the career of Alfred Duggan, whom Evelyn Waugh in 1964 recalled as an Oxford student who was always drunk:

> Little could have surprised me more forty, thirty, or even twenty years ago than the revelation that Alfred was to become the industrious, prolific historical novelist who is honoured today.... He was

very rich then with the immediate disposal of a fortune greater than any of our contemporaries. He was, moreover, the stepson of the Chancellor of the University, Lord Curzon. This connection irked the authorities, who otherwise would have summarily sent him down. . . . Whether in the saddle in the late mornings or at "the 43" (Mrs. Meyrick's night club . . .) in the early mornings, Alfred was always tight; never violent, always carefully and correctly dressed, always polite, he lived in an alcoholic haze. . . . Lord Curzon discerned his quality [however]. His memory was exceptionally retentive and in the shadowy years when he continued to drink very heavily and was seen sitting, apparently stupefied, turning the pages of an historical work in the library at Hackwood, his brain, like an electronic device, was in an inexplicable way storing up recondite information which became available when he heroically overcame this inherited disability.[36]

That Stringham is destined for literary distinction, as Alfred Duggan was, is not suggested by Powell, though he is, next to Moreland, the most articulate of Jenkins' friends. Nor would it be in Powell's style to make Stringham the center of the grand heroics that shower medals of honor upon the brave and the lucky. But that in warfare Childe Stringham may have redeemed his wasted life seems probable.

In form *The Soldier's Art* is the first volume in the series to have a three-part structure: one day of Jenkins' leave in London is sandwiched between two periods of duty as a staff officer in an infantry division headquarters. The first of these sections focuses on the abuses of power at the headquarters, abuses which Jenkins observes as Widmerpool's assistant. Widmerpool, the adjutant general (or DAAG), is of course at the center of the intrigue; he prevents a corporal in Jenkins' defense platoon from going to Officers Training School because he is a good clerk; and he schemes to get his own candidate made commander of a new reconnaissance unit. The larger intrigue ends in Widmerpool's discomfiture when Sunny Farebrother, now Widmerpool's "opposite number" at a higher headquarters, steps back into Jenkins' life after twenty years to announce that his own candidate has secured the coveted post (8.195). Farebrother has suavely and ruthlessly quoted Widmerpool's own words against him, and the volume ends with Widmerpool temporarily deflated, his machinations exposed. Some relief is brought to Jenkins and to Widmerpool, respectively, at the end, however, with the news that Germany has invaded Russia and that the general whom Widmerpool now has most reason to fear will be leaving to command a corps.

Like several of the previous volumes, *The Soldier's Art* traces the mysterious and therefore not wholly traceable path of a suicide. A vulgar captain in charge of physical training, an officer but no gentleman, finds Stringham's cool demeanor and cultivated accent offensive in the officers' mess; and Stringham is hounded without mercy. But it is the captain who is found hanging in the cricket pavilion: "Never thought Biggy would have done that. In the cricket pav, of all places, and him so fond of the game" (8.228).

The central section of *The Soldier's Art* takes us through only the first day of Jenkins' leave, a quiet day in London during the Blitz; but in it we have the only deaths attributable to enemy action. Jenkins dines with Moreland at the Café Royal, and Chips Lovell is with them for a while. In town unexpectedly, Chips hopes to meet his wife Priscilla at the Café de Madrid, where Bijou Ardglass is celebrating her fortieth birthday with a party to which Priscilla has been invited. Chips hopes to effect a reconciliation. He has barely departed for the Madrid when Priscilla arrives at the Café Royal on the arm of Odo Stevens, the commando with whom she is having an affair. The sound of a distant explosion, possibly that of a German tip-and-run raider dropping a single bomb, punctuates the conversation indistinctly; yet Priscilla grows nervous and leaves in agitation, almost breaking relations with Stevens on the spot. She returns to Lady Molly's, apparently hoping Chips will find her there, preferring Molly's family bastion to the nightclub atmosphere of the Madrid.

Later Moreland and Maclintick's wife (with whom Moreland is now living) take Jenkins to their apartment, and the talk is again punctuated with the sound of a distant explosion. Moreland's new lodger Max Pilgrim enters to tell them that the Madrid, where he was playing that night, has been bombed and that Chips Lovell is dead. When Jenkins tries to phone Molly to inform her, he fails to get through. After taking a taxi to Lady Molly's, he discovers that the other bomb has struck the rear of her house, leaving the façade intact, and that Priscilla is dead. Husband and wife, each in the mood for reconciliation, each having gone where he hopes to find the other, are killed in one quiet evening. Separate bombs falling on widely separated areas of London have ended another pattern. Was Priscilla's inexplicable fidgetiness at the Café Royal after the first muffled sound the result of some psychic contact with her husband in his agony? Powell leaves us with the possibility. The strange patterns of life continue. But Lady Molly has also been killed by the second bomb, and the patterns will never be the same.

IX The Military Philosophers

The "war trilogy" (as Anthony Powell calls this subset within *The Music of Time*) concludes with *The Military Philosophers* (1968). Jenkins, in his new role as liaison officer to allied military commands, is in the heart of London during the three years (1942-45) covered by the volume, except for a brief visit to the Continent. Widmerpool again is contiguous, but the focus is upon Peter Templer and Odo Stevens, both of whom parachute to join allied but bickering partisan troops in the Balkans. Templer finds death, and Stevens the clouded medals of a hero.

To the soldier in the foxhole who does not know what is going on in the war, though he has a front-line seat, so to speak, knowledge seems to lie in the rear—not on his periphery, where the action is, but at the central control. And the trajectory of Nick Jenkins has taken him steadily toward the center. There the wisest of military men should be, but the title is, at least in part, ironic.

As the novel opens, Jenkins is night-duty officer, as a member of the general staff in Whitehall (a name which combines the connotations of Pentagon and State Department); and he seems to be near the heart of British military intelligence. Indeed, the teletype is delivering just-decoded news of a potentially important break in the war: the Russians are allowing Polish troops to cross their frontier into Iran. This exodus may result in the doubling, at least, of Polish forces associated with the British army; yet it is odd in view of the earlier Russian "liquidation" of thousands of Polish officers in the Katyn Forest, an event about which there is only a growing sense of certainty, not certainty itself.

Powell's point seems to be that, even at the heart of things, uncertainty reigns. Whitehall is, of course, an immense international nerve center; and Jenkins is not exactly at the heart of Whitehall. But the volume opens on the day when he, fortuitously, is ushered into a bomb-proof command room deep under Whitehall where security clearances are so high that even Captain Jenkins is twice alluded to as a security risk. And there—in command of the situation, fresh from a Cabinet Minister's office (and from drafting memoranda that would be read by Churchill), and prepared to explain the complexities of the new Polish situation to all—is Colonel Widmerpool.

In one of those patterns of coincidence that are integral to Powell's ultimate purpose in *The Music of Time*, both Sunny Farebrother, a parachutist now, and Peter Templer, about to be dropped on a secret mission in the Balkans, join them for Widmerpool's briefing. His information that the new Polish integer in the puzzle, General Anders, is a bit of a swashbuckler awakens the old irony: "Still, I'm no enemy to a bit of dash. I like it" Widmerpool maintains (17).

The comedy thus continues at the heart of things but shaded with tragedy. The time is 1942; the Balkans have been occupied by the German army; and liaison is needed with the partisan factions within countries such as Yugoslavia. Odo Stevens adds to the complexities by joining the Communist partisans within Prince Theodoric's country (Tito's faction?); Templer (like Evelyn Waugh) joins the more conservative faction (Mihailovich's?). But Odo the stout is going to glory (Military Cross and bar); and Templer, as a result of a Widmerpool decision, is going to his death.

Jenkins through the ninth volume, which spans the years from 1942 to 1945, is a liaison officer with the military representatives of various governments in exile in London (and at field headquarters later on the Continent). The solemn presiding deities are, presumably, Lord Alanbrooke and Field-Marshal Montgomery; but on Jenkins' level the tone is seldom far from the comic. The book opens with reference to the myth and the symbols of the Nibelungs: "The curtain had obviously just risen on the third drama of *The Ring*—Mime at his forge—the wizened lieutenant revealed in his shirtsleeves, crouched over a table, while he scoured away at some object in an absolute fever of energy" (9.2). It is with ironic deflation that Jenkins notices that the lieutenant is actually polishing not the sword of Siegfried but his Sam Browne belt.

The spit-and-polish aspect of military decorum and protocol is personified, of course, by Widmerpool who meets his match, when it comes to the intricacies of red tape, in the person of professional staff officer Blackhead. On the other hand, the network of personal relations that has been seen as a part of the Establishment proves to be of military utility when it enables Jenkins to expedite the training, in England, of restless Belgian partisans (195) who are threatened by the Field-Marshal: "I'll shoot 'em up. Is that clear? I'll shoot 'em up" (179).

As officer in charge of liaison with the Belgians and Czechoslovaks, Jenkins meets an array of characters who bewilder the casual reader. Later, in 1944, he is promoted to major and charged with French and Luxembourg liaison as well. He finds Welsh-Breton links with the Free-French liaison officer Kernével, and an attempt is made to interweave other groups: Horaczko of Polish liaison marries Margaret Budd in the end, for instance, and setting the boys agog in the Free-French and the Polish legations is a niece of Charles Stringham.

Pamela Flitton, daughter of Stringham's sister Flavia, is first seen as a staff-car driver from the woman's transport auxiliary (ATS); and, though she leaves that boring job to work in Egypt, her sullen beauty shuttles through the whole novel. Umfraville is the first to peg her correctly: "Giving men hell is what Miss Flitton likes. . . . I know the sort" (74). Jenkins comes to see in her "a woman whose sexual disposition was vested in rage and perversity" (128). Pamela enters with the suggestion that she has had an affair with the nephew of her own mother's second husband, the American Milton Wisebite (72); but the stories of her affairs are legendary. Running through them, however, is a pattern: an "unvarying technique of silence, followed by violence" (74). Like many stunningly beautiful women, Pamela is also attractive to other women, such as Lady Norah Tolland (76) and Lady McReith (99) whom she similarly mistreats.

The men with whom Pamela Flitton is thought to have had affairs, although brief—Peter Templer (82), Prince Theodoric (102), and Bob Duport (190)—constitute a list which points to nymphomania, a word Powell does not use. Instead, he sees her as a figure of myth, the myth of Venusberg and his second novel, and as a scourge for Widmerpool. When told "the name of the girl in red who came in late," Widmerpool is interested: "So that's Pamela Flitton? . . . I've seen her before. With some Americans at one of Biddle's big Allied gatherings" (100). Though it was "unlikely Pamela had ever visited Widmerpool's underground office . . . she herself could be envisaged as one of the myriad incarnations of Venus, even if Widmerpool was not much of a Tannhauser" (203). Still, Widmerpool somehow does stumble "on the secret entrance to the court of the Paphian goddess," and another affair develops.

After V-E Day, Jenkins notices in the paper that "Colonel K. G. Widmerpool, OBE" has become engaged to Miss Pamela Flitton. At an embassy victory party, we are treated to a view of the conflict between Widmerpool and his fiancée that forebodes a marital life of pain. She arrives late, wearing the "oldest, most filthy garments she possessed" but looking "very pretty in spite of her disarray."

> "I think you ought to meet the Ambassador, dearest."
> "Stuff the Ambassador."
> "You really oughtn't to say things like that, darling. . . . Nicholas and I think it very amusing, but someone else might overhear. . . . I shall have to go now. I am late already."
> "Late for what?"
> "I told you—I'm dining with the Minister."
> "You're giving me dinner."
> "I only wish I was. Much as I'd love to, I can't. . . . Besides, I'm sure you told me you were dining with Lady McReith."
> "I'm going to dine with you."

From the struggle of wills, Widmerpool attempts to extricate himself by pointing out that "Nicholas used to be a friend of your uncle, Charles Stringham." " 'Yes,' she said, 'and Charles isn't the only one he knew. He knew Peter Templer too—the man you murdered' " (209-11). Widmerpool's attempts to evade this charge succeed only in showing how his swing to the Left politically, and his sympathy with the Communist partisans may indeed have been a factor in Templer's death. But, in another way, Pamela is the femme fatale for it was she who made it clear to Templer, whose first wife had deserted him and whose second is in an asylum, that he was "not so hot extra-matrimonially either" just before he insisted on participating in that dangerous mission behind the German lines (23,188).

Some philosophy is needed to get a person through such a life, but in *The Military Philosophers* Major David Pennistone is the only ostensible philosopher. In practical areas Pennistone's philosophy is exercised in shepherding temperamental liaison officers from Allied countries, as is that of Jenkins. Pennistone is devoting his spare time, however, to "writing a book about Descartes—or possibly Gassendi" (9.6), a book ultimately published under the title of *Descartes, Gassendi and the Atomic Theory of Epicurus* (10.240). By the end of the war, his interest in philosophy is reported to be so fatigued that he is joining Colonel Finn in Paris in the cosmetics business (9.237). It is Dicky Umfraville who alludes to the saying of that philosophic general, Marshal Lyautey, "that gaiety was the first essential in an officer" (140). Pennistone would not disagree, but he seems more stoic. " 'Not all the fruits of Victory are appetising to the palate,' said Pennistone, 'An issue of gall and wormwood has been laid on' " (197).

Part of the "gall and wormwood" comes with the victory celebration, with the news of Stringham's death in a Japanese prisoner-of-war camp (204). Part of it comes with the award of medals to representatives of countries who entered the war only after Allied victory is assured. One of these even arrives late at the victory service in St. Paul's Cathedral. Jenkins finds room for him among the liaison officers he has shepherded to St. Paul's and is afterward offered a ride by him back to Whitehall. Out of the car that has come to meet him step two ladies looking "incredibly elegant," the younger reminding Jenkins of Jean Templer. The colonel introduces Jenkins to his wife, but not until she begins to "laugh a lot" and exclaims "Nick . . . You look so different in uniform" (233) does he recognize Jean Templer and her daughter Polly Duport.

X Books Do Furnish a Room

Twenty years after the first volume of *The Music of Time* was published, the tenth volume appeared, *Books Do Furnish a Room* (1971). As the narrative begins the narrator is forty and has returned for a visit to his university; when the volume closes, he is forty-two and has returned for a visit to his public school. We move from the winter of 1945-46 to December 1947; and, holding the novel and its characters together, is the life story of a little magazine. Discharged from the army, Jenkins has returned to the London publishing world of *What's Become of Waring,* accepting a position as subeditor in charge of book reviews for the new magazine, *Fission,* which is "to strike the right note for the Atomic Age. Something to catch the young writers coming out of the services. . . ." (36). But initially the magazine, far from splitting up the world as its name might imply, draws characters together.

J. G. Quiggin, the literary critic met in *A Question of Upbringing,* returns to Jenkins' circle as co-founder, with Sir Howard Craggs, now married to Gypsy Jones, of the publishing firm of Quiggin and Craggs that sponsors the periodical. Though the firm has inherited the good will of Boggis & Stone and the Vox Populi Press, *Fission* is to be less dogmatically leftist, in theory at least, as befits the 1940's. The sudden death of Erridge threatens its economic foundations: "The magazine was to be Warminister's toy to do more or less what he liked with" (36). And we find that Widmerpool is also interested in *Fission,* as a Labour MP and a backbencher in the House of Commons: "He wants an organ for his own views" (95). The new financial backer of the magazine turns out to be Rosie Manasch (101) who has an affair with one of the contributors, Odo Stevens—just returned from the theater of war where Templer was killed—who wishes to publish his memoirs. Also getting memoirs in order for publication by Quiggin & Craggs (with excerpts to appear in *Fission*), is the don Sillery, now Lord Sillery, who has been threading his way through Jenkins' life since *A Question of Upbringing.* In short, the magazine serves to draw familiar characters together again in reasonable ways, thereby enabling Powell to return to the extended comic episode form of the earlier volumes, a form which the war-trilogy volumes tended to dissipate into anecdotage.

Although fewer new characters have to be coped with than in any of the war-trilogy volumes, three of the new characters are important; and all three are linked to *Fission*. Books-do-furnish-a-room Bagshaw is appointed editor by Erridge before his death; Bagshaw appeals to him perhaps because of his status as a professional revolutionary (30). Bagshaw gives *Books Do Furnish a Room* its title, of course, and there are several stories as to how he got his nickname—Books, for short. All of them are disreputable (33). The name contains multiple ironies for, like Peter De Vries' title *No, But I Saw the Movie*, it conveys an attitude toward culture that is both respectful and nugatory. Still, the ambivalence of Bagshaw's attitude toward literature makes him more, rather than less, promising as an editor.

"There was a chap called Max Stirner," Bagshaw would argue with friends like Moreland. "Stirner believed it would be all right if only we could get away from the tyranny of abstract ideas." "Whatever Bagshaw thought about abstract ideas when drunk," Jenkins adds, "he was devoted to them when sober. He resembled a man . . . familiar with the name of every horse listed in *Ruff's Guide to the Turf*, who has now ceased to lay a bet, even feel the smallest desire to visit a racecourse" (31). Bagshaw is thus an authority on the factions of the Left while remaining objective enough to use his knowledge to ease the course of *Fission*. And it is Bagshaw who hires Jenkins as book editor.

Jenkins occurs to Bagshaw as a candidate for the post when they meet in a railway station at the university where Bagshaw has just gone to recruit an executive secretary, Ada Leintwardine. Ada's family name is that of a village near Offa's Dyke on the border of Wales, not far from where the House of Powell first became prominent; and she appears to be a sympathetic character. She does so first by disconcerting Sillery: "It was in the Sillery tradition to brag of a great spy network, while keeping secret the names of individual agents. At the same time, with an audience like Short and myself, fullest advantage might be derived from Miss Leintwardine by admitting her as fount of that information, now that she was on the spot" (22). She comes to Sillery's rooms to collect a volume of his secret diaries, which she is helping him edit for their eventual appearance as *Garnered at Sunset: Leaves from an Edwardian Journal.* "'A masterpiece of dullness,' said Bagshaw" (210). She recognizes Jenkins as the novelist and is herself writing a novel, *I Stopped at a Chemist* which is to "upset several of the more old-fashioned reviewers who had survived the war" (239). Her role in Powell's novel is not large, but it is cohesive; for one thing, she is the only known friend of Widmerpool's wife.

The best new novel since the war is admitted to be *Camel Ride to the Tomb* and snaring its author for *Fission* is Bagshaw's biggest triumph. Its author is X. Trapnel, christened Francis Xavier; but he is a lapsed Catholic who can take a hint from Francis X. Bushman of the movies and give himself an "X" of distinction. Trapnel's long overcoat and his perpetual swordstick with a death's-head on its handle capture the imagination. In contrast to Bagshaw, his mind is subtle. Bagshaw argues: "All I said was, Trappy, that personally I preferred Realism—Naturalism, if you wish. . . . That's how Tolstoy came in. It's like life." "But Naturalism's only 'like' life if the novelist himself is any good," Trapnel replies in words Powell himself has used. "If he isn't any good, it doesn't matter whether he writes naturalistically or any other way. What could be less 'like' life than most of the naturalistic novels that appear?" (215-16).

What makes Trapnel most interesting is his internal contradictions—his confusion as to his own myth, as Powell has come to put it:

> Trapnel wanted, among other things, to be a writer, a dandy, a lover, a comrade, an eccentric, a sage, a virtuoso, a good chap, a man of honour, a hard case, a spendthrift, an opportunist, a *raisonneur*; to be very rich, to be very poor, to possess a thousand mistresses, to win the heart of one love to whom he was ever faithful, to be on the best of terms with all men, to avenge savagely the lightest affront, to live to a hundred full of years and honour, to die young and unknown but recognized the following day as the most neglected genius of the age. (144-45)

Trapnel seems misplaced in time, as do so many of Powell's favorite characters; for his time is "the Eighteen-Nineties, the *décadence*.... One could not help speculating whether an eye-glass would not be produced—Trapnel was reported to have sported one for a brief period, until broken in a pub brawl..." (106). He is a connoisseur of pubs, his favorite for a while being The Hero of Acre (156). His background is mythic too, for Trapnel vaguely suggests that his Middle East childhood was occasioned by his father's perigrinations there on secret service work. His career as a novelist has perhaps been influenced by "the resemblance between what a spy does and what a novelist does, the point being you don't suddenly steal an indispensable secret that gives complete mastery of the situation, but accumulate a lot of relatively humdrum facts, which when collated provide the picture" (229). Later, it turns out that Trapnel's father had been a jockey "whose professional career had been made largely in Egypt." Trapnel's panache had been the produce of myth; and the last words of the volume are those of Dicky Umfraville who has been asked if he has heard of a jockey of such a name: "Heard of him, old boy? When I was in Cairo in the 'twenties, I won a packet on a French horse he rode called Amour Piquant" (241).

What makes Trapnel's excursion into love especially "piquant" is that, when he first meets Pamela Widmerpool, she ignores him; and he is repelled by her lack of good manners. Yet at the christening party for *Fission* given by Rosie Manasch, love blossoms under the aegis of Ada Leintwardine, from whom Trapnel is cadging money for something he has written when Pamela arrives and admits she has read and liked *Camel Ride to the Tomb*. When Trapnel in despair asks Jenkins how he can see her again, Jenkins facetiously suggests he might return the quid that he borrowed from Widmerpool in order to be able to afford a taxi. And the next comic episode takes us, by way of a dinner at the House of Commons with Jenkins' brother-in-law Roddy Cutts, to Widmerpool's flat nearby. When the three men arrive the water is running full blast in the bathroom. The assumption is that Pamela is bathing there, until a neighbor appears to deliver a message that Pamela asked him to relay orally as she departed, carrying a walking stick, with a man carrying her suitcases and the Modigliani that Stringham had left her.

By brazen coincidence, Jenkins also happens to be present months later when Widmerpool, having traced Pamela and Trapnel by means of private detectives, arrives with a list of denunciations. "First . . . you borrow money from me. . . . Then you lampoon me in a magazine of which I am one of the chief supporters. . . . Finally, my wife comes to live with you" (201). Mixing the absurd with the deadly serious, as is Widmerpool's way, he proceeds to analyze the situation as he sees it: "You can keep my pound . . . I make you a present of it. . . . Secondly. . . . Your so-called parody is a failure. Not funny. Several people have told me so. . . . You may fear that I am going to institute divorce proceedings. Such is not my intention. Pamela will return in her own good time. I think we understand each other" (201-2). Nothing could seem more absurd than Widmerpool's understanding anybody; but, by the end of the novel, Pamela has returned to him.

The mechanism of her return is esthetic, or more accurately a struggle of wills esthetically colored. Pamela wants Trapnel's new novel *Profiles in String* to end differently: "I'd rather you burnt it than publish it as it stands. In fact you're not going to" (196).

In the book's final episode, Bagshaw phones Jenkins to ask his aid in getting Trapnel home from a pub. Trapnel, suspecting that Pamela has left him, and talking with brilliant extravagance, is trying to postpone the return, obviously afraid of what he will find. But they have not yet reached Trapnel's when the discovery is made: the manuscript of *Profiles in String* is floating down the Maida Vale Canal, and Trapnel in an extravagant gesture sends his famous death's-head swordstick into the canal after it. The odor in the lonely flat later reminds Jenkins of Maclintick's flat, and he thinks of suicide. "Trappy will never take that step," Bagshaw assures him, correctly. "He's too interested in his own myth" (228).

During the two years of *Fission*'s existence, Jenkins has been working on his own book, *Borage and Hellebore*, a study of the seventeenth-century antiquarian Robert Burton; and this tenth volume is striated with allusions to Burton's famous *Anatomy of Melancholy*, which is subtitled *What it is, with all the Kindes, Causes, Symptomes, Prognostickes, and severall cures of it. . . .*

With a Satyricall Preface.... Anno Dom. 1621 (2). Most of Powell's characters are somehow marked by "Burton's 'vile rock of melancholy, a disease so frequent, as few there are that feel not the smart of it'" (54). Burton feels that even the botanical world must feel the smart as "two trees bend and... stretch out their bows to embrace and kiss each other... sick for love, ready to die and pine away..." (230). Erridge is seen as "a subject for Burton if there ever was one" (28), but so are Moreland (119) and Trapnel, Widmerpool and Pamela.

Pamela, who is first seen in church at Stringham's wedding where she vomits into the baptismal font (48), outrages the family at Erridge's funeral by slamming noisily out of the middle of the funeral service and later by vomiting into one of Erridge's five-foot-high Chinese vases (82). Yet in the end Powell brings us sardonically into a kind of sympathy with the girl. "She wants it all the time, yet doesn't want it," Trapnel muses in his desolation. "She goes rigid like a corpse. Every grind's a nightmare. It's all the time, and always the same" (225). Jenkins wonders if "the Furies that had driven her into the arms of Widmerpool by their torments... at the same time invested her with the magnetic power that mesmerized Trapnel, operated in a manner to transcend love or sex, as both are commonly regarded. Did she and Widmerpool in some manner supplement each other, she supplying a condition he lacked—one that Burton would have called Melancholy?" (195-96). "Borage and Hellebore" are reputed herbal cures for the melancholy of love that has no cure.

No cure but death—and Pamela above all "seemed an appropriate attendant on Death" (46). From being a promising young novelist, Trapnel is reduced to a literary hack, doing bits and pieces for the cinema and radio as well as for literary magazines. The novel concludes in Victorian novel fashion by tracing the fates of the books the characters have written. Odo Stevens' memoir of the war in the Balkans is thought derogatory to the Communist party, and Gypsy Jones attempts to "liquidate" it by destroying the two known manuscripts. But landing on his feet as always, Odo has a third copy and arranges a better deal for *Sad Majors* with another publisher. Guggenbühl, who had become a Fellow at the university apparently on the strength of his book *Kleist, Marx, Sartre, the Existentialist Equation* (21), cements his position with *Bronstein: Marxist or Mystagogue?*; and his change of name to Vernon Gainsborough is presumably designed to establish him in the English landscape. Only Moreland, who has resisted Bagshaw's plea for an article about existential music, fails to produce the book contemplated, *The Popular Song from Lillibullero to Lilli Marlene,* (120). And Trapnel, whose *Profiles in String* is lost, does not write another novel, and his *Heresy of Naturalism* apparently never gets written. A very bad novel entitled *Sweetskin* with passages in it salacious enough to be thought obscene, like *Lady Chatterley's Lover,* after the preliminary injunction, becomes a best seller. Jenkins' *Borage and Hellebore: A Study* with, we presume, its more genuine contribution to our understanding of human nature, enters the world quietly "the following December"; and *Fission* and Quiggin & Craggs, having provided a pattern, stumble out of existence.

XI Temporary Kings

Nicholas Jenkins is listening to the singing of a Venetian gondolier in the opening scene of *Temporary Kings* (1973), both amused that the man is singing with joy a Neapolitan song (*Funiculì-Funiculà*) and sobered by the reflection that the aged singer might be the same one that he had heard in Venice with his parents forty years before. Now in 1958 an international festival of the arts has drawn to Venice also two Americans, a university professor named Russell Gwinnett and a film producer named Louis Glober. Opposites in almost every respect, Gwinnett and Glober are both drawn richly and truly, redeeming the occasional flaws in Powell's earlier portraits of Americans.

Gwinnett is American gothic, descendant of a Welsh signer of the Declaration of Independence, "at once intensely American and allergic to American life" (11.49). Reticent and candid, naïve and shrewd, knowledgeable about the English life he is dedicated to studying and ignorant of its subtler details, Gwinnett attracts Jenkins' sympathy, and needs it, for he is engaged in research for a biography of the elusive X. Trapnel. "Let's hope he treats Trapnel's own Romanticism in a Classical manner," a mutual friend remarks. Since Gwinnett shares Edgar Allan Poe's preoccupation with death—or stands, as Jenkins puts it, "halfway between Henry Adams and Charles Addams" (84)—there is cause for concern. On the one hand he has come into possession of Trapnel's cryptic *Commonplace Book,* which reveals more about Trapnel's affair with Pamela Widmerpool and the manuscript of his last novel, thrown into the canal by Pamela, than Jenkins had known (189); and on the other, although he had resided in London, an admirer of Trapnel when Trapnel was still alive, he had not known how easy it would have been to meet him (23). Thus confronted with a welter of conflicting stories about Trapnel, Gwinnett must rely upon those who did know him, such as Jenkins and Pamela Widmerpool.

The other American, the son of Jewish immigrants who changed their family name to Glober, has roots so shallow that he might be called "at once pseudo-American and intensely devoted to American life." As a publisher, Glober had attracted Jenkins in London thirty years before, and now a playboy-tycoon, "a noted rider, shot, golfer, yachtsman," a racing-car fan, film producer, and still a collector of pubic souvenirs, he has been in the international gossip columns ever since. Neither American much likes the other, yet both diffident scholar and flamboyant film-producer are liked by Jenkins (269) and both are drawn toward the sexual maelstrom that is Pamela Widmerpool.

Growing older and obsessed by death too (102), Pamela wants to try being a film star and hopes the last novel of X. Trapnel may be the vehicle (149). In the pattern we have come to expect, Glober who may produce the film has "something of Trapnel about him—a Trapnel who brought off being a Complete Man" (74) and Gwinnett grows to resemble Trapnel more the more he studies him (201).

A larger pattern emerges when the Venice Film Festival draws Polly Duport to Venice, as the star of a Thomas Hardy film. In a sense the four schoolboys of *A Question of Upbringing* cross paths again, exchanging partners, for although Peter Templer and Charles Stringham have died during the war, Polly is Templer's niece, Pamela is Stringham's niece, and Widmerpool arrives in pursuit of Pamela. When first seen by Jenkins, however, Pamela is being pursued by Glober; and she leaves Venice, indeed, leaves the world, in pursuit of Gwinnett. Polly and Pamela are linked in other patterns: Polly "lived almost as a nun" (52) and Pamela seems to have some yearning for the religious life, comic or pathetic (158). Also about the time Pamela takes up the pursuit of Gwinnett, Glober meets Polly and "it was an instantaneous click" (220). Not that Pam cared: "she was already mad about that other American. . . ."

The title of the volume comes from the oratory used to persuade Jenkins to attend the festival where, Mark Members assures him, he will be treated like a king. "One of those temporary kings in *The Golden Bough*," Jenkins asks rhetorically, "everything at their disposal for a year or a month or a day—then execution? Death in Venice?" The title encompasses more than the regal feeding of the intellectuals and their access to normally unvisited Venetian palaces, of course. Polly Duport reveals that her stepfather might be considered a king, having become military dictator of his country in South America (235). Glober too, the movie king who has won and lost several fortunes, is to meet his final death within the year in a racing car on the Riviera. But the shock Powell seems to prepare us for most royally is the arrival in Venice of Lord Widmerpool. Elevated to the House of Lords for services rendered to the Labour Party, after losing his seat in the House of Commons in the Tory victory of 1955, Lord Widmerpool is on the other hand only a Life Peer. No peerage for a son to inherit is his, but then he has no son either. Moreover his figurative assassination by Lady Widmerpool is foreshadowed by a painting usually hidden from the public in the Bragadin Palace, Tiepolo's *Candaules and Gyges*. Appropriately Pamela and Glober, both house-guests of Jacky Bragadin, are supine, corpse-like, contemplating the painting on the ceiling when Jenkins and Gwinnett arrive. The painting (apparently one invented by Powell) depicts Candaules, King of Lydia, unclad and supine awaiting his wife at the moment when she glances aside to see Gyges, the king's chief officer, who has been coerced by the king into a voyeur's role, sidling away. In the sequel the queen, shocked that more than one man alive should have known her in the nude, confronts Gyges with a choice: kill the king and marry me or be killed. Gyges takes the first option and lives to rule Lydia well for forty years (87). Pamela's fascination with the myth is fully explained, however, only when she effects the symbolic execution of Candaules-Widmerpool, as Hugh Moreland defines him, near the end of the volume.

While chapters one to three cover three successive days in Venice, the last three record events spread over the following year in London. Gwinnett on sabbatical leave to write his book arranges to room with another Trapnel authority, Books-Do-Furnish-a-Room Bagshaw—now converted into the television personality Lindsay Bagshaw. Bagshaw's eccentric ménage includes nubile stepdaughters who take a fancy to Gwinnett, and when Pamela finally tracks him down at Christmas time and is discovered nude in the hall, locked out of Gwinnett's room, a row ensues. Gwinnett insists on leaving the next day.

"To express how things fell out is to lean heavily on hearsay," Jenkins admits (190), but as the winter progresses he pieces together clues as to Gwinnett's progress: "We had a talk. . . . I was not sure he was up to tackling so picturesque a figure as Trapnel" (215). At a military reunion dinner he also learns a bit more about Stringham's death in a Japanese prison camp after the fall of Singapore—"Stringham . . . behaved very well there" (206)—and of the developing "Widmerpool case." Rumor has it, he learns at a literary luncheon at the Soviet Embassy, that Widmerpool is to be tried for espionage or treason, perhaps given twenty-five years in prison (215), but few facts have reached the papers.

Truth is revealed with time, but what quickens the rhythm to an almost unbearable degree is a charity production of Mozart's *Abduction from the Seraglio* given at the home of the former Rosie Manasch and Odo Stevens. "Am I to be suffocated by nostalgia?" Moreland demands. "Will that be my end?" And Jenkins talks to Polly Duport, thinking of his old love for her mother Jean, while Glober, who has brought Polly, talks to Jenkins' wife Isobel. Moreland is acutely aware that his former wife Matilda, now Sir Magnus Donners' widow, is there and demands to know if Jenkins has noticed, hanging on the wall, "Barnby's drawing . . . of Norma, that little waitress at Casanova's Chinese Restaurant? All this and Mopsy Pontner too. I can't bear it." But at that moment, Carolo, Matilda's first husband, arrives as substitute violinist, and Audrey Maclintick, Moreland's current mistress, forces recognition upon him—"I lived with the man for three years, didn't I?"—quickening Moreland's progress to the grave. When Myra Erdleigh the clairvoyant also turns up with Jimmy Stripling and reminds Jenkins of their first meeting when, under the wing of his Uncle Giles, she had forecast his marriage to Isobel, and of their second, at Peter Templer's, when her planchette board had broken up the party with its eerie predictions, even Jenkins grows appalled: "Better reminiscence should stop there" (243). As the party ends, Jenkins hears that Moreland has blacked out. "I told you nostalgia would get me," Moreland laughs on his way to the hospital.

The orchestration that began with wondering where the hands are now, "Pale hands I loved . . ." is drawing to a close. The crescendo is reached out of Jenkins' earshot, however, on the terrace before Stevens' house when Glober, unwittingly perhaps, offers the Widmerpools a ride home in his vintage car and Pamela (who once had had an affair with Stevens) accosts Polly—"I hear you're going to be the star in Louis's new film" (256)—then accosts Glober regarding the existence of his "little cushion" of pubic souvenirs. Failing to rattle either, she turns on Widmerpool: "Anyway it's a cheaper hobby than his." Myra Erdleigh, who had been chatting about the occult with Moreland, now attempts to intervene. "My dear, beware. You are near the abyss" (260). Her effect is uncanny; Pamela pauses, for a moment. "Court at your peril those spirits that dabble lasciviously with primeval matter . . . sperm of the world. . . ." Myra continues, but Pamela goes into a frenzy. "He thought I didn't spot he was watching through the curtain. . . . Watching your wife being screwed. Naturally it wasn't the first time. It was just the first time with a blubber-lipped Frenchman, who couldn't do it, then popped off." She reveals that Widmerpool has been "playing games" with a former mistress of Trapnel's too (from whom she has just received Gwinnett's new address) and that Widmerpool escaped the charge of treason only by betraying his dead communist friend, the "blubber-lipped Frenchman" (263). Goaded to violence, Widmerpool attacks her physically, is staggered by Glober's fist and hustled away.

The departure of Pamela was "most mysterious," Moreland reports, with "some parting shot to the effect that none of us would ever see her again."

The last chapter is brief. Jenkins visits the hospital to see Moreland and they discuss Widmerpool, as Candaules, and the fate of his queen. Pamela had visited Gwinnett's hotel that night: "You really think she took the overdose, told him, then.... Literally dying for love" (270). Moreland links power-seeking to voyeurism in a philosophic ramble, Widmerpool to Donners, Pamela to his own lost love Matilda. He mentions an Elizabethan title, *Cambises, King of Percia: a Lamentable Tragedy mixed full of Pleasant Mirth,* that he enjoys because it "does summarize life" (275) and finally muses with cheerful rue about an opera he might have composed, "about Candaules and Gyges perhaps."

"That morning was the last time I saw Moreland," Jenkins concludes. "It was also the last time I had, with anyone, the sort of talk we used to have together. Things drawing to a close, even quite suddenly, was hardly a surprise."

As Jenkins walks back across Westminster Bridge, observing a parade of vintage cars, wondering if one might be the car driven by General Conyers in 1914, his path intersects that of Widmerpool who is walking crisply along the Thames. At that moment a car with Glober and Polly Duport is passed by another carrying Odo Stevens and Jimmy Stripling. The hooting horn is read by Widmerpool as mockery of himself and he glares at the cars with "enraged surprise." The encounter unavoidable, he and Jenkins exchange a few banalities. "In the Upper House ... I shall continue ... to expose the bankruptcy of cold-war propagandists." Jenkins thinks he sounds "more than a little unhinged" and offers, as they part, a final "platitude about the evenings drawing in."

The symbolism behind the platitude is of course lost on Widmerpool, but *Temporary Kings* has been put together so beautifully that Powell's success in drawing things to a close, "even quite suddenly," in one more volume of *The Music of Time* seems to have passed finally into the realm of the probable, leaving us with confidence that Powell, like Jenkins, will "get home before dark."

CHAPTER 8

Conclusion

LOOKING back over the career of Anthony Powell from *Afternoon Men* (1931) to *Temporary Kings* (1973), we view one of the most fruitful careers in the history of the modern novel. The fruitfulness is all the more surprising in as much as Powell never gives the impression of having worked frenetically. From beginning to end we see the work of an honest craftsman, yet never do we get the impression of dedicated esthetic piety, as we do with Virginia Woolf or James Joyce. His craftsmanship has been that of a younger generation that honored art more than Victorian novelists had, but not to the point of sanctification.

In the course of time Powell's generation itself must come to the bar of judgment, and the question well may be: Why should not you, as a generation, take only second honors, since you did not try harder? But it may be that his generation's esthetic insouciance has been accompanied by greater experience in the nether worlds of life and thus by a greater breadth of understanding, greater integrity of dramatization, and greater interest from the reader's point of view. Whatever the verdict of time, Powell's position seems clearly to be in the forefront of his generation.

Joyce's concept of the writer as a devout scientist of letters, forever experimenting with his media to push back the frontiers of expression, is too romantic for Powell's taste. The experiments Powell makes are few but respectable. They have been made casually too, without any trumpeting of their virtues, which may have resulted in their being undervalued, for a time. Experiment for experiment's sake has not been a major goal of the next generation of novelists either, and among the novelists of the Kingsley Amis-William Golding generation Powell's popularity seems to be greater than that of Virginia Woolf or James Joyce.[1] Perhaps it will be with the public at large in years to come.

Not that Powell has sought or would much value the kind of popularity that is measured by best-seller lists. With his contemporaries Henry Green and Evelyn Waugh, he accepts the notion that a limited audience—readers "fit . . . though few," as Milton phrased it—may be all that a craftsman of taste and sensitivity can hope for in certain epochs. Perhaps to an excessive degree Powell's subject matter has been the people who constitute such an audience. Including as this audience does the more significant people of the twentieth century in Great Britain, the subject area Powell limits himself to is not without world importance, however. Moreover, it is the world he knows best and can write about with the greatest authority.

Nor has Powell limited himself, as Henry Green has, to the peculiarities of the group. Recognizing fundamental constants in human nature, Powell's characters are first of all men, then Englishmen. No doubt much of their universality can be attributed to Powell's greater scholarship—to his wide and profound readings in the memoirs, biographies, and novels of the more psychologically minded figures of Switzerland, Germany, Russia, Italy, and especially France. Part of his universality must be attributed to his own world view that, despite his deep love of England, he regards England as only one of the patterns of history. More than Henry Green, or Evelyn Waugh for that matter, Powell transcends national boundaries. He is a man to whom the subtle American mind of Henry James is more attractive than the scientific English mind of H. G. Wells.

When we compare Anthony Powell to George Orwell, his classmate at Eton, we see that the currently more famous writer, despite his prophetic and verbal gifts, is a less satisfactory artist. Orwell wrote his novels because he thought he knew England and wanted to explain it to his benighted countrymen, as in *Keep the Aspidistra Flying* (1936), or because he thought he understood the present well enough to predict the future, as in that literary klaxon *1984* (1949). Leaving aside the small masterpiece *Animal Farm* (1942), the humor of which is attributed by some friends to the collaboration of his wife, Orwell's career as an artist stars only his intense honesty. But his honesty is of a limited kind, that of acidic self-examination in social and political spheres; only Albert Camus gives the impression of being as desperately in pursuit of naked candor. And possibly Powell is not Orwell's rival in calling a spade a spade. Yet Orwell's novels tend to corrupt our view of the world by oversimplifying reality; they are not true to life itself. Fidelity to the history of changes in the way people talk, for instance, must follow careful observation of how they talk; and Orwell impresses us as being more eager to talk himself than to listen, more eager to tell people what their motives are in the dirty bourgeois world than to examine their motivation in all its actual subtlety. Fittingly, Orwell's essays are more forceful than Powell's; but his characters lack the inner strength which alone can give long life to a novel.

Powell's Oxford contemporary Evelyn Waugh has also created characters of tremendous inner vitality, it is true; and perhaps he even surpasses Powell in regard to the bounce with which his characters come alive in our minds. Captain Grimes in Waugh's first novel *Decline and Fall* (1928), for instance, is a character as vitally conceived as Erridge or Widmerpool. Waugh's more immediate success was due in some measure to the larger-than-life effect of these characters, to their Dickensian verve, coupled of course with a radically different set of attitudes. Yet the bounce was accomplished at the cost of caricature, and caricature militates against the ultimate acceptance of novels such as *Black Mischief* (1934) or *Scoop* (1938). Nearly half of Waugh's work in fact is a step beyond reality, brilliant, but of a different category. Only *Agents and Patients* among Powell's novels falls into this category. It was the least successful of the novels even there, as we have mentioned; and Powell quickly returned to his own specialty—the acute and humorous depiction of society.

"My own books set out to be naturalistic, that is to say [,] never to describe anything that could not have happened in everyday life," Powell has been quoted as saying. "It is always difficult to know how human beings really live. If you describe it, you often appear to be a humorous writer, even if it is no more than mere reporting of exactly what has happened. Very few people can believe the routine of their lives when it is shown to them."[2] The extent of Powell's area of observation is far from all-embracing, however; and, when we compare his output to that of Balzac or Dickens, we detect an additional limitation.

Many a course in sociology has used a novel in its study of society—a *Grapes of Wrath* to show, better than any textbook, how the dust-bowl evacuees became transient laborers in California, or a *Studs Lonigan* to show how immigrant groups and their children are assimilated in the maw of the American city. This documentary importance cannot be claimed for the novels of Anthony Powell. When information is passed on by Powell about the daily routine of people, the data is always peripheral, casual—as when museum officials are "interrupted" from their personal concerns by the intrusion of a bore who wants to discuss museum business in *Afternoon Men*, or when Jenkins mentions inspecting the defense platoon in *The Soldier's Art*. This novel would never serve as a manual on the art of soldiering; it leaves too much unspoken; it eschews the documentary technique of *Père Goriot* or *Moby Dick*. It assumes an audience aware of the diurnal chores in a multitude of fields, an audience that has already perused the sociological novels and found them, in other respects, lacking.

What Powell's novels give the reader instead is what most documentary novels lack: subtleties of dialogue and psychology, and an understanding of the way human beings actually behave. Here Powell has no master in the modern novel. He supplements his details of observation with few deductions or theories, it is true; and we may miss the tidy generalizations in which many a novel is wrapped. If we close the volumes of Powell only a bit wiser about the mysteries of human nature, we have at least not been misled. And we carry away a memory of the world of social relations observed with wit and good humor. *The Music of Time*, even if it should not reach the twelve volumes now projected, will rank in this area as one of literature's most valuable works.

This projected completion of *The Music of Time* poses another question. "After the war, when I came out of the Army and returned to the writing of novels," Powell recalled in 1961,

"I decided that the thing to do was to produce a really large work about all the things I was interested in—the whole of one's life, in fact. . . . Such a scheme has great advantages, but you pay a price. . . . You cannot write about everybody. . . . If one lived a thousand years, one might bring everything in, but then you would have to cope with a thousand years of experience rather than the normal span."[3] If Powell has been quoted correctly, and if his remark is considered rather than flippant, the length of *The Music of Time* may be determined by Powell's own longevity; its shape, by vicissitudes of health and accident.

Critical judgment on such a projection would tend automatically to be negative. The esthetic creed seems betrayed. Form is the essence of a work of art, and *The Music of Time* would seem destined to have a form shaped not by the artist but by chance. All that saves Powell from such a threatening appraisal is the theme of the work, and the primary esthetic tenet that theme and form should be in correspondence. What may be the key to Powell's notion of the work's form then may be found in *The Acceptance World* when Jenkins speculates that, "in a sense, nothing in life is planned—or everything is—because in the dance every step is ultimately the corollary of the step before; the consequence of being the kind of person one chances to be" (3.63). Therefore, the formal integrity of *The Music of Time,* whatever its ultimate length, will derive no doubt in part from its author's having been the person of family and tradition that we have just met.

Notes and References

For the early novels of Anthony Powell, references are made to the Heinemann reissues (London, 1953-58); for *John Aubrey and His Friends,* the first edition (London, 1948); and for *The Music of Time,* the first editions (London, 1951-73). To reduce the number of footnotes, page references to books clearly identified in the text are given parenthetically—(42). For *The Music of Time* sequence, the number of the volume is also given, before the decimal—(5.42). Items below from *Punch* and the *Daily Telegraph* (London) are by Anthony Powell unless otherwise noted.

Chapter One

1. *Daily Telegraph,* August 25, 1961, p. 14.
2. *Daily Telegraph,* March 24, 1951, p. 18.
3. *Daily Telegraph,* June 26, 1959, p. 14.
4. Arthur Mizener, *The Sense of Life in the Modern Novel* (New York, 1961), p. 79; Walter Allen, *Tradition and Dream* (London, 1964), p. 223.
5. *John Aubrey and His Friends,* p. 20.
6. *Aubrey's Brief Lives,* ed. by Oliver Lawson Dick (Ann Arbor, Michigan, 1962), p. 174.
7. *Times* (London), January 5, 1960, p. 11.
8. *Punch,* CCXXVI (February 3, 1954), 187.
9. Captain Jenkins is also invalided out in 1928 (6.126).
10. *Daily Telegraph,* October 6, 1961, p. 18.
11. *Daily Telegraph,* December 2, 1960, p. 18.
12. Louis Auchincloss, *Partisan Review,* XXVII (Fall, 1960), 690-701.
13. *Daily Telegraph,* May 22, 1959, p. 14.
14. *Daily Telegraph,* March 4, 1960, p. 16.
15. *Daily Telegraph,* September 22, 1961, p. 18.
16. *Daily Telegraph,* March 4, 1960, p. 16.
17. Evelyn Waugh, *Tourist in Africa* (Boston, 1960), p. 199.
18. Anthony West, *New Yorker,* XXXVII (February 16, 1963), 159.
19. *Daily Telegraph,* August 11, 1961, p. 14.
20. *Daily Telegraph,* September 18, 1959, p. 14.

21. Aldous Huxley, "Selected Snobberies," *Music at Night* (New York, 1930), pp. 197-202.

22. *Daily Telegraph,* November 3, 1963, p. 19.

23. *Spectator,* CLXI (December 16, 1938), 1056.

24. Beverley Nichols, *The Sweet and Twenties* (London, 1958), p. 57.

25. *Daily Telegraph,* December 20, 1961, p. 18.

26. *Daily Telegraph,* October 12, 1962, p. 19.

27. *Daily Telegraph,* March 23, 1962, p. 19.

28. *Times,* March 18, 1960, p. 15.

29. Evelyn Waugh, "Father and Son," *Atlantic,* CCXI (March, 1963), 50.

30. Samuel Lodge, *Scrivelsby: The Home of the Champions, with Some Account of the Marmion and Dymoke Families* (London, 1893), p. 42.

31. Samuel Pepys, "23d April 1661, Coronation Day," *Diary and Correspondence,* Vol. I (Philadelphia, 1887), p. 177.

32. Quoted by Lodge, pp. 146-47. See also Sir Walter Scott's novel *Redgauntlet.*

33. Quoted by Lodge, p. 201.

34. Lodge, p. 115. An attenuated form of the ritual was reinstituted in the twentieth century, and a Dymoke stood as King's Champion at the coronations of Edward VII, 1902; George V, 1911; and George VI, 1937.

35. *Daily Telegraph,* September 21, 1962, p. 18.

36. Norreys Jephson O'Conor, *Godes Peace and the Queenes: Vicissitudes of a House, 1539-1615* (Cambridge, Massachusetts, 1934), p. 125.

37. *Daily Telegraph,* June 22, 1962, p. 18.

38. *Punch,* CCXXXV (November 26, 1958), 705.

39. A dramatization of his first novel *Afternoon Men* was produced in London in 1963, however. Riccardo Aragno did the dramatization, in eight scenes, after Powell had declined.

Chapter Two

1. "The Wat'ry Glade," *The Old School,* edited by Graham Greene (London, 1934), p. 149.

2. *Ibid.,* pp. 150-52.

3. *Ibid.,* pp. 152-53. Henry Green on the other hand recalls the masters as "a poor lot." *Pack My Bag* (London, 1940), p. 157.

4. Graham Greene, "The Last Word," *The Old School,* p. 247. See also Christopher Hollis, *Eton: A History* (London, 1960), p. 295.

5. *Time,* LXXXIII (May 22, 1964), 96.

6. *Times Literary Supplement,* August 17, 1962, p. 632.
7. Henry Green, *Pack My Bag,* p. 156.
8. Cyril Connolly, *Enemies of Promise* (London, 1938), pp. 317-19. See also John Lehmann, *The Whispering Gallery* (London, 1955), pp. 105-96.
9. Harold Acton, *Memoirs of an Aesthete* (London, 1948), pp. 90-101, 111, 119. Powell and Acton have an ancestral connection, a great-aunt of Powell's having married Sir John Acton, "an English cavalry officer in the Army of the Two Sicilies." *Punch,* CCXXI (December 12, 1956), 730.
10. John Wain, "A Voice from the Grave," *New Republic,* CXLIII (November 28, 1960), 24.
11. Cyril Connolly, *Sunday Times* (London) (July 15, 1956), 5, and Anthony Powell, *Punch,* CCXXXIII (October 30, 1957), 518.
12. Evelyn Waugh, *Ronald Knox* (London, 1959), p. 83.
13. John Betjeman, *New Yorker,* XXXVI (April 23, 1960), 174.
14. Sir Laurence Jones, *An Edwardian Youth* (London, 1956), pp. 39, 54, and Frank Pakenham, *Born to Believe* (London, 1953), p. 59.
15. *John Aubrey,* p. 246.
16. Christopher Sykes, *Four Studies in Loyalty* (London, 1946), p. 88.
17. Acton, *Memoirs of an Aesthete,* pp. 112-13.
18. Daphne Fielding, *Mercury Presides* (New York, 1954), p. 105.
19. Earl of Birkenhead, *Lady Eleanor Smith* (London, 1953), pp. 54-55, 86.
20. Acton, *Memoirs of an Aesthete,* pp. 122-24, and Claud Cockburn, *A Discord of Trumpets* (New York, 1956), pp. 60-63.
21. Nancy Mitford, *The Pursuit of Love* (London, 1945), pp. 41-43.
22. "Nancy Mitford," *Twentieth Century Authors: First Supplement* (New York, 1955), p. 678.
23. Fielding, *Mercury Presides,* pp. 129-30.
24. Evelyn Waugh, *P.R.B.* (London, 1926), p. 17, and *Dante Gabriel Rossetti* (London, 1928), pp. 46-47.
25. Evelyn Waugh, *A Little Learning* (London, 1964), p. 201.
26. Christopher Hollis, *The Road to Frome* (London, 1958), p. 65.
27. Waugh, *A Little Learning,* p. 213.
28. *Punch,* CCXXXII (April 10, 1957), 480.

Chapter Three

1. *New York Times Magazine,* November 30, 1952, p. 72.
2. *Daily Telegraph,* May 27, 1960, p. 18.

3. *Daily Telegraph*, August 5, 1960, p. 14.
4. Osbert Sitwell, *Noble Essences* (London, 1950), pp. 149-50.
5. *Daily Telegraph*, May 3, 1963, p. 20.
6. *Daily Telegraph*, May 18, 1962, p. 18.
7. See Arthur Calder-Marshall, *The Magic of My Youth* (London, 1951), pp. 106-36.
8. *Punch*, CCXXXI (September 19, 1956), 346.
9. Waugh, *A Little Learning*, p. 201. See also *The Early Years of Alec Waugh* (London, 1962), p. 203.
10. *Memoirs of an Aesthete*, p. 202.
11. Preface, *The Complete Ronald Firbank*, p. 10.
12. *Spectator*, CCVIII (June 29, 1962), 863.
13. *Daily Telegraph*, September 21, 1962, p. 18 and *Spectator*, CCVII (October 27, 1961), 594.
14. *A Little Learning*, p. 196.
15. *Memoirs of an Aesthete*, p. 127.
16. *Daily Telegraph*, September 18, 1959, p. 14.
17. Frederic Warburg, *An Occupation for Gentlemen* (London, 1959), pp. 106-8.
18. *Punch*, CCXXXIII (July 31, 1957), 138, and *Daily Telegraph*, October 30, 1959, p. 16.
19. *Punch*, CCXXXIII (October 16, 1957), 460, and CCXXIX (November 16, 1955), 585.
20. W. K. Rose, ed., *The Letters of Wyndham Lewis* (London, 1963), pp. 244-45.
21. Watson Lyle, "Modern Musicians-II–Constant Lambert," *Bookman*, LXXXI (March, 1932), 342.
22. "Constant Lambert, 1905-[1951]," *Composers Today* (New York, 1934), pp. 157-59.
23. Hermon Ould, "English Music of the Year," *Bookman*, LXXX (December, 1931), 181. In a similar fashion the musician Moreland is taken up by the fashionable Mrs. Foxe in *The Music of Time* (5.133).
24. Cecil Gray, *Peter Warlock* (London, 1934), pp. 223-28.
25. Harry T. Moore, *The Intelligent Heart: The Story of D. H. Lawrence* (London, 1954), pp. 212-19.
26. Jocelyn Brooke, *Aldous Huxley* (London, 1954), p. 15.
27. *Peter Warlock*, pp. 223-28. See *Antic Hay* (London, 1948), pp. 49-54.
28. *Peter Warlock*, p. 250.
29. *Daily Telegraph*, July 27, 1962, p. 16.
30. Nina Hamnett, *Is She a Lady?* (London, 1955), pp. 28-35.
31. Gray, *Peter Warlock*, pp. 289-96.

32. *Punch,* CCXXXIX (August 3, 1960), 18.
33. *Daily Telegraph,* March 18, 1960, p. 16.
34. Adrian Daintrey, *I Must Say* (London, 1963), pp. 13, 155-56.
35. Gray, *Musical Chairs* (London, 1948), p. 291.
36. Hamnett, *Is She a Lady?,* pp. 128 ff.
37. Critic, *New Statesman,* LVI (December 22, 1956), 812.
38. *John Aubrey,* pp. 100, 131, and Introduction, *Brief Lives,* pp. x-xii.
39. Waugh, *A Little Learning,* p. 201.
40. *Spectator,* CCVII (July 26, 1961), 96.
41. Longford, *Country Places* (London, 1932), p. 274.
42. *Times,* December 3, 1934, p. 17.
43. *Punch,* CCXXXI (September 26, 1956), 384.
44. *Spectator,* CLXXVI (May 3, 1946), 460, and *Punch,* CCXXIV (May 27, 1953), 640.
45. *Daily Telegraph,* July 24, 1959, p. 5.
46. *Daily Telegraph,* November 2, 1962, p. 21.
47. *Punch,* CCXXVIII (February 23, 1955), 271, and CCXXVI (January 20, 1954), 114.
48. *Times,* February 22, 1946, p. 8.
49. *Times Literary Supplement,* February 16, 1951, p. 100.

Chapter Four

1. T. S. Eliot, *For Lancelot Andrews* (London, 1928), p. ix.
2. *Daily Telegraph,* July 27, 1962, p. 16.
3. *The Writings of Oscar Wilde,* VIII (London, 1907), 43.
4. *The Works of Oscar Wilde,* IV (New York, 1909), 403.
5. Aldous Huxley, *Jesting Pilate* (London, 1948), p. 91.
6. *Times Literary Supplement,* June 10, 1960, p. 371.
7. *Punch,* CCXXX (June 27, 1956), 775.
8. Aldous Huxley, *The Realist,* I (June, 1929), 111.
9. *Punch,* CLXXVIII (January 5, 1955), 72.
10. *Punch,* CCXXX (April 4, 1956), 389.
11. *Daily Telegraph,* October 21, 1960, p. 18.
12. *Daily Telegraph,* June 21, 1963, p. 20.
13. *Daily Telegraph,* September 7, 1962, p. 16 and September 30, 1959, p. 16.
14. *Daily Telegraph,* February 8, 1963, p. 14.
15. *Daily Telegraph,* January 26, 1962, p. 18.
16. *Daily Telegraph,* December 15, 1961, p. 18.
17. *Daily Telegraph,* August 17, 1962, p. 14.
18. *Daily Telegraph,* September 21, 1962, p. 18.
19. *Daily Telegraph,* August 7, 1959, p. 14.

20. *Daily Telegraph,* December 14, 1962, p. 16.
21. *Cornhill,* CLXI (December, 1945), 481-88 and CLXII (April, 1946), 78-81.
22. Aldous Huxley, *Athenaeum,* 4697 (May 7, 1920), 607, and 4713 (August 27, 1921), 274.
23. *Daily Telegraph,* December 14, 1962, p. 16.
24. *Punch,* CCXXVII (December 29, 1954), 828.
25. *Daily Telegraph,* April 12 1962, p. 18.
26. *Punch,* CCXXXII (June 5, 1957), 722.
27. *Cornhill,* CLXII (April, 1946), 81.
28. Joseph Conrad, *Under Western Eyes* (New York, 1958), p. 89.
29. Albert J. Guerard, *Conrad the Novelist* (Cambridge, Mass., 1962), p. xi.
30. *Daily Telegraph,* January 29, 1960, p. 16.
31. *Punch,* CCXXVIII (May 25, 1955), 657.
32. *Punch,* CCXXVI (March 3, 1954), 301.
33. *Punch,* CCXXXIV (May 7, 1958), 619.
34. *Punch,* CCXXVII (August 26, 1954), 268.
35. *Punch,* CCXXVI (March 3, 1954), 301.
36. *Daily Telegraph,* September 9, 1960, p. 19. Yet he praises Woolf's memoirs as "extraordinarily well done."
37. Quoted by J. K. Johnstone, *The Bloomsbury Group* (New York, 1954), p. 30.
38. *Punch,* CCXXIX (November 2, 1955), 529.
39. *Punch,* CCXXV (November 18, 1953), 614. When General Conyers, having read Virginia Woolf's *Orlando,* insists "The Woman can write, you know," the narrator replies: "Yes, I can see that. I still don't like it" (4.80).
40. *Daily Telegraph,* March 10, 1961, p. 18; *Punch,* CCXXXIII (October 30, 1957), 518; *Daily Telegraph,* April 5, 1963, p. 9.
41. Arthur Mizener, *The Sense of Life in the Modern Novel,* pp. 192-93.
42. *Daily Telegraph,* December 28, 1962, p. 13.
43. *Spectator,* CLXXVIII (March 7, 1947), 244.
44. *Daily Telegraph,* January 11, 1962, p. 17.
45. *Daily Telegraph,* March 6, 1959, p. 17.
46. *Punch,* CCXXXI (September 12, 1956), 315.
47. *Punch,* CCXXV (November 18, 1953), 614.
48. *Punch,* CCXXXI (July 4, 1956), 24.
49. *Punch,* CCXXVII (September 1, 1954), 295.
50. *New Statesman,* XIX (February 17, 1940), 204. Reprinted in *The New Statesman: The History of the First Fifty Years 1913-1963,* by Edward Hyams (London, 1963), p. 221.

51. *Daily Telegraph,* May 24, 1961, p. 18.
52. Paul Johnson, *Nation,* CLXXXIII (September 1, 1956), 178-80.
53. "The New Conservatism," *Times Literary Supplement,* July 29, 1955, p. 429.
54. Jack Lindsay, *After the 'Thirties: The Novel in Britain and Its Future* (London, 1956), p. 26.
55. *Lectures on the English Comic Writers,* 1819 (London, 1951), p. 5.
56. Albert Camus, *The Myth of Sisyphus and Other Essays* (New York, 1955), pp. 21, 34-35. Note Powell's admission: "I would be hard put to deny that theorists are distasteful to me. People get me down who claim, you know, to have the answer to life." *College English,* XXIV (April, 1963), 535.

Chapter Five

1. *Times Literary Supplement,* June 29, 1962, p. 476 and July 13, 1962, p. 509.
2. V. S. Pritchett, *New York Times Book Review,* January 12, 1958, p. 22.
3. See Charlotte Bingham, *Coronet Among the Weeds* (New York, 1963), and *Musical Chairs,* p. 285.
4. In the Neo-Classic vein, when Powell does touch Nature, the touch is cool, as in this view of the Camberley countryside: "The grass looked parched. Some charred gorse marked the limits of a heath fire. The unspeakable pines gave off a medicinal odour." *What's Become of Waring,* p. 200.
5. Richard J. Vorhees, *Dalhousie Review,* XLII (Autumn, 1962), p. 313.
6. Several critics have treated Powell with hostility apparently because he mentions that Verelst is a Jew. But in the 1920's, before Hitler turned the clock back, Jews were so widely accepted in British society that critical views taken of individual Jews did not automatically carry the smack of intolerance they came to later. Today one can at last depict unsavory Irishmen without making Irishmen angry, and that day will no doubt come again for the Jews. As for Powell's general attitude, one might note his dedication of *Casanova's Chinese Restaurant* to the Chairman of the Anglo-Israel Bank.
7. "The roast-beef-English atmosphere" of the boxing arena Comrades' Hall, in Camden Town, was a favorite with Roy Campbell, Nina Hamnett, and others of the Heseltine circle. *Is She a Lady?,* pp. 49-54.
8. With her Chinese tea-gowns, books with such titles as *God's*

Failures, exotic liqueurs, kindly, misguided patronage, and aristocratic absence of sham, "Naomi Race" seems to owe something to Lady Ottoline Morrell.

9. Possibly a touch of Evelyn Waugh enters Pringle's portrait at this point. In his autobiography, Waugh confesses that, while in despair as a schoolmaster in Wales, he had left a farewell note (among his clothes, and in Greek) as he swam out to sea, only to be stung by jellyfish to the point where life on shore seemed more desirable. *A Little Learning,* p. 230.

10. Robert Flaherty's documentary films about Eskimos ("Nanook of the North") and Irish peasants ("The Man from Aran") were being widely hailed in the mid-1930's, though Graham Greene scorned them as "phoney." *Spectator,* CLV (October 25, 1935), 663.

11. *A la Vache enragée* seems based on the famous *Boeuf sur le Toit* where Cole Porter composed "Let's Do It."

12. Powell has commented on the Berlin cinema world of Eric von Stroheim and Alfred Hitchcock as if personally acquainted with it, *Punch,* CCXXVI (January 20, 1954), 114-15.

13. John Lehmann, *The Whispering Gallery* (London, 1955), p. 176.

14. Gérard de Nerval's sonnet about the knight returning to find the land in ruins, which the Count recites at the emotional focus of the novel (174), struck a responsive chord in Powell and Cecil Gray as well as in Eliot. Count Robin de la Condamine, who acted on the London stage under the name of "Robert Farquharson," is a possible model here. See Laver, *Museum Piece,* pp. 119-20.

15. Robert Browning's poem "Waring" seems to have led Powell rather than his character Alec Pimley (who is not much of a reader of poetry) to the alias "T. T. Waring." Yet Alec Pimley shares the melancholy of E. M. Forster: "A hundred years ago Browning's Waring could give all civilization the slip and vanish from the midst of his friends into the unknown," but our era is more brutal, Forster complains. "Waring, today, couldn't slip off in his little boat . . . ," *Atlantic,* CLXIII (January, 1939), 54.

Chapter Six

1. *Spectator,* CLXII (June 30, 1939), 1134 and CLXXVI (March 8, 1946), 247-48.

2. *Punch,* CCXXVIII (June 1, 1955), 688.

3. *John Aubrey and His Friends,* pp. 128, 131, 242.

4. R. G. G. Price, *A History of Punch* (London, 1957), pp. 277, 327-31.

5. *New Yorker,* XXXVIII (June 2, 1962), 119. See also Michel

Mohrt, "Un Proust anglais: Anthony Powell," *Arts* (Paris), March 16, 1955, p. 7.

6. Elizabeth R. Jackson, *Publications of the Modern Language Association,* LXXVI (December, 1961), 588, and Germaine Brée, *Marcel Proust and Deliverance From Time* (New York, 1955), p. 19.

7. "History has got in," as Elizabeth Janeway observes. *New York Times Book Review,* January 21, 1962, p. 1.

8. James Hall, *The Tragic Comedians* (Bloomington, Indiana, 1963), p. 133.

9. See Evelyn Waugh's *A Little Learning,* pp. 202-3.

10. *Times Literary Supplement,* August 15, 1958, p. iii.

11. *Daily Telegraph,* March 16, 1962, p. 18.

12. John Lehmann, *The Whispering Gallery,* p. 37.

13. G. B. Stern, *Monogram* (New York, 1936), pp. 28-29.

14. Cecil Gray, *Musical Chairs,* pp. 12, 105, 235, 243, 268.

15. *A Little Learning,* p. 201.

16. Marvin Mudrick, *Hudson Review,* XVII (Spring, 1964), 119.

17. Almost all critics of *The Music of Time* have made similar errors about the motivation of characters, viz. James Hall's supposition that Jean Templer left her husband because she preferred the "artistic temperament" of Jenkins when her motives were quite ruthlessly sensual, *The Tragic Comedians,* p. 142. This critic undoubtedly has erred too.

18. *Times Literary Supplement,* September 13, 1947, p. 464.

19. Wyndham Lewis, *Tarr* (New York, 1948), p. 53.

Chapter Seven

1. Frank Pakenham, *Born to Believe,* pp. 101-2.

2. *Ibid.,* pp. 23-48.

3. *Ibid.,* pp. 50-83.

4. *New Yorker,* LXXXIII (May 22, 1964), 96.

5. Flavus, "London Diary," *New Statesman,* LXIII (June 29, 1962), 934.

6. *Times,* December 1, 1939, p. 11, and May 25, 1940, p. 9.

7. *Punch,* CCXXXIV (January 22, 1958), 160. See also *The Memoirs of Lord Chandos* (London, 1963), *passim.*

8. *Sunday Times,* April 28, 1963, p. 8.

9. *Times Literary Supplement,* June 29, 1962, p. 476.

10. *Daily Telegraph,* October 7, 1960, p. 18.

11. *Times,* April 22, 1938, p. 16.

12. *New Statesman,* LIX (February 22, 1958), 248.

13. A portrait of Evelyn Waugh by Henry Lamb is reproduced in *The Bookman* (London), LXXX (October, 1931), 40.

14. John Russell, *A Portrait of Logan Pearsall Smith* (London, 1950), p. 13. See also Robert Gathorne-Hardy, *Recollections of Logan Pearsall Smith: The Story of a Friendship* (London, 1949), and Cyril Connolly, "Logan Pearsall Smith," *Atlantic Monthly*, CLXXVII (June, 1964), 129-30.

15. Russell, pp. 2, 26, 30.

16. *Punch*, CCXXI (September 26, 1956), 384.

17. Lovat Dickson, *The House of Words* (London, 1963), p. 82.

18. James Laver, *Museum Piece*, p. 93.

19. *Time and Tide*, XLI (July 2, 1960), pp. 764-65, and (July 9, 1960), pp. 808-9.

20. Waugh, *A Little Learning*, p. 202.

21. Lady Warminster in some respects resembles the Countess of Longford, as has been pointed out; in other respects she resembles Lady Burghclere, the mother of Evelyn Heygate to whom Powell dedicated his third novel. See her obituary, *Times*, October 3, 1933, p. 7.

22. Pakenham, *Born to Believe*, pp. 69-70, 81-84. See also Philip Toynbee, *Friends Apart* (London, 1954), pp. 109-11, 139-40.

23. Pakenham, *Born to Believe*, pp. 173, 215-20.

24. *Ibid.*, pp. 16, 73, 169.

25. *Ibid.*, pp. 14, 114.

26. Cecil Gray, *Musical Chairs*, p. 290.

27. Gray, *Peter Warlock*, p. 291.

28. Gray, *Musical Chairs*, p. 289.

29. Gray, *Peter Warlock*, pp. 12-13.

30. Gray, *Musical Chairs*, p. 285.

31. See Arthur Calder-Marshall, *The Magic of My Youth*, pp. 106-36.

32. *Punch*, CCXXXI (September 19, 1956), 346.

33. *Daily Telegraph*, October 25, 1963, p. 20.

34. Evelyn Waugh, *Spectator*, CCVII (June 24, 1962), 864.

35. James Laver in *Museum Piece* reports that, when his book on Nostradamus was published, he received a letter from Aleister Crowley beginning "Do what thou wilt shall be the whole of the Law. . . ." The letter invited him for a visit at his hotel in Hastings in 1947. See pp. 226-31. So similar is the description, from heroin to Tarot cards, that Powell almost certainly based his account of Dr. Trelawney on someone's visit to Crowley there.

36. Waugh, *A Little Learning*, pp. 202-3.

Chapter Eight

1. See for instance Kingsley Amis, "Afternoon World," *Spectator*, CXCIV (May 13, 1955), 619-20.
2. "Taken From Life," *Twentieth Century*, CLXX (July, 1961), 51.
3. *Ibid.*, p. 53.

Selected Bibliography

PRIMARY SOURCES

1. The Comic Novels and John Aubrey (chronologically listed)

Afternoon Men. London: Duckworth, 1931; New York: Holt, 1932; London: Heinemann, 1952; Boston: Little, Brown, 1964.

Venusberg. London: Duckworth, 1932; New York: Periscope-Holliday, 1952, under the title *Two Novels*. London: Heinemann, 1955.

From a View to a Death. London: Duckworth, 1933; New York: Vanguard, 1934, under the title *Mr. Zouch, Superman*. London: John Lehmann, 1948; London: Heinemann, 1954.

Agents and Patients. London: Duckworth, 1936; New York: Periscope-Holliday, 1952, under the title *Two Novels*; London: Heinemann, 1955.

What's Become of Waring. London: Cassell, 1939; London: Heinemann, 1953; Boston: Little, Brown, 1963.

John Aubrey and His Friends. London: Eyre and Spottiswoode, 1948; New York: Scribner's, 1948; London: Heinemann, 1963, revised edition; New York: Barnes and Noble, 1963.

2. *The Music of Time* Sequence (chronologically listed)

A Question of Upbringing. London: Heinemann, 1951; New York: Scribner's, 1951; Boston: Little, Brown, 1962: *A Question of Upbringing*, *A Buyer's Market*, and *The Acceptance World* reissued collectively under the title *A Dance to the Music of Time: First Movement*.

A Buyer's Market. London: Heinemann, 1952; New York: Scribner's, 1953.

The Acceptance World. London: Heinemann, 1955; New York: Farrar and Strauss, 1956.

At Lady Molly's. London: Heinemann, 1957; Boston: Little, Brown, 1958; Boston: Little, Brown, 1964: *At Lady Molly's*, *Casanova's Chinese Restaurant*, and *The Kindly Ones* reissued collectively under the title *A Dance to the Music of Time: Second Movement*.

Casanova's Chinese Restaurant. London: Heinemann, 1960; Boston: Little, Brown, 1960.

The Kindly Ones. London: Heinemann, 1962; Boston: Little, Brown, 1962.

The Valley of Bones. London: Heinemann, 1964; Boston: Little, Brown, 1964; Boston: Little, Brown, 1971: *The Valley of Bones, The Soldier's Art,* and *The Military Philosophers* reissued as *A Dance to the Music of Time: Third Movement.*

The Soldier's Art. London: Heinemann, 1966; Boston: Little, Brown, 1967.

The Military Philosophers. London: Heinemann, 1968; Boston: Little, Brown, 1968.

Books Do Furnish a Room. London: Heinemann, 1971; Boston: Little, Brown, 1971.

Temporary Kings. London: Heinemann, 1973.

3. Other Books by Powell

Caledonia. A Poem. Privately Printed. Alluded to by Auberon Waugh, *Spectator* (December 8, 1967).

The Garden God and *The Rest I'll Whistle.* The text of two plays, with four set designs by Osbert Lancaster. London: Heinemann, 1971; Boston: Little, Brown, 1972.

4. Books with Sections by Powell

Barnard Letters, 1778-1824. London: Duckworth, 1928. Powell edited this selection from the letters of Sir Andrew Francis Barnard (1773-1855), Thomas Barnard, Bishop of Limerick (1728-1806), and Lady Anne Barnard Lindsay (1750-1825), and wrote an introduction, pp. 9-16.

The Old School: Essays by Divers Hands. Edited by Graham Greene. London: Jonathan Cape, 1934. Contains Powell's memoir of Eton, "The Wat'ry Glade," pp. 147-62.

Novels of High Society from the Victorian Age. London: Pilot Press, 1947. Powell selected the novels—*Henrietta Temple,* by Benjamin Disraeli; *Guy Livingstone,* by G. A. Lawrence; and *Moths,* by Ouida (Marie Louise de la Ramée)—and supplied an introduction, pp. vii-xv.

John Aubrey. *Brief Lives and Other Selected Writings.* Edited by Anthony Powell. London: Cresset Library, 1949; New York: Scribner's, 1949. Powell edited these selections from manuscripts in the Bodleian Library and elsewhere, supplying notes, pp. xxiii-xxx and 387-97, and an introduction, pp. ix-xxii.

The Pick of Punch: An Annual Selection. Edited by Nicholas Bentley. London: Deutsch, 1957; New York: Dutton, 1957. Powell's skit, "Leaves from Notable New Diaries–Kingsley Amis," appears on p. 22.

The Complete Ronald Firbank. London: Duckworth, 1961; New York: New Directions, 1961. Powell supplied the Preface, pp. 1-16.

The Compleat Imbiber. Edited by Cyril Ray. London: Vista Books, 1963. Powell's article on Rosa Lewis and the Cavendish Hotel is said to supplement the picture of that fabulous London hotel proprietress in Evelyn Waugh's novel *Vile Bodies* (1930) and books by Daphne Fielding and Michael Harrison, q.v.

The Compleat Imbiber. Edited by Cyril Ray. London: Studio Vista, 1964. Article on John Aubrey and seventeenth-century drinking practices.

Burke's Genealogical and Heraldic History of the Landed Gentry. London: Burke's Peerage, 1965. Powell contributed one of the three introductions, "Reflections on the Landed Gentry," pp. xxv-xxviii.

Winter Tales 12. Edited by A. D. Maclean. London: Macmillan, 1966. Contains "A Reference to Mellors," a story related to *Lady Chatterley's Lover.*

5. Articles, Stories, Reviews

Articles and reviews by Powell published in periodicals number in the thousands and cannot be given here. The curious should check especially the London *Daily Telegraph* (1936, 1958-72), the *Spectator* (1937-39, 1946), and *Punch* (1953-58).

SECONDARY SOURCES

ALLEN, WALTER. *Tradition and Dream: The English and American Novel from the Twenties to Our Time.* London: Dent, 1964. One of the first general surveys to treat Powell as a major novelist.

BERGONZI, BERNARD. *Anthony Powell* (following Paul Bloomfield's *L. P. Hartley*). London: Longmans, Green, 1962. Writers and Their Work Pamphlet 144. Brief but intelligent survey of Powell's novels.

BOSTON, RICHARD. "A Talk with Anthony Powell," *New York Times Book Review,* March 9, 1969, pp. 2, 36. On his home life and methods of composition.

BRENNAN, NEIL. "At Lady Molly's," *Epoch,* IX (Fall, 1958), 126-29. On the fourth volume of *The Music of Time.*

———. "The Aesthetic Tradition in the English Comic Novel," *Dissertation Abstracts,* XIX (June, 1959), 1780-81. Relates Powell to Oscar Wilde, Ronald Firbank, Aldous Huxley, and others.

DAVIS, DOUGLAS M. "An Interview with Anthony Powell, Frome, England, June, 1962." *College English,* XXIV (April, 1963), 533-36. Some personal details not elsewhere revealed.

ELLIS, G. U. *Twilight on Parnassus.* London: Michael Joseph, 1939. First book to recognize Powell's genius.

"From a Chase to a Death," *Times Literary Supplement,* February 16, 1951, p. 100. Essay on the novels before *A Question of Upbringing.*

GLAZEBROOK, MARK. "The Art of Horace Isbister, E. Bosworth Deacon and Ralph Barnby." *London Magazine,* VII (November, 1967), 76-82. Relates the painters of *The Music of Time* to Walter Sickert, Augustus John, and others.

GUTWILLIG, ROBERT. "A Walk Around London with Anthony Powell," *New York Times Book Review,* September 30, 1962, pp. 5, 30. Witty interview focused upon the London of Powell's novels.

HALL, JAMES. "The Uses of Polite Surprise: Anthony Powell," *Essays in Criticism,* XII (April, 1962), 167-83. On Powell's techniques in *The Music of Time.*

———. *The Tragic Comedians: Seven Modern British Novelists.* Bloomington: Indiana University Press, 1963. Contains study of the first four volumes of *The Music of Time.*

HOWARTH, HERBERT. "Discords in the Music of Time," *Commentary,* LIII (January, 1972), 70-75. Indignant critique of Powell for not satirizing adequately the society he depicts.

KARL, FREDERICK R. *A Reader's Guide to the Contemporary English Novel.* New York: Farrar, Strauss, and Cudahy, 1962. Describes the first five volumes of *The Music of Time.*

KERMODE, FRANK. *Puzzles and Epiphanies: Essays and Reviews 1958-1961.* London: Routledge and Kegan Paul, 1962. Contains a review of *Casanova's Chinese Restaurant.*

LEE, JAMES WAR. "The Novels of Anthony Powell," *Dissertation Abstracts,* XXV (March, 1965), 5281-82. Summary of an Auburn University doctoral thesis.

LEWIS, WYNDHAM. "Satire in the Twenties," *Times Literary Supplement,* September 27, 1947, p. 493, and October 4, 1947, p. 507. Letters objecting to Powell's article on his comic novels.

MCCALL, RAYMOND G. "Anthony Powell's Gallery," *College English,* XXVII (December, 1965), 227-32. On the painter's eye of the narrator in *The Music of Time.*

MACLAREN-ROSS, J., *Memoirs of the Forties.* London: Alan Ross, 1965. Memories of bohemian London by a reputed original of the character X. Trapnel in *Books Do Furnish a Room.*

MIZENER, ARTHUR. "A Dance to the Music of Time: The Novels of Anthony Powell," *Kenyon Review,* XXII (Winter, 1960), 79-92. First major article about Powell in the United States.

———. *The Sense of Life in the Modern Novel.* Boston: Houghton, Mifflin, 1964. Sympathetic evaluation of Powell's contribution.

MORRIS, ROBERT K. "The Early Novels of Anthony Powell: A Thematic Study," *Dissertation Abstracts,* XXV (January, 1965), 4152-53. Summary of a University of Wisconsin doctoral thesis.

———. *The Novels of Anthony Powell.* Pittsburgh: University of Pittsburgh Press, 1968. Survey of Powell's novels through *The Soldier's Art.*

POWELL, LADY VIOLET. *Five Out of Six.* London: Heinemann, 1960. Memoirs of her youth, by Powell's wife.

PRITCHETT, V. S. *The Working Novelist.* London: Chatto and Windus, 1965. On the "bored barbarians" of the later novels.

QUESENBERY, W. D., JR. "Anthony Powell. The Anatomy of Decay," *Critique,* VII (Spring, 1964), 5-26. Misreading of Powell's intent in *The Music of Time.*

RUOFF, GENE W. "Social Mobility and the Artist in *Manhattan Transfer* and *The Music of Time,*" *Wisconsin Studies in Contemporary Literature,* V (Winter-Spring, 1964), 64-76.

RUSSELL, JOHN. "Quintet from the '30s: Anthony Powell," *Kenyon Review,* XXVII (Autumn, 1965), 698-726. On the early novels.

———. *Anthony Powell: A Quintet, Sextet, and War.* Bloomington: Indiana University Press, 1970. Best in-depth study of Powell to date.

"A Who's Who of 'The Music of Time,' " *Time and Tide,* XLI (July 2, 1960), 764-65, and (July 9, 1960), 808-9. Helpful glossary of the characters in the first four volumes.

ZIGERELL, JAMES J. "Anthony Powell's *Music of Time*: Chronicle of a Declining Establishment," *Twentieth-Century Literature,* XII (October, 1966), 138-46. The breakdown of society as seen in volume seven.

Index